Criminal Justice
Recent Scholarship

Edited by
Marilyn McShane and Frank P. Williams III

A Series from LFB Scholarly

Restorative Justice
Theories and Practices of Moral Imagination

Amy Levad

LFB Scholarly Publishing LLC
El Paso 2012

Library of Congress Cataloging-in-Publication Data

Levad, Amy, 1979-
  Restorative justice : theories and practices of moral imagination /
Amy Levad.
     p. cm. -- (Criminal justice: recent scholarship)
  Includes bibliographical references and index.
  ISBN 978-1-59332-486-5 (hbk. : alk. paper)
  1. Restorative justice. 2. Criminal justice, Administration of--Moral
and ethical aspects. I. Title.
  HV8688.L48 2012
  364.6'8--dc23
                                    2011026580

ISBN 978-1-59332-486-5

Printed on acid-free 250-year-life paper.

Manufactured in the United States of America.

Table of Contents

List of Figures and Tables

FIGURES

TABLES

Acknowledgements

I have been truly fortunate in the companions that have journeyed with me on the road to completing this book. First, I am thankful for having supportive friends and colleagues at Emory University, including Liz Bounds, Robert Agnew, Pamela Hall, Nancy Eiesland, John Senior, Katherine Shrout, and Matthew Bersagel Braley during the writing of this book.

Much of the work of this book involved real journeying, traveling from Georgia to Colorado. Although I cannot name them for the sake of their privacy, I deeply appreciate all of the people who agreed to participate in the ethnographic portion of this study. These are people who do what they can, where they are, with what they have in order to change the world—truly a virtuous way of being that deserves deep respect.

Of course, a person cannot go on a journey without traveling money and a place to stay. I am grateful to Emory University for five years of generous funding, support, and opportunities for research and teaching. I also thank the Initiative in Religious Practices and Practical Theology, funded by Lilly Endowment Inc. and directed by Tom Frank at the time of writing, for financial support of travel, research, and transcription that made my work in Colorado possible. A few people who let me stay at their homes also merit gratitude: Ashley and Dan Chase, Mike and Jan Henwood, and Lisa and Andy Levad. Thank you.

I would also like to thank Leo Balk from LFB Scholarly Publishing for his support, as well as Marilyn McShane and Frank P. Williams III—editors of the Crime and Justice series—for this opportunity.

Thanks particularly to my family, especially my sister, Katy, who inspired my concern with the topic of this book in the first place. Thanks also to my husband, Mark DelCogliano. He is a great partner, a fine intellectual, and a kind man. My mother, Karen, saw me through difficult times and read through several drafts; she has become one of my best friends and strongest supports. And thanks to my father, Richard. As my high school English teacher, he taught me to write. As my dad, he taught me to pay close attention to the world around me. These skills and attitudes have been important for creating this book; I dedicate it to his memory.

CHAPTER 1

Introduction: A Crisis of Justice

[M]oral change for the better happens, if at all, slowly, as new modes of outlook (metaphor) and new desires come into being. Sudden conversions and dramatic new starts can be significant if a new external regime can be established, which then gradually assists the inward change, which cannot happen all at once, upon its way.... One escapes (often) from really seductive temptation, not by a sudden violent inward "act of will" which redirects the character, but by an external change such as literally running away, making something impossible, winning time to develop other attachments, *to imagine how things might be different.*

Iris Murdoch
Metaphysics as a Guide to Morals
(Penguin Books 1992: 330-331)

C riminal justice systems in the United States are in crisis. Currently over 7.3 million adults in the U.S. are under some form of supervision, including probation, jail, prison, and parole, by state, local, or federal criminal justice systems.[1] At midyear 2009, nearly 1.6

---

[1] Heather C. West, "Prison Inmates at Midyear 2009—Statistical Tables," Bureau of Justice Statistics, U.S. Department of Justice, posted June 2010, http://bjs.ojp.usdoj.gov/content/pub/pdf/pim09st.pdf (accessed on July 21, 2010). In what follows, I draw on statistics that highlight the plight of prison and jail inmates. However, a larger proportion of the population of the United States experiences criminal justice systems through probation or parole. When we see statistics about incarceration rates, we really see only the proverbial tip of the iceberg of criminal justice systems.

1

60million of these people were in prison, and nearly 800,000 were in jail.[2] These numbers represent a gross increase in the rate of incarceration in the U.S. over the last several decades. In 1980, the rate of incarceration in prisons was 139 people per 100,000 U.S. residents. Over thirty years, this rate has increased by more than 360 percent; it was 504 people per 100,000 U.S. residents in 2008 (these rates do not include jail inmates, who bring the overall rate of incarceration up to 762 people per 100,000).[3] Although the U.S. has less than five percent of the world's population, it holds nearly twenty-five percent of the world's people incarcerated in jails and prisons.[4] The U.S. incarcerates its residents at higher rates than any other nation, and by over 700,000 people behind bars, we incarcerate more people than any other nation (China incarcerates the second highest number of people at 1.6 million inmates).[5] In short, we have more people locked up in the U.S. and at higher rates than at any other time in our history and than any other national jurisdiction.

While these numbers are troubling enough to raise serious questions about our criminal justice systems, discrepancies related to race and ethnicity among prison and jail populations add greater urgency to addressing this crisis. Racial and ethnic minority

---

[2] Ibid. Jails differ from prisons in that the former typically confine only people prior to trial or sentencing and those who have been convicted of a misdemeanor, usually resulting in a sentence of less than one year. That is, jails are used for holding and restraining people temporarily while prisons generally have more permanent populations.

[3] Ibid. Bureau of Justice Statistics, "Key Facts at a Glance: Correctional Populations," U.S. Department of Justice, posted July 2010, http://bjs.ojp. usdoj.gov/content/glance/tables/corr2tab.cfm (accessed on July 21, 2010).

[4] Adam Liptak, "U.S. Prison Population Dwarfs that of Other Nations," *New York Times,* April 23, 2008.

[5] Roy Walmsley, "World Prison Population List," 8th edition, International Centre for Prison Studies, King's College London, posted January 2009, http:// www.kcl.ac.uk/depsta/law/research/icps/downloads/wppl-8th_41.pdf (accessed on July 21, 2010).

populations are incarcerated at astounding rates in comparison with whites.[6] At mid-year 2009, the incarceration rate of black non-Hispanic males (4,749 per 100,000 black non-Hispanic U.S. resident males) was six times that of the incarceration rate of white non-Hispanic males (708 per 100,000 white non-Hispanic U.S. resident males) and nearly three times that of Hispanic males (1,822 per 100,000 Hispanic U.S. resident males). Although about 93 percent of people in state and federal prisons in 2009 were men, in recent years the incarceration rate of women has increased twice as quickly as that of men. While women are incarcerated at a much lower rate than men (131 versus 1398 per 100,000 U.S. resident females and males, respectively), the population of incarcerated women reflects similar racial and ethnic disparities as the male inmate population. Black non-Hispanic females (333 per 100,000 black non-Hispanic U.S. resident females) are incarcerated at a rate nearly four times that of white non-Hispanic females (91 per 100,000 white non-Hispanic U.S. resident females) and over two times that of Hispanic females (142 per 100,000 Hispanic U.S. resident females). Increasing incarceration has hit racial and ethnic minority populations in the U.S. especially hard.

In addition to racial and ethnic disparities, criminal justice systems in the U.S. are also marred by disparities related to the socio-economic status of inmates. Measures of the socio-economic status of people in jail or prison are difficult to find; a person's income and wealth are not noted upon incarceration as are his or her sex and race. However, according to Marc Mauer, "a 1997 survey of state inmates conducted by the Justice Department found that 68 percent of prisoners had not completed high school, 53 percent earned less than $1,000 in the month prior to their incarceration, and nearly one half were either unemployed or working only part-time prior to their arrest."[7] Another measure of socio-economic status of prison and jail inmates is whether they need

---

[6] The following statistics are found in West, "Prison Inmates at Midyear 2009."

[7] Marc Mauer, *Race to Incarcerate*, 2nd edition (New York: New Press, 2006), 178.

publicly-financed counsel, and the most recent data recording this statistic are also from over a decade ago.[8] In 1998, about two-thirds of federal felony defendants required public defense. In 1996, more than four-fifths of felony defendants in the 75 most populous counties in the United States required public defense. While conviction rates did not vary according to whether defendants had privately- or publicly-financed counsel, defendants with public defense were incarcerated at higher rates and for longer sentences than those with private defense. Criminal justice systems not only disproportionately incarcerate racial and ethnic minorities; they also tend to hold high numbers of poor people behind bars as well.

These trends within adult criminal justice systems in the U.S. are also apparent within juvenile justice systems, which in many ways feed our prisons and jails through what the Children's Defense Fund calls the "cradle-to-prison pipeline."[9] On February 22, 2006, the last date of a census by the Office of Juvenile Justice and Delinquency Prevention (OJJDP), over 92,000 juvenile offenders were held in "residential placement facilities."[10] According to the OJJDP, this number represents roughly how many juveniles occupy these facilities on "any given day." So on any given day, we could expect about fifteen percent of juveniles in these facilities to be girls. We could also expect about 767 per 100,000 black non-Hispanic juveniles living in our country to be in a residential placement facility. The rate for Hispanic juveniles

---

[8] Bureau of Justice Statistics, "Indigent Defense Statistics," U.S. Department of Justice, posted October 1, 2001, http://www.ojp.usdoj.gov/bjs/id.htm#defendants (accessed on November 14, 2007).

[9] Children's Defense Fund, "America's Cradle to Prison Pipeline," October 2007, http://www.childrensdefense.org/child-research-data-publications/data/cradle-prison-pipeline-report-2007-full-highres.html (accessed on January 21, 2011).

[10] For comprehensive statistics on juvenile justice in the United States, see Office of Juvenile Justice and Delinquency Prevention, "Statistical Briefing Book," U.S. Department of Justice, Office of Justice Programs, http://ojjdp.ncjrs.gov/ojstatbb/ (accessed on January 21, 2011).

was 326, and the rate for white non-Hispanic juveniles was 170. That is, the rate at which black juveniles are placed in these facilities is about four-and-a-half times that of whites; the rate for Hispanics is about twice that of whites—statistics that echo patterns among adults.

More sixteen-year-olds than any other age group occupied residential placement facilities—about 25,000.[11] Sixteen-year-olds edged out seventeen-year-olds because thirteen states send seventeen-year-olds directly to criminal courts, and many other states allow for seventeen-year-olds to be sent to criminal courts via statutory exclusion or concurrent jurisdiction provisions. As a result, every year, over 200,000 youth under age eighteen are tried as adults.[12] During the 1990s, every state except Nebraska expanded the number of juveniles it sends through criminal justice systems rather than treat as juveniles. Thus, not only do our criminal justice systems disproportionately affect minority and impoverished individuals and communities; they also increasingly affect young people within these communities, blurring once well-established lines between youth and adults.

Together, these data suggest that as the reach of criminal and juvenile justice systems in the U.S. continues to expand, these systems grip certain groups of people in our society—especially racial and ethnic minorities and socio-economically disadvantaged people, and increasingly, women and young people—more tightly than other groups. As these systems have grown, however, they have not necessarily decreased incidents of crime, made our communities safer, or resulted in the return of offenders prepared to be fully integrated

---

[11] Ibid.

[12] The Annie E. Casey Foundation, "2008 KIDS COUNT Message FACT SHEET: A Road Map for Juvenile Justice," The Annie E. Casey Foundation, posted 2009, http://www.aecf.org/KnowledgeCenter/Publications.aspx?pubguid ={29CFCA70-348B-416B-8546-63C297710C5D} (accessed on May 14, 2009).

members of society again.[13] Furthermore, the demographics of people in our prisons and jails do not necessarily correspond with the demographics of people who are violating the law; being poor and black greatly increases the likelihood that a person will be incarcerated.[14]

Due to the repeated failure of criminal and juvenile justice systems to realize their purported goals not only over the last several decades, but at least over the last two centuries, many observers of these systems in the U.S. (as well as the people most directly involved in them as staff or inmates) have questioned the "overall direction and basic legitimacy" of modern punishments, especially incarceration.[15] Sociologist David Garland argues that beneath the more apparent aspects of the current crisis in criminal and juvenile justice systems is a "crisis of self-definition," largely between retributive and rehabilitative ideologies:

> What seems to have come into question now, after the acknowledged failure of the most developed form of correctionalism…is a basic principle of modern punishment—

---

[13] Increases in incarceration rates *did coincide* with drops in crime rates during the 1990s, although, at best, only about 25% of decreasing crime rates could be attributed to locking up offenders. Nevertheless, increases in incarceration rates *also coincided* with *increases* in crime rates in the 1980s. The relationship between incarceration and crime rates is complex, and often the interpretation of this relationship reflects selective interpretation of the data. For a thorough, yet brief, discussion of this relationship—and why throwing more people in jails and prisons will not necessarily result in less crime—see Ryan S. King, Marc Mauer, and Malcolm C. Young, "Incarceration and Crime: A Complex Relationship," The Sentencing Project, posted January 2005, http://www.sentencingproject.org/doc/publications/inc_iandc_complex.pdf (accessed on July 21, 2010). For a more detailed discussion, see Mauer (2006).
[14] Mauer (2006), 177-186.
[15] David C. Garland, *Punishment and Modern Society: A Study in Social Theory* (Chicago: University of Chicago Press, 1990), 6.

namely the presumption that crime and deviance are social problems for which there can be a technical institutional solution.[16]

Garland argues that the radical scope of the crisis is due in part to the lack of a "working ideology" in criminal justice systems, or rather, the layering of multiple, often conflicting, ideologies upon one another throughout the history of these systems that have helped to justify locking more and more people up for longer and longer time periods. These systems have moved away from a commitment to rehabilitation to touting retributive principles of "just deserts," "penal harm," "selective incapacitation," and "humane containment."[17] This identity crisis suggests that addressing high rates of incarceration as well as the disparities that riddle criminal and juvenile justice systems requires reconsideration of basic ideologies and practices of justice. Among the questions that must arise is this process of reconsideration is whether justice is being realized in any meaningful sense. True, people must face the consequences of their crimes. But *what do we understand "justice" to mean, and how can we know if it is being realized? What should the nature of our criminal and juvenile justice systems be? What consequences do our interpretations of justice entail for victims, offenders, and our communities in the wake of crime? How should our ideologies of justice be instituted in practice?*

RESTORATIVE JUSTICE: AN ANSWER TO THE CRISIS?

In the midst of conversations about whether our criminal and juvenile justice systems should operate with rehabilitative or retributive ideologies and practices, a third response to these questions has

---

[16] Ibid., 7.

[17] For further discussion of each of these ideologies, see Garland (1990), 6-7, n. 7.

garnered significant support: restorative justice. This movement has developed over the last four decades in several locations around the world, including South Africa, Brazil, Australia, New Zealand, Canada, Great Britain, and parts of the United States such as Minnesota and Colorado.[18] It includes programs that use practices as wide-ranging as

---

[18] Many restorative justice advocates argue that this movement is rooted in ancient practices of addressing conflict from indigenous peoples throughout the world. This claim is quite common throughout restorative justice literature; an exhaustive citation of everyone who makes it is impossible. For some examples, see Denise Breton and Stephen Lehman, *The Mystic Heart of Justice: Restoring Wholeness in a Broken World* (West Chester, PA: Chrysalis Books, 2001); Daniel W. Van Ness and Karen Heetderks Strong, *Restoring Justice*, 2nd edition (Cincinnati: Anderson Publishing Company, 2002); Gordon Bazemore and Mara Schiff, *Juvenile Justice Reform and Restorative Justice: Building Theory and Policy from Practice* (Portland, OR: Willan Publishing, 2005); Elmar Weitekamp, "The History of Restorative Justice," in *Restorative Juvenile Justice: Repairing the Harm of Youth Crime*, ed. Gordon Bazemore and Lode Walgrave (Monsey, NY: Criminal Justice Press, 1999); and Howard Zehr, *Changing Lenses: A New Focus for Crime and Justice* (Scottdale, PA: Herald Press, 1990) and *The Little Book of Restorative Justice* (Intercourse, PA: Good Books, 2002). Kathleen Daly has offered an important critique of this claim as often reflecting ethnocentrism and as contributing to a restricted history of the movement that fails to attend to the various streams of thought and action that came together in the construction of restorative justice as it is used in the context of Western legal systems whether in North America, Europe, or Australia and New Zealand. See "Restorative Justice: Moving Past the Caricatures" (paper presented at the Institute for Criminology, Sydney Law School, Sydney, Australia, April 1998). I find Daly's history of restorative justice more convincing, and I believe it is important to distinguish between contemporary practices of restorative justice in these contexts and many indigenous justice practices, although in some circumstances, they do overlap. It is because of this view of the history of restorative justice that I maintain that the ethnographic study in chapter four of this text is a unique contribution to discussions of this movement. Of course, sociologists and anthropologists have produced numerous studies of indigenous justice practices that may prove helpful for restorative justice advocates. However, more work must still be

victim-offender mediation and dialogue, truth-and-reconciliation commissions, family-group conferencing, citizen- and neighborhood-accountability boards, and community conferencing as well as hybrids of each of these practices. Advocates of restorative justice argue for the use of these practices to address several levels of conflict, from interpersonal and family quarrels, to community and school disputes, to large-scale clashes that affect entire nations. Although most efforts to implement restorative justice programs have focused on conflicts associated with crime, restorative justice advocates suggest that these practices are useful for addressing a variety of other kinds of conflict as well. The goal of restorative justice in addressing various conflicts is to empower the people with a direct interest in a particular conflict to participate in an inclusive procedure that enables them to come to an agreement about how to "repair the harm" caused by the conflict.

In terms of conflicts associated with crime, advocates maintain that restorative justice represents a "paradigm shift" from the predominant retributive and rehabilitative models of criminal and juvenile justice, which they view as underlying the crises in these systems today. Rehabilitative approaches in our criminal and juvenile justice systems focus on "treatment" of offenders for ailments—whether emotional, mental, social, spiritual, or physical—that contributed to their crime. Rehabilitation views crime as a symptom of a larger disease suffered by an offender, and thus, concludes that the way to put an end to crime is to cure offenders of the various illnesses that led to their wrongdoing. This model of criminal and juvenile justice prevailed in the United States from the times of early penitentiaries and reformatories until about the 1970s, when a retributive model became ascendant. Retributive approaches to crime instead focus on "punishment" of wrongdoers who willfully choose to violate the law, thereby undermining the legitimate authority of the state. In contrast to rehabilitation, retribution views crime as a disruption of a balanced

---

done to understand practices of restorative justice in the context of Western legal systems.

moral order preserved by the state, and thus, concludes that the appropriate response to offenders is punishment proportionate to the severity of the offense.

For restorative justice advocates, these two models of criminal justice have helped create the current crises in our criminal and juvenile justice systems, particularly as retributive justice has become more predominant, resulting in increasingly punitive sentencing. Advocates describe several flaws with rehabilitative and retributive models of criminal justice. First, both attend solely to offenders and ignore the needs of victims and communities affected by crime. Second, while focusing on offenders, neither model enables or requires offenders to take responsibility or to assume accountability for their wrongdoing, although for different reasons. With rehabilitation, offenders are "pathologized" so their behavior cannot be their fault; it is the result of their illness, not their will. Although a retributive framework acknowledges the "free will" of offenders, the stakes of punishment are so high in our current systems that offenders avoid admitting what they did and hide behind lawyers in adversarial courtroom procedures, often feeling that they have actually been victimized by criminal or juvenile justice systems. Finally, restorative justice advocates find the sanctions entailed in rehabilitative and retributive responses to crime to be essentially meaningless. With rehabilitation, sanctions do not correspond to offenses because the real problem is understood to be the underlying ailment, not the offense, which is a mere symptom. As a result, the wrongfulness of an offense is never communicated to an offender. With retribution, sanctions address the violation against the state, and so punishments are abstracted from the actual harm caused to victims and communities. Because these problems with rehabilitative and retributive responses to crime have contributed to our criminal and juvenile justice crises, restorative justice advocates suggest that solutions to these crises depend on "changing lenses"[19] through which we view crime and the people affected by it.

Restorative justice can be defined as "every action that is primarily oriented to doing justice by *repairing the harm* that is caused by crime."[20] Through a restorative lens, advocates view crime primarily as an offense committed by one person against another person that injures specific victims and communities as well as offenders themselves. To realize justice, they suggest that we ought not necessarily to punish or treat offenders; rather we should bring victims, offenders, and community members together in small conferences, circles, or meetings to reach an agreement about the steps needed to repair the harms caused to these stakeholders by a crime. These practices, advocates suggest, generate meaningful responses to wrongdoing, encourage offenders to assume accountability and take responsibility for their actions, address some of the underlying causes of crime, provide victims with satisfaction that they have received justice, and empower communities to transform some of the conflicts in

---

[19] Howard Zehr originated the argument for "changing lenses" with respect to visions of crime and criminal justice in his foundational text, *Changing Lenses: A New Focus for Crime and Justice* (Scottdale, PA: Herald Press, 1990). Gordon Bazemore and Mark Umbreit capture the distinctions made by restorative justice advocates between rehabilitation, retribution, and restoration in juvenile justice systems in their article "Rethinking the Sanctioning Function in Juvenile Court: Retributive or Restorative Responses to Youth Crime," in *Crime and Delinquency* 41.3 (1995): 296-316.

[20] Gordon Bazemore and Lode Walgrave, "Restorative Juvenile Justice: In Search of Fundamentals and an Outline for Systemic Reform," in *Restorative Juvenile Justice: Repairing the Harm of Youth Crime*, ed. Gordon Bazemore and Lode Walgrave (Monsey, NY: Criminal Justice Press, 1999b), 48. I will discuss the sources and strengths of this definition compared to alternatives in chapter three. For now, let it suffice to say that this is not the only definition of restorative justice prevalent within the literature, that this definition is highly disputed, and that some advocates dispute the need for any definition at all.

their midst.[21] On the whole, then, advocates find that restorative justice corrects the flaws of rehabilitative and retributive models of criminal and juvenile justice.

Although each stage in the processes of our criminal and juvenile justice systems—from arrest to re-entry—requires attention in our efforts to reform these systems, the restorative justice movement concentrates primarily (although not exclusively) on sentencing (or, in the cases of minors, adjudicating), the stage in which the legal consequences for an offense are decided. Sentencing is an especially important stage for reform because it informs every subsequent response of criminal and juvenile justice systems to offenders. By emphasizing the sentencing stage, restorative justice advocates suggest that both rehabilitative and retributive sentencing processes and outcomes, especially those involving incarceration, fail to repair the harm caused by crime and to bring about healing for stakeholders. The practices of restorative justice differ dramatically from more common sentencing procedures. Rather than passively relying on judges to deliver sentences, which are increasingly pre-determined by legislated sentencing guidelines, restorative justice participants actively seek consensus on an agreement to repair the harm caused by crime. Participants represent themselves; lawyers play a minimal role in most restorative justice practices. Facilitators foster a non-adversarial environment of collaboration and at least a minimum level of respect. Advocates of restorative justice express hope that by humanizing and personalizing our practices of sentencing and by seeking responses to crime that repair harm, our criminal and juvenile justice systems as a whole will become more humane, personal, and restorative.

Before advocating restorative justice as a solution to crises in our criminal and juvenile justice systems, we ought to explore this movement on its own terms, examining the claims and experiences of

---

[21] Restorative justice has been evaluated by respected criminologists, and it has shown promising results in many of these areas. See chapter three for a more thorough discussion of the evaluation literature of restorative justice.

its advocates and participants. Restorative justice includes a much more diverse and complex set of ideologies and practices than the discussion thus far has indicated. Any recommendations of restorative justice must attend to this diversity and complexity, or else risk presenting either a too idealistic picture of restorative justice or an overly pessimistic view. Indeed all discussions of criminal and juvenile justice reforms should bear in mind Charles Dickens's mixed reviews of 19th-century penitentiaries in the U.S. On the one hand, restorative justice seems "kind, humane, and meant for reformation," to borrow Dickens's words.[22] On the other hand, anyone familiar with the history of criminal and juvenile justice in the United States should rightly ask whether we really "know what [we] are doing"[23]—whether we are fully aware of the consequences of our ideologies and practices of justice. Any attempt to overcome the injustices of our current systems is susceptible to the danger that we will simply recreate the problems that we find so abhorrent now.[24] Supporters of restorative justice must attend to both the strengths and weaknesses of this movement for reform of these systems as it has taken shape as an alternative justice theory and practice. A time in which we have more people under state supervision than any other nation in the world and in which impoverished and minority groups disproportionately bear the brunt of that supervision is no time for casual idealism about the next best thing in criminal and juvenile justice reform. If we are to try to influence these systems, then we must also engage in serious reflection about the possibilities and dangers of any of our recommendations, including

---

[22] Charles Dickens, *American Notes*, introduction by Christopher Lasch (Gloucester, MA: Peter Smith, 1842/1968), 120.

[23] Ibid.

[24] Todd R. Clear helpfully discusses some of the historical challenges of criminal justice reform. His insights are particularly useful for reminding reformers—including restorative justice advocates—to be humble about our assumptions that our reforms will be panacea to all of the problems of criminal justice systems. See "Thoughts About Action and Ideology in Criminal Justice Reform," *Contemporary Justice Review* 7.1 (March 2004): 69-73.

restorative justice. Such reflection requires dialogue with participants in our criminal and juvenile justice systems (both those who work within and those who are constrained by them) as well as with scholars in a variety of disciplines studying these problems, especially sociologists and criminologists, but also, I would suggest, philosophers and scholars of religion.

ETHICAL DISCERNMENT IN RESTORATIVE JUSTICE PRACTICES

In this book, I aim toward a charitable, yet critical, assessment of restorative justice as a criminal and juvenile justice reform based on a comprehensive understanding of this movement. I will draw upon the perspectives of participants in and advocates of restorative justice as well as work from the disciplines of sociology and criminology. Of course, this text will not answer every question about restorative justice; my disciplinary training as a Christian social ethicist will shape the questions that I will attempt to answer and the methods that I will use to answer them. Nevertheless, I believe that the answers generated in this inquiry, because they are informed by an interdisciplinary effort to understand restorative justice, will be of interest not only to Christian social ethicists, but also to other religious and philosophical ethicists, advocates of and participants in restorative justice, criminologists and sociologists, and others concerned with crises in our criminal and juvenile justice systems.

As a Christian social ethicist trained in theology, ethics, and sociology, I am particularly interested in the processes of ethical discernment among participants (regardless of their religious backgrounds) in practices of restorative justice and how these processes reflect their understanding of justice. Because practices of restorative justice differ from the sentencing procedures more commonly used in our criminal and juvenile justice systems, the processes of ethical discernment within them differ as well. By "processes of ethical discernment," I mean processes through which we understand, interpret, and judge moral situations. "Moral situations" are situations in which questions about self, others, and our relationships arise, usually because of some ambiguity, conflict, or disturbance. Ethical discernment requires the use of several faculties, such as reason, emotion, perception, and imagination. Crime is a quintessentially moral situation because it inevitably raises questions about just relationships among victims, offenders, and members of communities affected by wrongdoing. Efforts to realize justice in response to crime are therefore a subset of processes of ethical discernment. Participants in restorative justice practices use various faculties, especially imagination, in their processes of ethical discernment differently than participants in more common sentencing procedures. Advocates of restorative justice tell stories of participants beginning to empathize with one another. They argue that participants begin to see themselves and others in ways other than stereotypical images of victims, offenders, and bystanders in our culture allow. They are creative about possible responses to crime. They see justice from a variety of perspectives in conversation with each other, and they imagine moral situations precipitated by crime in new ways. Participants often come away with new tools to engage broader life challenges. These distinctive characteristics of ethical discernment among participants in restorative justice practices suggest that implementing these practices more broadly to replace or supplement more common sentencing procedures would fundamentally transform the sentencing stage of our criminal and juvenile justice systems.

This insight about the differences of ethical discernment in practices of restorative justice versus more common sentencing procedures provides the basis of the contribution of this book to discussions about crises in criminal and juvenile justice systems. While many other possible responses to these crises also merit study, the strength of the restorative justice movement suggests that this topic deserves more sustained attention. And while many other aspects of restorative justice still require scrutiny, my training as a Christian social ethicist has prepared me to examine particularly the processes of ethical discernment used in restorative justice. Despite my hesitation to recommend any response to our criminal and juvenile justice crises without a great deal of circumspection, I argue that *restorative justice entails processes of ethical discernment that encourage vivid and expansive moral imagining among their participants, which then better enables them to realize justice (defined in terms of equity) in response to particular cases of crime.*

Two terms within this statement require more precise definition to clarify my argument: "justice as equity" and "moral imagination." Two bodies of theoretical literature, namely, Aristotelian virtue ethics and works on moral imagination, provide the basis for my definition of these terms. These sets of literature illuminate the role and meaning of moral imagination in processes of ethical discernment generally, including efforts to realize justice. Their discussions of moral imagination also highlight the importance of this faculty in the processes of ethical discernment specific to restorative justice. In turn, consideration of moral imagination in efforts to realize justice in restorative justice practices may likewise clarify the importance of this faculty in ethical discernment more broadly considered. That is, by placing these two bodies of literature in dialogue with restorative justice in this book, theory and practice may mutually inform and improve each other.

The first body of theoretical literature, Aristotelian virtue ethics, clarifies the meaning of "justice." This concept is certainly difficult to define, and contributors to different sets of theoretical literature— whether philosophical, theological, or legal—would offer differing perspectives on the meaning of justice. Even Aristotle provides varying descriptions of justice depending on the situation. Various traditions would contest that justice is a function of establishing fair procedures; others that it is a matter of outcomes that give each person her due. Among the latter, even more questions arise about whether due should be determined by need or merit or some other factor. In our everyday moral lives, we often draw on all of these conceptions of justice without much worry or reflection about being inconsistent in our treatment of others, and thus in some way unjust. Ideally legal interpretations of justice would agree with philosophical or theological interpretations and common usage, but different concerns often result in varying conceptions that usually, but not always, coincide or overlap. One consequence of this complexity is that no definition will address all of the relevant ways in which we understand justice in ethical or legal theory, let alone in our mundane efforts to realize justice in practice. For my purposes, I therefore find it more interesting and useful to explore more openly different conceptions of how justice can be realized and what the nature of our criminal and juvenile justice systems should be, than to provide an *a priori* definition of justice through which we could evaluate these systems. Aristotle's discussion of justice is especially helpful for this project because he allows for some openness in his definition of justice, while also illuminating the processes of ethical discernment and the faculties that we need in order to exercise this virtue.

Aristotle's description of "justice as equity" will therefore guide my argument, even though his definition speaks more to interpretations in philosophical and theological ethics than to interpretations in legal theory. I also find that his description also speaks to experiences of ethical discernment in our everyday moral lives. According to Aristotle, justice cannot be reduced to strict compliance with the law, or a legalistic interpretation of justice. He argues that law is inherently limited because of its necessary generality, which causes law sometimes to make mistakes or to inspire overly harsh responses to its violation in particular circumstances. While law is essential to any functioning society as a summary of its norms, Aristotle finds that a form of justice higher than strict legal justice requires equity to supplement and correct the law. Although Aristotle's definition of justice as equity is vague at points, he indicates that equity is a virtue that apprehends the just response in situations when the rules set out by legislators fail, while still respecting the intentions of legislators in setting out those rules. Equitable people realize justice by attending to particular details of specific cases that law in its generality tends to obscure. To do so, they engage in certain activities in their processes of ethical discernment: empathizing with others, locating specific incidents within broader contexts, and considering possibilities outside of the strict limitations of legal codes. Efforts to realize justice as equity, therefore, are processes of ethical discernment that draw upon well-developed faculties of emotion, perception, and imagination in addition to reason.

The second body of theoretical literature clarifies the meaning of "moral imagination." It is composed by a diverse group of authors—writing in fields ranging from anthropology to public policy, business to peace-building (often without awareness of each other's work)—who have lamented the reliance of their disciplines in recent decades upon principles and procedures in their respective discernment processes. For the sake of convenience, I will refer to these authors as "moral imagination authors" and this body of literature as "works on moral imagination." These authors suggest that dependence upon general rules has stunted the abilities of participants within their areas of work and study to respond adequately to the nuance and complexity of particular circumstances. In response to this problem, these authors suggest a common answer: the cultivation of moral imagination. Although this body of literature offers several definitions and descriptions of moral imagination, contributors to this conversation commonly hold that this faculty enables human beings to consider a variety of images of both the world as it is and possibilities for what it could become. Furthermore, they hold that vivid and expansive moral imagining improves the abilities of participants in their disciplines to respond more appropriately to specific cases than if they depended on principles and procedures alone, thereby enhancing processes of discernment generally and ethical discernment specifically.

An example may clarify the arguments made in works on moral imagination. I first encountered the term "moral imagination" in John Paul Lederach's *The Moral Imagination: The Art and Soul of Building*

Peace.[25] In this text, Lederach argues that transforming conflict depends upon moral imagination to enliven the skills and techniques associated with the profession of peace-building. He describes "moral imagination" as "the capacity to imagine something rooted in the challenges of the real world yet capable of giving birth to that which does not yet exist."[26] This capacity is necessary, Lederach avers, to bring about the social change envisioned by peace-builders because without it, we cannot comprehend our interrelationship with enemies, embrace the complexity of conflicts, seek creative resolutions, or accept the risk of moving beyond violence into new peaceful, and often vulnerable, relationships. Examples from Lederach's text detail numerous cases in which skills and techniques of peace builders failed until one party in a conflict engaged the moral imagination of the other. About these cases, Lederach writes,

[I]t was not the techniques used by the mediators nor the nature and design of the process that created the shift.... It was not a particular religious tradition: the stories in fact cut across religions. It was not political, economic, or military power in any of the cases. What then, created a moment, a turning point, of such significance that it shifted whole aspects of a violent, protracted setting of conflict? I believe it was the serendipitous appearance of the *moral imagination* in human affairs.[27]

Lederach's description of moral imagination highlights the significance of capacities in addition to reason necessary for addressing moral problems in communities, especially problems of justice, and including problems that arise from conflicts such as those in the wake of crime.

---

[25] John Paul Lederach, *The Moral Imagination: The Art and Soul of Building Peace* (New York: Oxford University Press, 2005).

[26] Ibid., ix.

[27] Ibid., 19. Emphasis in original.

His work reveals that building peace and transforming conflict cannot be processes simply of reasoning together; they must be processes of re-imagining ourselves, others, and our relationships together in ways that appreciate interrelationship, complexity, creativity, and risk. Although Lederach does not discuss restorative justice theories and practices, or even processes of ethical discernment, it seems that the importance of moral imagination for conflict transformation and peace-building at least suggests that this faculty may also be significant for understanding processes of ethical discernment in restorative justice.

Notably, none of the other moral imagination authors writes within disciplines concerning restorative justice or ethical discernment either. Nevertheless, their insights about the need for moral imagination in the discernment processes of various disciplines indicate that consideration of this faculty might improve our understanding of processes of ethical discernment in restorative justice—especially because principle-based and procedural modes of assessing cases have dominated all of these disciplines.

Building upon the contributions of these authors, I define moral imagination as *the cognitive faculty that empowers human beings to create images of our world and its possibilities.* These images are moral because they inform our understandings, interpretations, and judgments of ourselves, others, and our relationships—key factors in ethical discernment. Our images of the world and its possibilities help us to organize and give meaning to our experience; they are a primary component of our knowledge of the world. Moral imagination is schematic in that it helps us to map our world and its possibilities, drawing connections between various experiences. As individuals are formed and sustained through engaging in practices within certain cultural, social, and institutional locations, they use the narratives, metaphors, and symbols around them to create images of their world and what it could become. Because of this schematic character, we can describe different types of moral imagination based on their narrative, metaphorical, and symbolic schemes used for organizing and interpreting experience. An example of types of moral imagination can be found particularly within religious traditions, which cultivate practices from which narratives, metaphors, and symbols arise in participants' interpretations of the world and its possibilities.

The cognitive faculty "moral imagination" entails several activities: entering others' stories and appreciating their perspectives, making connections across a variety of experiences, and considering myriad possibilities for what the world could become. One's moral imagining may be described as more or less vivid and expansive depending upon one's facility with these activities. Types of moral imagination and activities of moral imagining are tightly interwoven. Xenophobic types of moral imagination, for example, may deaden and narrow the moral imagining of individuals who draw upon these images of the world, particularly with respect to encounters with people deemed "other." In turn, vivid and expansive moral imagining in such an encounter may change the narratives, metaphors, and symbols that one uses to understand the other. Because of the interrelationship between types of moral imagination and activities of moral imagining, and because the types of moral imagination we draw upon are influenced by our engagement in practices within certain social, cultural, and institutional locations, the vividness and expansiveness of our moral imagining depends in part upon the types of moral imagination prevalent in the practices of our cultural interactions, social arrangements, and institutional structures.

These two bodies of theoretical literature undergird a central premise of my argument: *the realization of justice as equity requires vivid and expansive moral imagining in our processes of ethical discernment.* Justice as equity demands that we attend to the particular details of specific cases. To do so, we must empathize with others, locate specific incidents within broader contexts, and consider possibilities outside of the strict limitations of legal codes. Similarly, vivid and expansive moral imagining in our processes of ethical discernment requires that we enter into others' stories and appreciate their perspectives, make connections across a variety of experiences, and consider myriad possibilities for what the world could become.

The demands of justice as equity coincide with the activities of vivid and expansive moral imagining.

Since vivid and expansive moral imagining depends in part upon the types of moral imagination that we use to organize and interpret our experience, the realization of justice as equity depends in part upon the types of moral imagination that inform our responses to crime. To improve the realization of justice within sentencing procedures of our criminal and juvenile justice systems, we therefore need interactions, arrangements, and structures that support types of moral imagination that foster vivid and expansive moral imagining among people making sentencing decisions. As participants in restorative justice practices endeavor to understand, interpret, and judge moral situations arising from crime and try to respond justly, they imagine these situations in manners that allow them to appreciate others' stories and perspectives, draw connections across as variety of cases, and consider myriad possibilities for the future. By engaging in these activities of vivid and expansive moral imagining, participants are more able to attend to the particularities of the cases before them, and thus, more able to respond equitably than other sentencing procedures typically allow. This premise, supported by these sets of literature, thus, underlies my thesis: *restorative justice entails processes of ethical discernment that encourage vivid and expansive moral imagining among its participants.* As a result, *participants in restorative justice are better enabled to realize justice as equity in their responses to particular cases of crime.* Insofar as restorative justice can result in more equitable sentencing, it may provide one answer to the complicated crises of our criminal and juvenile justice systems.

METHODS AND OUTLINE

I write as a Christian social ethicist, and I hope that this book will be useful to other ethicists who are interested in processes of ethical discernment and the faculties necessary for it, such as reason, emotion, perception, and imagination; the meaning of justice; crises in our criminal and juvenile justice systems; and the potential of restorative justice as one answer to these crises. But as I have engaged these topics, I have found the work of other disciplines invaluable, particularly criminology and sociology, which offer important resources for understanding the causes of crime, its effects, and methods of its control as well as the impacts of massive criminal and juvenile justice systems on society at large. Furthermore, fair representation of restorative justice demands thorough immersion in the work of its advocates and critics in order to understand the diversity and complexity of this movement. My engagement with this work outside of Christian social ethics has enlarged my understanding of the problems set forth here and should make this text of interest to people outside of my discipline as well.

In addition to valuing interdisciplinarity, I also maintain a methodological commitment to placing theory and practice into dialogue within the discipline of Christian social ethics—a commitment that is embodied in my inclusion of an ethnographic study with five restorative justice programs in Colorado in chapter four. This commitment stems from an epistemological assumption that all knowledge, including moral knowledge, is located within experience. A corollary of this axiom is that any construction of theory must draw upon what human beings actually do, that is, our practices. Many Christian social ethicists and theologians have recently begun to appreciate practices as independent sources of knowledge that should be put into conversation with academic theorizing.[28] Christian

---

[28] Richard Miller, Traci West, and Todd Whitmore have particularly informed my understanding of the incorporation of practical knowledge into theology and ethical theory, and vice versa, and thus, their observations have shaped the construction of this text. Each of these authors emphasizes different justifications for methodology that attends to practices alongside theory. Despite these differences, they also share common perspectives about the relationship between theory and practice, and thus, how we should go about

theologian Rebecca Chopp, drawing on David Kelsey and Craig Dykstra, defines "practice" as "a pattern of meaning and action that is both culturally constructed and individually instantiated." She continues by indicating that practices involve "shared activities of groups of persons that provide meaning and orientation to the world, and that guide action."[29] The practices of the restorative justice programs in Colorado, for example, include the activities associated with a group of facilitators, victims, offenders, and community members seeking consensus on an agreement to repair the harm caused by crime. For Chopp, practices are aspects of the life of people engaged in common activities, and we generate knowledge through participating in practices. If this is the case, then practices must always inform theory in any discipline, including Christian social ethics. For instance, it is insufficient for me merely to read about restorative justice to gain my knowledge of this movement; my methodological commitments compel me to see people practicing restorative justice in order to understand the knowledge they generate in practice more fully. And because our participation in practices cultivates our images of the world and its possibilities (as primary components of our knowledge), my interpretation of moral imagination must not only account for the two bodies of theoretical literature discussed above, but also attend to the experiences of moral imagining among people engaged in processes of ethical discernment.

"doing ethics." See Richard B. Miller, "On Making a Cultural Turn in Religious Ethics," *Journal of Religious Ethics* 33.3 (2005): 409-443; Traci C. West, *Disruptive Christian Ethics: When Racism and Women's Lives Matter* (Louisville: Westminster John Knox Press, 2006); and Todd David Whitmore, "Crossing the Road: The Case for Ethnographic Fieldwork in Christian Ethics," *Journal of the Society of Christian Ethics* 27.2 (2007): 273-294. Furthermore, theologian Rebecca Chopp has particularly influenced my understanding of practices. See especially *Saving Work: Feminist Practices of Theological Education* (Louisville, KY: Westminster John Knox Press, 1995), 15-18.

[29] Chopp (1995), 15.

Theory that remains aloof from practice, therefore, is practically useless to the moral life, which always entails a practical component as we go about our lives in interaction with one another in social, cultural, and institutional contexts. Too often, theory that does not attend adequately to practice cannot generate knowledge that corresponds with human experience or provide the motivation for people to act on the basis of the principles or procedures suggested by it. My musings on Aristotle's interpretation of justice as equity or on definitions of moral imagination do not serve much purpose unless they pertain to actual efforts on the part of real human beings to be equitable or to imagine morally. Practices of restorative justice are one arena in which I can observe and participate in these efforts.

Another corollary to the axiom that all knowledge is located within experience is that all experience, and thus all knowledge, is shaped by our social locations. As discussed above, the same holds true for our moral imaginations. We all tend to create images of the world and how it works (that is, theories) based upon our own limited realms of experience. We generate our theories in response to our encounters within certain cultural interactions, social arrangements, and institutional structures, and our responses depend in large part on where we stand within them. Catholic social ethicist Todd Whitmore argues that "epistemological particularity" inhibits any one person or group of people[30] from generating theory that does not reflect social location. The theories created by one person or group of people from one position will not necessarily account for the empirical realities faced by people in other positions, unless theorists conscientiously work to include alternative perspectives. Likewise, the types of moral imagination readily available to us depend in part upon our social locations. People who are paid to theorize, whether in books or classrooms, tend to occupy relatively privileged positions within their societies. As a result, the choices to overemphasize theory and to

---

[30] Whitmore refers primarily to the membership of the Society of Christian Ethics.

ignore practice as sources of knowledge elevate the perspectives of privileged groups and neglect those of the marginalized.[31]   Whitmore summarizes this problem well: "For the Christian ethicist to only read texts is for him (*sic*) to access only the most powerful people."[32]   It is also for him or her to access a few, relatively limited images of the world and its possibilities.   If Christian social ethicists are to attend to the experiences and perspectives of marginalized people, then we must value practice as much as we value theory.   Because of this setting of priorities, I include and value the voices of participants in restorative justice practices as much as—if not sometimes more than—the literature produced by restorative justice advocates, Aristotelian virtue ethicists, and moral imagination authors.   Without their perspectives, uncovered through participant observation and interviews, this book would provide only partial interpretations of restorative justice and moral imagination.

Despite the limitations of theory alone, overvaluing practice without theoretical reflection runs the risk of failing to recognize that what human beings actually do is often "'disturbed, troubled, ambiguous, confused, full of conflicting tendencies, obscure, etc.'"[33] As human beings go about our ordinary lives, we often do not know the best course of action or we find that long-established patterns of behavior are no longer sufficient in light of new experiences or we recognize that we are failing to bring our visions of what the world could become into reality.   We do things without necessarily knowing

---

[31] Whitmore (2007), 284, 287-290. West concurs with this conclusion. See West (2006), xiv-xviii.

[32] Whitmore (2007), 275. West's first chapter in *Disruptive Christian Ethics* proves Whitmore's point well. She discusses the difference reading Reinhold Niebuhr alongside examining the practices of African-American women activists working in Harlem at the same time that he wrote makes for understanding the effects of community contexts on theories and practices.

[33] Quoting John Dewey. See Steven Fesmire, *John Dewey and Moral Imagination: Pragmatism in Ethics* (Bloomington: University of Indiana Press, 2003), 35.

why or whether our actions will help us to realize our goals. In many conversations with participants in restorative justice practices, I found that they struggled in their processes of ethical discernment and found no clear paths to realizing justice as equity. They were uncertain in some of their moral imagining, unable to find the right images to encapsulate and guide their experiences. In instances of doubt, confusion, interruption, or ambiguity, human beings may turn to theory in order to find clarity about what to do next. Theory can restore some level of predictability, constancy, and stability to our practices. Participants in restorative justice may have found some guidance in theories that discussed the meaning of justice as equity or processes of ethical discernment or restorative images of the world and what it could become.

While attending to practice may help to elevate the perspectives of marginalized people within theory, a non-critical approach to practice risks not only confusion and ambiguity, but also may reinforce demeaning or inhumane patterns of interaction. Racism, sexism, homophobia, and class bias all take shape in our private and social relationships through our practices. Theory can help to correct dangerous practices. Black feminist ethicist Traci West writes, "[T]heory provides critical analysis that reveals subjugating assumptions in social and religious practices. At the same time, attention to concrete practices is necessary to reveal the rehearsal of those subjugating assumptions within the patterns of our everyday lives."[34] In addition to clarifying what to do next, theory—especially ethical theory—can shed light on what we *ought* to do morally. Where the participants that I encountered expressed doubts about whether practices were fraught with difficulties because of racial and ethnic differences, they may have found in theory resources for correcting their practices. Describing the narratives, metaphors, and symbols that compose a racist type of moral imagination, for example, may have better enabled them to recognize when those images infringe upon

---

[34] West (2006), xvii.

restorative justice practices and how to foster those activities of moral imagining that could help them overcome that imagery in their practices.

Because of the limitations of theory and practice alone, and the potential that they have for challenging, illuminating, and correcting each other, the methodology of ethics is best conceived in terms of putting theory and practice in what West calls "a fluid conversation": "Theory needs practice in order to be authentic, relevant, and truthful. Practice needs theory so that practices might be fully comprehended."[35] In order for this conversation to be most fruitful, we must envision theory and practice as equal contributors to knowledge. Even when theorists describe practices within their writing, frequently they use them as mere case studies, illustrations, or examples of what they would have said anyway, regardless of what people actually do. Or if ethicists mention theory in their discussion of practices, they often do so "to add prestige"[36] to their arguments. By placing theory and practice in conversation, ethicists must be open to the possibility that either one might challenge, illuminate, or correct the other; only with this openness can we improve either theory or practice.

In sum, I assume first that all knowledge is located within experience. Based upon this assumption, the methodology of ethics entails placing theory and practice in dialogue that involves mutual critique so that theory and practice can challenge, illuminate, and correct each other. This methodology not only permits, but values and demands the inclusion of perspectives other than those of ethical theorists. Furthermore, it seeks the rectification of subjugating, demeaning, and inhumane practices. In order to understand the broader value of principles, virtues, and goals, ethicists must be capable of readily appreciating the stories and perspectives of diverse groups of people trying to discern the right or the good in particular situations. We must be skilled at making connections across various experiences

---

[35] Ibid.

[36] Miller (2005), 417.

and recognizing the morally salient features of each and how they relate to each other. We must be able to use theory as a tool for critique of imperfect practices, as well as capable of seeing ways in which particular practices create the knowledge that informs our theories. And ethicists must be able to generate diverse and creative visions of the good if we ever hope to change the world for the better. The methodology of ethicists is enhanced both by being aware of the types of moral imagination used in practice by participants in various processes of ethical discernment and by developing our own capacities to imagine morally in vivid and expansive ways.

A methodology that puts theory and practice into dialogue structures my argument as a whole—particularly its conversation among restorative justice advocates and participants, works of moral imagination authors, and Aristotelian virtue ethics. Chapter two, entitled "Justice as Equity and Moral Imagining," draws on the two bodies of theoretical literature discussed above to construct a framework for understanding the role moral imagination plays in ethical discernment generally and efforts to realize justice specifically. After describing moral imagination in detail, I draw Aristotelian virtue ethics and works on moral imagination together to establish my premise that the realization of justice as equity requires vivid and expansive moral imagining in our processes of ethical discernment.

From this theoretical framework, I explore restorative justice in chapters three and four, especially concentrating on the relationship between justice as equity and moral imagination among it advocates and participants. Chapter three, "Restorative Moral Imagination," examines the content of a "restorative moral imagination" as presented by advocates in seminal works of restorative justice literature. Through this description, it will become apparent that advocates believe that drawing on the schemes of restorative moral imagination encourages participants to enter into others' stories and appreciate their perspectives, to draw connections across several cases, and to consider myriad possibilities of what the world could become. By encouraging these activities, restorative justice practices have the potential of vivifying and expanding the moral imagining of participants, and thus better enabling them to realize justice as equity in their processes of ethical discernment than either retributive or rehabilitative moral imaginations could allow.

Chapter four, "Moral Imagining in Restorative Justice Practices," shifts from the arguments of advocates in restorative justice literature to look at the experiences of participants in restorative justice practices. Over the course of about eighteen months,[37] I conducted an ethnographic study of restorative justice programs in five counties in Colorado. Using methods of participant-observation, semi-structured interviewing, and examination of primary documents such as training manuals, case records, and program evaluations given to me by program coordinators, I consider in this chapter, first, how participants in restorative justice use and negotiate the types of moral imagination described by restorative justice advocates; second, whether this use and negotiation connects to activities of vivid and expansive moral imagining; and third, if these activities then better enable participants to realize justice as equity in the processes of ethical discernment in response to particular cases.

My approach throughout the ethnographic study is appreciative, rather than evaluative, in the sense that I strive "to gain an understanding of social action *in context* based on a non-judgmental, descriptive account of events, processes, and theories of participation in the terms and frame of reference of those applying them."[38] That is, I am less concerned, for example, with reproaching participants as non-restorative for occasionally drawing on retributive or rehabilitative imagery than with trying to grasp how they understand the relationships among retribution, rehabilitation, and restoration in response to

---

[37] I traveled to Colorado for research between January and June 2007, between November 2007 and March 2008, and between July and August 2008.

[38] Gordon Bazemore and Mara Schiff, *Juvenile Justice Reform and Restorative Justice: Building Theory and Policy from Practice* (Portland, OR: Willan Publishing, 2005), 138. Emphasis in original.

particular cases. And I am more interested in understanding why they sometimes struggle with activities of moral imagining than in deeming them failures because they sometimes do not enter fully to another's story or because their specific responses at times lacked creativity. By taking an appreciative stance, I allow the complexity of putting restorative justice into practice to come to light and value the participants of this study as people who are trying in good faith to realize justice as equity. Their experiences in many ways illuminate, challenge, and correct the interpretations of the theoretical literature presented in previous chapters on processes of ethical discernment, the faculty of moral imagination, crises in criminal and juvenile justice systems, and the potential of restorative justice to realize justice as equity. In turn, examining their experiences in light of these theories may indicate ways in which their practices may be improved.

In my use of qualitative methods, I am borrowing from the disciplines of sociology and criminology, but I am not necessarily trying to meet their standards of evidence for the hypotheses that I make. As a Christian social ethicist, I cannot claim that the data I collected through these methods are either representative or generalizable. I did not use an experimental model through which I could compare experiences of participants in more common sentencing procedures with those of participants in restorative justice. I did, however, draw on sampling methods used in other disciplines, such as generating a snowball sample with multiple starts, which enabled me to access a wide range of participants in restorative justice practices. While the sample of programs, conferences, and participants in this study does not represent all restorative justice programs, conferences, and participants, I find that these methods allowed me to encounter people with various experiences, with both criminal and juvenile justice systems and restorative justice, whose voices are not generally heard and appreciated in much of the literature on these topics. Using the tools of other disciplines thus helped me to address some of my methodological commitments as a Christian social ethicist to put theory and practice into dialogue as well as my normative commitments to include a diverse set of perspectives aside from those of other ethicists, or even myself. To say that my data are not representative, generalizable, or comparative, therefore, is not to say that this study does not provide insights into the topics discussed here. Rather I find that my observations of these programs, conferences, and participants at least suggest that processes of ethical discernment in restorative justice encourage vivid and expansive moral imagining in practice.

The last chapter, "The Moral Imagination of Restorative Justice," draws out the most significant contributions of this discussion from the previous four chapters and articulates a qualified hope in restorative justice as a response to our criminal and juvenile justice crises. Placing theory and practice in dialogue, I seek to integrate the insights of restorative justice advocates and participants, Aristotelian virtue ethicists, and moral imagination authors. I conclude that because restorative justice practices encourage activities of vivid and expansive moral imagining, they better enable participants to realize justice as equity in their processes of ethical discernment. I also offer reflections on the cultural, social, and institutional shifts necessary to support the implementation of restorative justice in criminal and juvenile justice systems, including reassessment of the relationships among restoration, rehabilitation, and retribution. Together these reflections lead me to a qualified hope in restorative justice for offering space for vivid and expansive moral imagining that can foster justice as equity in order to respond to the crisis in our criminal and juvenile justice systems.

CHAPTER 2

Justice as Equity and Moral Imagining

A warning to the reader: if we were to look over the bulk of Western moral philosophy and theology, we might conclude that introducing imagination into discussions of ethical discernment generally, and of efforts to realize justice specifically, would be gravely misguided. Moral imagination has never been a favorite topic in Western thought. Although the towering philosopher Immanuel Kant, for example, developed a theory of imagination as the mental faculty that provides spatial, temporal, and categorical coherence to our empirical experience, he denied a role for imagination in morality, which resides for him in the realm of pure reason. Imagination, it seems, was too contaminated with the empirical for it to be moral, and it certainly could not help realize justice.[39] Kant both carried forth and

---

[39] Much of Kant's moral philosophy can be found in *Groundwork of the Metaphysics of Morals*, first published in 1785, in which Kant argues for a need to focus upon the rational aspects of morality based on *a priori* knowledge and pure reason in exclusion of the empirical aspects of morality. See the work edited and translated by Mary Gregor (Cambridge: Cambridge University Press, 1998). Iris Murdoch offers an interesting discussion of imagination in Kant's philosophy, particularly the role that imagination *does not* play in his

helped transmit a predominant tradition of ignoring imagination in Western moral philosophy, particularly in deontological and consequentialist thinking.[40]   Since Kant's contributions, in Hide

---

moral philosophy. See "Imagination," in *Metaphysics as a Guide to Morals* (New York: Penguin Books, 1992). For other discussions of Kant's theory of imagination, see James Engell, *The Creative Imagination: Enlightenment to Romanticism* (Cambridge, MA: Harvard University Press, 1981), chapter 10; Hide Ishiguro, "Imagination," in *British Analytical Philosophy*, ed. Bernard Williams and Alan Montefiore (London: Routledge, 1966); P.F. Strawson, "Imagination and Perception," in *Experience and Theory*, ed. Lawrence Foster and J.W. Swanson (Amherst: University of Massachusetts Press, 1970), 31-54; Mary Warnock, *Imagination* (Berkeley: University of California Press, 1976); and Alan White, *The Language of Imagination* (Oxford: Blackwell, 1990). For a dissenting view of Kant's theory of imagination, see Bernard Freydberg, *Imagination in Kant's Critique of Practical Reason* (Bloomington: Indiana University Press, 2005). Freydberg argues that although Kant never mentions imagination in the *Critique of Practical Reason* and he explicitly eschews imagination in his discussion of the categorical imperative, he still saw an indispensable role for imagination to play in the moral life.

[40] Summarizing the history of the general concept of imagination in philosophical thought is a complicated endeavor that must span both a wide stretch of Western history and a broad array of philosophical schools from Aristotelianism to 20th-century developments in phenomenology. This history can be pieced together somewhat with a collection of texts that explore various philosophical treatments of imagination. On Aristotle, see Nancy Sherman, *The Fabric of Character: Aristotle's Theory of Virtue* (Oxford: Clarendon Press, 1989). White (1990) also discusses imagination in Aristotle's thought, but he further explores the development of this concept in later authors, including Hume, Kant, Sartre, Ryle, and Wittgenstein. For more discussion of these later figures, see Ishiguro (1966), Strawson (1970), and Warnock (1976). Several authors deal with the concept of imagination in Anglo-American thought from the 16th century onwards. See Engell (1981); Gertrude Himmelfarb, *Poverty and Compassion: The Moral Imagination of the Late Victorians* (New York: Alfred A. Knopf, 1991) and *The Moral Imagination: From Edmund Burke to Lionel Trilling* (Chicago: Ivan R. Doe, 2006); Thomas McFarland, *Originality and Imagination* (Baltimore: The John Hopkins

Ishiguro's words, moral imagination has been "an ugly duckling" in the philosophical world.[41] Adjectives applied to imagination by various scholars in recent years include "mysterious,"[42] "ambiguous" and "nonrational,"[43] "elusive and private,"[44] "powerful, complex, and subtle,"[45] and "a knot of contradictions."[46] Whereas most people would often prefer black-and-white answers to ethical questions, especially questions of justice, these words suggest that imagination is too gray to help us face the moral problems of a broken world. The general conclusion in Western thought has been that reason, not imagination (or any other cognitive faculty, such as emotion or perception), ought to be our primary (if not sole) guide in processes of ethical discernment and our efforts to realize justice.

Given this warning, this chapter defies the bulk of Western thought by proposing that imagination plays a major role in ethical discernment generally and efforts to realize justice specifically. I argue that the realization of justice requires expansive and vivid moral imagining in our processes of ethical discernment, a premise that I introduced in chapter one. The argument proceeds in four parts, beginning with a return to Aristotle, who suggests that equity is necessary to supplement

---

University Press, 1985); and Christopher Tilmouth, *Passion's Triumph over Reason: A History of the Moral Imagination from Spenser to Rochester* (Oxford: Oxford University Press, 2007). For a discussion of imagination in the history of Christian theology, see Philip S. Keane, *Christian Ethics and Imagination* (New York: Paulist Press, 1984).

[41] Ishiguro (1966), 153.

[42] McFarland (1985), xiii.

[43] Ishiguro (1966), 153.

[44] Ibid., 177.

[45] Engell (1981), 136.

[46] Paul Ricoeur, "Imagination in Discourse and in Action," in *Rethinking Imagination: Culture and Creativity*, ed. Gillian Robinson and John Rundell (New York: Routledge, 1994), 119-120.

and correct strict legal justice.[47] Based upon Aristotle's philosophy, I then explore the work of recent virtue ethicists, especially Nancy Sherman and Martha Nussbaum,[48] who have argued that we must attend to the particulars of cases through imagination, perception, and emotion in addition to reason if we are to be equitable, although these authors often neglect imagination in comparison with emotion, perception, and reason. We must then move beyond Aristotelian virtue ethicists to appreciate moral imagination fully in processes of ethical discernment and efforts to realize justice as equity. Thirdly, I turn to recent works on moral imagination to explore further the role of this faculty in processes of ethical discernment generally and efforts to realize justice as equity specifically. Finally, I bring these two bodies of theoretical literature together to establish the underlying premise of this text: being equitable depends in large part on vivid and expansive moral imagining in our processes of ethical discernment. To reach this conclusion, let us begin by considering Aristotle's interpretation of justice.

---

[47] For my use of Aristotle, I depend upon *The Basic Works of Aristotle*, trans. and ed. Richard McKeon (New York: Modern Library Classics, 2001). In following citations, I refer to this translation as *Nicomachean Ethics* or *Rhetoric*.

[48] I follow Pamela M. Hall here in rejecting the view that "there is some trans-historical project which is an ethics of character." See "Limits of the Story: Tragedy in Recent Virtue Ethics," in *Studies in Christian Ethics* 17.3 (2004), 1, footnote 1. I do not want to suggest a unified group of theological and philosophical ethicists who share the same interpretation of virtues and their roles in the moral life. Rather when speaking of recent virtue ethics, I refer to a common interest among several theological and philosophical ethicists since the mid-20th century in the significance of virtues. These ethicists typically turn to Platonic or Aristotelian interpretations of virtue, although they do not often agree about various issues surrounding the virtues such as the unity and hierarchy of the virtues, the formation of character, or the nature of moral luck. For a helpful selection of essays in virtue ethics, see Roger Crisp and Michael Slote, eds., *Virtue Ethics* (Oxford: Oxford University Press, 1997).

JUSTICE AS EQUITY

Understanding the role of moral imagination in efforts to realize justice as equity requires first understanding what justice involves. For the purposes of this text, I limit the discussion to just responses to violations of the law, or criminal justice, and I discuss these responses largely from the perspective of ethical, rather than legal, theory. I do not suppose that other forms of justice (for example, distributive or commutative justice) are unrelated to criminal justice. Quite the contrary: the distribution of goods and resources in our communities and societies and the processes by which we accomplish those distributions often impact crime, its causes and effects, and our understanding of just responses to it.[49] But the precise connections

---

[49] As previously mentioned, defining "justice" is a complex affair. A classical definition is *suum cuique*, or giving each person his or her due. Of course, determining what a person is due and why is one of the basic problems of ethics, and several different types of justice offer answers. One way to determine due is by using a fair procedure to which all parties in a question of justice can freely agree. An example of this model is John Rawls's use of the "original position" in constructing fundamental principles of justice. Rawls assumes that by entering into the original position, people deliberating about these principles can take on an impartial point of view that will enable them to realize fair outcomes in the ordering of society. See John Rawls, *A Theory of Justice: Original Edition* (Cambridge, MA: The Belknap Press of Harvard University, 1973). Procedural justice assumes that whatever the outcome, the decision resulting from a fair procedure is just. This sort of justice is relevant to questions of criminal justice because it is the basis for procedures such as trial-by-jury. All parties presumably agree before a jury trial that if everyone follows the proper procedures, then whatever the jury decides is just. Commutative justice is one type of procedural justice that uses contracts as the procedure for determining justice. If all parties agree that a contract is fair and they enter into it freely, then justice demands that all parties abide by the terms of the agreement. In contrast to procedural and commutative justice, distributive justice determines what is due to someone based upon a fair allocation of goods throughout society. It therefore focuses on outcomes rather

between these different forms of justice are not the focus of my argument here.

In common usage, criminal justice is often equated with retribution, where appropriate levels of punishment for particular crimes are enumerated in the law. This interpretation of justice—I will call it a "legalistic interpretation" or "strict legal justice"—depends on a few, somewhat dubious assumptions. It assumes, first of all, that justice requires the return to offenders of pain for pain, harm for harm in order to reinstate some sort of moral balance that the offense has upset. The task of law is to restore the order that balances the forces of good and right against those of evil and wrong. Law does so by assigning to each category of offense the correct amount of punishment, and judges are the only people with the legitimate power to discern the appropriate application of the law. Strict legal justice also assumes that the particulars of every case readily fit into the categories outlined in law and that the law provides a comprehensive, universal, and accurate accounting of all types of wrongdoing. This

---

than procedures in realizing justice. The factors that determine the fairness of an allocation, however, vary. Some people, for example, have argued that each person is due whatever would satisfy their basic *needs*. See Martha C. Nussbaum and Amartya Sen, eds., *The Quality of Life* (Oxford: Clarendon Press, 1993). Others have argued that we serve justice when we give each person what she *deserves* based upon her merits that she has earned through skill, hard work, or some other achievement. Robert Nozick, in *Anarchy, State, and Utopia* (Oxford: Blackwell Publishers, 1978), exemplifies this position. At different points, each of these arguments appropriately addresses questions of justice, although they may come into conflict. Finally, criminal justice usually concerns what someone is due when he or she violates the law. As the discussion below will demonstrate, determining what is criminal and what is due when someone commits a crime is a complex issue involving the negotiation of ideals of retribution, rehabilitation, and restoration. Nevertheless, each of these types of justice is relevant in different circumstances; they overlap with each other; and the realization of justice of one type often depends upon the realization of justice of the other types.

interpretation abides with a black-and-white understanding of the moral world, admitting little or no room for the nuance of a grayscale. Insofar as the law effectively reflects the balance of the moral order, justice is served by the strict application of the law in all cases regardless of the particular characteristics of the offense, offender, victims, or communities in which the crime took place. The just response to crime is that which is enumerated in the law; deviations from the law are patently unjust.[50]

If this interpretation is a correct assessment of the meaning of justice, it seems that moral imagination has little or nothing to do with justice (although I believe that, even here, moral imagining plays its part, even if often deadened and narrowed by certain legal restrictions). Being just can be reduced to the seemingly "mechanical application of an abstract general rule to a concrete situation."[51] The primary faculty involved in delivering this form of justice is reason, and justice is best served if reason is not disturbed by the sway of other faculties such as perception, emotion, and especially imagination. These other faculties may cause reason to become biased by passion, and according to this interpretation, justice is best served when "law is intelligence without desire"[52] so that it may be meted out impartially. The best judges then

---

[50] Andrew Skotnicki presents a view similar to this portrayal of strict legal justice in his article, "How is Justice Restored?" See especially pp. 195-197, 201-203. He argues that justice must be grounded in an ontological foundation, rather than merely a procedural foundation. An ontological foundation, Skotnicki maintains, requires the pre-eminent agency of the state in "a necessary role in the processes of trial, sentencing, and remission" (195). He locates the ontological foundation within the Catholic tradition of natural law. In his view, punishment of violations of the law is required by justice to regain "the moral 'equilibrium'" (196).

[51] Constantine Georgiadis, "Equitable and Equity in Aristotle," in *Justice, Law, and Method in Plato and Aristotle*, ed. Spiro Panagiotou (Edmonton, Alberta: Academic Printing and Publishing, 1987), 167.

[52] Sherman (1989), 14. See also Martha Nussbaum's discussion of the role of emotions in criminal sentencing procedures in *Upheavals of Thought: The*

are those who are most reasonable in their strict application of the law—not the most perceptive, emotive, or imaginative. Their reasoning is supposedly unbiased by the irrelevant particulars of cases. Instead they assume a distanced and neutral view of how to apply the law in all circumstances.

Of course, I have painted this interpretation of justice in broad strokes that may miss the nuanced presentations of some of its advocates. Despite the simplicity of my description, I do not believe that I have misrepresented the basic tenets of this interpretation or its presence in our culture. A modern example of this interpretation of justice can be found in the use of sentencing guidelines, which provide charts and logarithmic calculations that equate the severity of a crime, the prior record of an offender, and aggravating or mitigating circumstances with a sentencing range that determines the proper allotment of punishment for each offender, usually in terms of months to be served on probation or in prison.[53] Originally formulated in the United States in the 1980s, sentencing guidelines were legislative efforts to decrease disparities in sentencing. Disparities could be the result either of judges differing from each other in the severity of the sanctions they impose on offenders or of individual judges giving unequal punishments to offenders for the same types of crime based upon any number of prejudices, particularly racial and ethnic discrimination.

Intelligence of Emotions (New York: Cambridge University Press, 2001), 441-453.

[53] For more detailed descriptions of sentencing guidelines, see Richard S. Frase, "State Sentencing Guidelines: Diversity, Consensus, and Unresolved Policy Issues," *Columbia Law Review* 105.4 (2005): 1190-1232; Jennifer F. Reinganum, "Sentencing Guidelines, Judicial Discretion, and Plea Bargaining," *The RAND Journal of Economics* 31.1 (2000): 62-81; and Max M. Schazenbach and Emerson H. Tiller, "Reviewing the Sentencing Guidelines: Judicial Politics, Empirical Evidence, and Reform," *The University of Chicago Law Review* 75.2 (2008): 715-760.

Undoubtedly, these disparities are a danger with judicial discretion. These dangers became especially apparent in the wake of the civil rights movement and prisoners' right movements in the 1960s and 1970s, which revealed gross injustices of harsh treatment of African Americans versus whites in U.S. judicial systems. In practice, however, many sentencing guidelines have been found to reify aspects of unequal treatment in the law (for example, with different sentences for powder and crack cocaine possession and distribution), rather than to correct the disparities found among judges. Furthermore, in some jurisdictions, they seem to result in harsher sentences and larger prison populations.[54] Apart from these problems, sentencing guidelines also restrict possibilities for judges to offer alternatives when the law would seem mistaken or overly harsh in particular cases.[55] In some instances, sentencing guidelines and their outcomes might seem good, or at least, acceptable compared to judges in different jurisdictions varying in sentencing severity or individual judges allowing prejudices to sway

---

[54] Regarding the relationship between sentencing guidelines and prison populations, see Albert W. Alschuler, "The Failure of Sentencing Guidelines: A Plea for Less Aggregation," *The University of Chicago Law Review* 58.3 (1991): 901-951; Thomas B. Marvell, "Sentencing Guidelines and Prison Population Growth," *The Journal of Criminal Law and Criminology* 85.3 (1995): 696-709; Norval Morris and Michael Tonry, *Between Prison and Probation: Intermediate Punishments in a Rational Sentencing System* (New York: Oxford University Press, 1990), 31-35; and Michael Tonry, "Intermediate Sanctions in Sentencing Guidelines," *Crime and Justice* 23 (1998): 199-253. Relevant U.S. Supreme Court decisions about sentencing guidelines include *Apprendi v. New Jersey (2000)*, *United States v. Booker (2005)*, and *Cunningham v. California (2007)*. For a fascinating, but frustrating, example of an effort to find the moral balance supposedly upheld by sentencing guidelines, see *Koon v. United States (1996)*.

[55] Although federal sentencing guidelines established in the Sentencing Reform Act of 1984 were initially "mandatory," the U.S. Supreme Court decision in *U.S. v. Booker (2005)* made them "advisory." If a judge departs from the guidelines, however, he or she must justify the decision in open court or in a written opinion. The departure is then reviewed by appellate courts.

their discernment. But in other instances, sentencing guidelines may deaden and narrow judges' opportunities to imagine morally in response to pitfalls in the law that would result in mistakes or excessive harshness.[56]

Even though a legalistic interpretation of justice is common in our culture and its antecedents in Western thought can be traced all the way back to ancient Greece,[57] it suffers from some inherent flaws. I will name only two. First, a legalistic interpretation of justice presupposes a faulty model of ethical discernment in which reason reigns without influence from other faculties such as perception, emotion, and imagination. However, as I will demonstrate in more detail below, processes of ethical discernment always require more than sound reasoning. We cannot begin to know how to apply general rules or laws to particular situations without accurate perception, appropriate emotion, and vivid and expansive moral imagining as well. By trying

---

[56] Former U.S. Supreme Court Chief Justice William Rehnquist, among other judges, complained about the increasing legislative restrictions placed upon federal judges who would "depart downward" from the requirements of sentencing guidelines. See Linda Greenhouse, "Chief Justice Attacks as Law as Infringing on Judges," *New York Times,* January 1, 2004; also, Lynette Clemetson, "Judges Look to New Congress for Changes in Mandatory Sentencing Laws," *New York Times,* January 9, 2007. Max Schazenbach and Emerson Tiller have observed that judicial hostility to sentencing guidelines is apparent not only in public statements, but also in survey data and the speed of retirement among federal judges. They note that a survey conducted by the Federal Judicial Center in 1996 found that almost three-quarters of trial judges and over two thirds of appellate judges believed that mandatory federal guidelines are unnecessary. Furthermore, federal judges now retire about two-and-a-half years earlier than they had prior to the passing of the Sentencing Reform Act of 1984, which instituted the United States Sentencing Guidelines. See Schazenbach and Tiller (2008), 715-717.

[57] Martha Nussbaum discusses this interpretation of justice as it appears in the writings of 6th-century B.C.E. philosopher Anaximander. See Nussbaum (1999), 157-159. I do not wish to imply here that ancient Greeks used anything like modern sentencing guidelines.

to exclude these faculties, practices that fit within a legalistic interpretation of justice tend to elide central aspects of the moral life.

The second problem with this interpretation is that it denies inherent limitations of law, and so fails to account adequately for the complexities of human life. Legal codes cannot attend to the particulars of all possible cases. They will inevitably miss some possibilities and in some cases, will get things wrong because of the necessary generality of law. Laws are mere summaries—even if indispensable summaries—of particular societies' assessments of right and wrong, good and evil. While law is necessary and in most instances, good, justice requires more than the mechanical application of the law according to the mandates of reason, more than charts and logarithmic calculations. It demands discernment of the intent of the law in concrete situations in light of particular circumstances, a process that entails the use of faculties such as perception, emotion, and imagination in addition to reason.

Fortunately, an alternative—but also common and ancient—interpretation of justice likewise suggests that justice in its fullest sense reaches beyond strict legal justice. In his discussion of law, justice, and equity, Aristotle gives an interpretation of justice that offers a fuller model of ethical discernment and gives a better account for the complexities of human life. He recognizes the limitations of law and the need for discretion in its application as well as the need for faculties in addition to reason in processes of ethical discernment and efforts to realize justice. The virtue of equity, he argues, provides resources for discerning what ought to be done when law fails to address the particular circumstances of concrete situations.[58]

---

[58] Aristotle's understanding of equity should be distinguished from sociological and psychological theories of equity that began to gain attention in the 1960s and 1970s. For introductions to these theories, see Michael R. Carrell and John E. Dittrich, "Equity Theory: The Recent Literature, Methodological Considerations, and New Directions," *The Academy of Management Review* 3.2 (1978): 202-210; Karen S. Cook and Karen A. Hegtvedt, "Distributive Justice,

Aristotle offers perhaps the earliest critique of a legalistic interpretation of justice as the deliverance of retribution against wrongdoers according to the exact stipulations of the law. To be clear, though, he does not entirely reject retributive responses to crime, as is apparent in his discussion of "corrective justice" or "rectificatory justice" in the *Nicomachean Ethics*, Book V, Chapter 4.[59] Corrective justice, in contrast with distributive justice (Chapter 3), is concerned

---

Equity, and Equality," *Annual Review of Sociology* 9 (1983): 217-241; Gerald S. Leventhal, "What Should Be Done with Equity Theory?: New Approaches to the Study of Fairness in Social Relationships," in *Social Exchange: Advances in Theory and Research*, ed. Kenneth J. Gergen, Martin S. Greenberg, and Richard H. Willis (New York: Plenum Press, 1980): 27-55; and Elaine Walster, G. William Walster, and Ellen Berscheid, *Equity: Theory and Research* (Boston: Allyn and Bacon, 1978). Theories of equity in these disciplines concern fairness in the distribution of rewards and resources (and correlatively, punishments) in social relationships, from one-on-one exchanges between two individuals to large-scale, society-wide allocations. The underlying assumption of these theories is that "human beings believe that rewards and punishments should be distributed in accordance with recipients' inputs or contributions" (Leventhal, 28). As a result, the study of equity involves determining outcomes for each participant in a distribution that are proportional to their inputs, and examining reasons for inequity (for example, gender or racial discrimination) and the effects on relationships when outcomes and inputs are not proportional. Aristotle's conception of equity differs on several points from this understanding, but only two bear mentioning here. First, sociological and psychological theories of equity focus on merit as the primary determinant of justice. Aristotle's understanding of equity conscientiously avoids associating this higher form of justice with merit alone, as the following paragraph demonstrates. Second, equity theory concentrates on the final distribution and its effects, and not procedures through which distributions are attained. For Aristotle, the process of ethical discernment in which an individual engages to perceive the limitations of the law in a particular case are fundamental to understanding equity as a virtue, not merely an adjective for certain distributions. Both the process and the decision need to be equitable in Aristotle's thought.

[59] See *Nicomachean Ethics*, 1131b, 25-1132b, 20.

with rectifying unequal transactions between two parties in which one party has taken unfair advantage of the other. The task of corrective justice is to remove the ill-gotten gain from the wrongdoer and to return it to the injured party: "The judge tries to equalize things by means of the penalty, taking away from the gain of the assailant."[60] Although this discussion of corrective or rectificatory justice seems to advocate some sense of retribution, in Chapter 5, Aristotle rejects a view of justice that would hold that "Should a man suffer what he did, right justice would be done."[61] He proceeds to describe situations in which corrective justice and this form of "reciprocity" do not coincide and to suggest that the harmony of the city depends not upon "precisely equal return,"[62] but upon return mitigated or qualified by "grace."[63] So Aristotle in part agrees that corrective justice requires the restoration of balance between right and wrong, good and evil, but he also in part finds that a draconian interpretation of this balance may result in discord. Right justice, according to Aristotle, cannot be reduced to inflicting upon a wrongdoer the suffering of what he did.

The tenth chapter of the *Nicomachean Ethics*, Book V expands upon this criticism of a legalistic interpretation of justice. Here Aristotle discusses the relationship between justice and equity. He introduces the chapter with a quandary arising in Platonic philosophy. In *The Laws*, Plato holds, "Equity and forgiveness, whenever they are applied, are always enfeeblements of the perfection and exactness that belong to strict justice."[64] This Platonic interpretation of justice shares

---

[60] Ibid., 1132a, 8-10.

[61] Aristotle here quotes "the justice of Rhadamanthus." Ibid., 1132b, 27.

[62] Ibid., 1132b, 34.

[63] Ibid., 1133a, 1-4. With his emphasis on grace rather than precisely equal return, Aristotle presents an interpretation of equity that differs from the emphasis on proportionally equal inputs and outcomes in modern sociological and psychological equity theories.

[64] See *The Laws of Plato*, trans. Thomas L. Pangle (Chicago: The University of Chicago Press, 1980), 757e. For discussion of connections between Aristotle's discussion of justice and equity and Plato, see Georgiadis (1987), 159-161.

much in common with a legalistic interpretation.[65] Aristotle challenges the Platonic view by describing a paradox in any view that puts equity and justice in opposition:

> For on examination they appear neither to be absolutely the same nor generically different; and while we sometimes praise what is equitable and the equitable man...at other times, when we reason it out, it seems strange if the equitable, being something different from the just, is yet praiseworthy; for either the just or the equitable is not good, if they are different; or, if both are good, they are the same.[66]

The problem for Aristotle is that if both justice and equity deserve praise (and both receive praise in common parlance), then they must be the same thing. But equity often departs from the demands of strict legal justice, so they must actually be different and only one can truly deserve its praise. Aristotle's answer to this quandary is that strict legal

---

[65] In the section of *The Laws* where the previous quotation occurs, Plato does not discuss recompense for wrongdoing (Aristotle's concept of corrective justice). Rather his argument resembles Aristotle's discussion of distributive justice and the proportionate allotment of goods according to the varying states of members of the city. Cf. *The Laws*, 756e-758a and *Nicomachean Ethics*, 1131a, 10-1131b, 24. Although Plato is concerned here with distributive justice instead of some version of corrective or rectificatory justice, his interpretation of justice in this section is similar to the interpretation above that the laws of the city ought to uphold some sort of natural (or even, cosmic; see reference to Zeus in 757b) balance among its members and that this balance best approximates justice. Most of Plato's discussion in *The Laws* of the need for recompense for wrongdoing comes in Book X (884a-910d). He enumerates several crimes, all of which disturb the natural balance of good against evil in the city, and suggests appropriate punishments that would restore the balance. Particularly in this section, Plato's allegiance with a legalistic interpretation of justice becomes apparent.

[66] *Nicomachean Ethics*, 1137a, 33-1137b, 4.

justice is not justice itself and that equity must supplement and correct the law in order to realize the fullest sense of justice: "Hence the equitable is just, and better than one kind of justice [that is, legal justice]—not better than absolute justice but better than the error that arises from the absoluteness of the statement [of the law]."[67]

Someone who held to a legalistic interpretation of justice might respond to Aristotle by claiming that law needs no supplement or correction to achieve absolute justice provided that it effectively reflects the balance of the moral order. Aristotle, however, would answer that law will always fail to meet this standard because of its inherent generality.[68] What he means by the generality of law is

---

[67] Ibid., 1137b, 24-26.

[68] Some authors might further argue against using Aristotelian philosophy to understand law in modern times because the nature of law has shifted since ancient Greece. See, for example, Roger A. Shiner, "Aristotle's Theory of Equity," in *Justice, Law, and Method in Plato and Aristotle*, ed. Spiro Panagiotou (Edmonton, Alberta: Academic Printing and Publishing, 1987): 173-191, particularly his discussion of "gaps" in the law. The argument basically is that law has so proliferated in modern society that the gaps in the law have sufficiently closed to make equity unnecessary. While Aristotle's society may not have had enough time to have written specific and complete enough laws to cover all possible cases, Western societies have now had a few millennia to generate a thorough body of law. While law has certainly proliferated, I think we could still safely say with Aristotle that law is inherently general and will inevitably leave gaps—and sometimes get things wrong. Consider the discussion in Nussbaum (2001), 441-453. One example of continuing gaps in the law is the recent effort to restrict "sexting," the practice of sending sexually-explicit pictures on cell phones through text and picture messaging, among minors. Some jurisdictions have begun charging minors, usually teenagers, who "sext" pictures of themselves to boyfriends or girlfriends with distribution of child pornography, an offense that requires listing offenders on sex-offender registries. Critics have argued that this response is harsh and falls outside of the intent of child pornography laws. But prosecutors respond that the child pornography laws are their only legal recourse for addressing this issue; they suppose that a more just response

elucidated both in the remainder of Book V, Chapter 10 and in his discussion of law, justice, and equity in *Rhetoric*, Book I, Chapter 13.[69] In the latter, Aristotle acknowledges that law is necessary for the good ordering of communal life, but also that it "must be expressed in wide terms."[70] Legislators are not able to pass laws that apply to all particular cases because of the infinite number of possibilities presented by human life, and so they "legislate as if that held good always which in fact only holds good usually."[71] Situations will always arise that defy the usual and therefore do not readily fit within the bounds of legal codification. Equity discerns the just response in particular situations that are exceptions to the rules set out by legislators. But equity also respects the intent of those rules:

> When the law speaks universally, then, and a case arises on it which is not covered by the universal statement, then it is right, where the legislator fails us and has erred by over-simplicity, to correct the omission—to say what the legislator himself would have said had he been present, and would have put into his law if he had known.[72]

Of course, legislators are human and cannot possibly know all possible cases beforehand,[73] and so justice will always require equity to supplement and correct the law.

---

requires more specific laws, not greater equity in applying the law. See Sean D. Hamill, "Students Sue Prosecutor in Cellphone Photos Case," *New York Times*, March 25, 2009.

[69] *Rhetoric* 1373b, 1-1374b, 23. For more on Aristotle's view of law and justice, see W. Von Leyden, "Aristotle and the Concept of Law," in *Philosophy* 42.159 (1967): 1-19.

[70] *Rhetoric*, 1373a, 34-35.

[71] Ibid., 1374a, 31-32.

[72] Ibid., 1137b, 19-24.

[73] Cf. *Rhetoric*, 1137a, 26-31 on the limits of human knowledge.

To say that equity is a higher form of justice than strict legal justice and that it supplements and corrects the law, however, does not yet tell us much about this virtue. Aristotle does not present a detailed definition of equity as he does with other virtues, which he describes generally as habits of character that strike a balance between two opposing vices (for example, courage is the mean between fear and recklessness; friendliness between churlishness and obsequiousness). He never clarifies the vices for which equity is the mean; nor does he describe how we obtain this virtue. Nevertheless, Aristotle provides a brief sketch of equity in two passages where he describes what this virtue looks like in practice. Each of these passages ends his chapters on justice in the *Nicomachean Ethics* and *Rhetoric* respectively, in a sense laying down Aristotle's final words on the nature of justice as equity. In *Nicomachean Ethics*, Aristotle writes that the man who "is no stickler for his rights in a bad sense but tends to take less than his share though he has the law on his side, is equitable, and this state of character is equity, which is a sort of justice and not a different state of character."[74] Here Aristotle indicates that equitable actors do not demand all that is due to them by law. They do not require precisely equal return as mandated by corrective justice, but allow their judgments to be mitigated or qualified by a certain amount of grace and reciprocity.

The second passage offers more detail about equity than the first, but also apparently serves as background for Aristotle's later comments in the *Nicomachean Ethics*. In *Rhetoric*, Aristotle writes,

> Equity bids us be merciful to the weakness of human nature; to think less about the laws than about the man who framed them, and less about what he said than about what he meant; not to consider the actions of the accused so much as his intentions, nor this or that detail so much as the whole story; to ask not what a man is now but what he has always or usually

---

[74] *Nicomachean Ethics,* 1137b, 34-1138a, 3.

been. It bids us remember benefits rather than injuries, and benefits received rather than benefits conferred; to be patient when we are wronged; to settle a dispute by negotiation and not by force; to prefer arbitration to litigation—for an arbitrator goes by the equity of a case, a judge by the strict law, and arbitration was invented with the express purpose of securing full power for equity.[75]

According to this passage, equity requires that we recognize that human beings are prone to "errors of judgment" and "misfortunes" that contribute to wrongdoing and that acts stemming from these causes (as opposed to "criminal acts") are forgivable.[76] Discerning whether acts are forgivable entails more than the strict application of the law; we must look to the intentions of the legislator. We must also try to understand the acts of the wrongdoer within the context of an entire story that reveals the intentions underlying the act. Furthermore, equity calls us to give more weight to the positive aspects of our relationships, to concentrate on what we owe rather than what we are owed, and to seek ways to continue relationship with patience and negotiation rather than depending on the swift and certain force of strict law administered by judges.[77]

---

[75] *Rhetoric,* 1374b, 10-22.

[76] Cf. *Rhetoric,* 1374b, 4-10.

[77] Reasonable questions might arise with respect to this aspect of equity: why does attention to the particulars usually result in giving more weight to the positive aspects of relationships, in mercy, forgiveness, and grace? Why wouldn't knowing the details of a particular case more often result in more harshness? Nussbaum addresses these questions from an Aristotelian perspective in her essay, "Equity and Mercy," in *Sex and Social Justice* (New York: Oxford University Press, 1999), chapter 6. She asks this question in these terms: "How do the exceptionless and inflexible mandates of law as justice come to be seen as harsh in their lack of fit to the particulars, rather than just imprecise?" (157). One answer that she offers is that when we attend to the particulars and see the situation from others' perspectives, the tragic aspects of

Aristotle, in sum, offers an alternative to a legalistic interpretation of justice based upon his observations of the limitations of the law. I will call it an "equitable interpretation of justice" or "justice as equity." Because law cannot account for all possible cases beforehand and so sometimes makes mistakes or responds too harshly, justice cannot be restricted to strict legal justice, which must at times be corrected and supplemented by equity. As a higher and more complete form of justice, equity attends to the complexities of human life and offers resources for discerning appropriate responses in certain circumstances where the law fails to account fully for their particulars. Some general characteristics of justice as equity, according to Aristotle, include compassion, reciprocity, forgiveness, gracefulness, and patience. Equitable people attend to the particulars before them by empathizing with others, locating specific incidents within broader contexts, and considering possibilities outside of the strict limitations of legal codes. That is, the most equitable people possess well-developed faculties of perception, emotion, and imagination, not merely reason.

---

another's circumstances often come to light. In seeing the tragic, we come to see ways in which people have already been punished or otherwise hindered by their circumstances, and so feel that a punishment deemed proportionate by the law would in fact go beyond proportionality. We then often conclude, with Seneca, that "It is a fault to punish a fault in full" (quoted in Nussbaum (1999), 165). Of course, if we attend to the particular circumstances of a wrongdoer and find that they have not experienced any tragedy in their lives that contributed to their wrongdoing, that their wrongdoing was purely a function of bad will, then we might not be so forgiving. But due to the tragic nature of our world, such cases seem to be relatively rare. Attending to the particulars and seeing from another's perspective tend to lead us to more mercy and forgiveness in general, then, because of the complex effects of tragedy upon our actions.

THE FACULTIES NECESSARY FOR EQUITY: PERCEPTION, EMOTION, AND IMAGINATION

If we want to pursue an alternative to strict legal justice and its contemporary manifestations in practices such as sentencing guidelines and the restriction of judicial discretion, then it seems, based on this interpretation of Aristotle, that we must try to understand how people come to respond equitably in specific situations. That is, we must consider the various faculties involved in ethical discernment generally and efforts to realize justice as equity specifically. By understanding these faculties, we can then consider how to foster them among people who make sentencing decisions in our criminal and juvenile justice systems. Encouraging and developing the use of these faculties in sentencing procedures may then contribute to more equitable systems as a whole.

Some modern virtue ethicists drawing from Aristotle's philosophy have laid out the significance of the faculties of perception, emotion, and imagination for being equitable. Nancy Sherman and Martha Nussbaum have especially made these connections apparent, emphasizing for the most part the role of perception, although recognizing emotion and imagination as well. Their discussions highlight the complexity of processes of ethical discernment and indicate the necessity of these other faculties in addition to reason for efforts to realize justice as equity. In this section, I draw on Sherman and Nussbaum in order to highlight ways in which perception, emotion, and imagination undergird our efforts to be equitable. But I also suggest that they underplay the significance of moral imagination relative to perception and emotion, and I call for greater understanding of this faculty and its role in ethical discernment.

Perception, according to Nussbaum, is the sensitive appreciation of the particulars of each situation and of each person one encounters. It is "complex responsiveness"[78] in light of the "richness and

---

[78] Nussbaum (1990), 55.

concreteness"[79] of the particulars. Nussbaum describes the perceptive person, borrowing from Henry James, as someone who is "finely aware and richly responsible."[80] Sherman similarly defines perception as the ability to know "how to construe the case, how to describe and classify what is before one."[81] It requires appreciation of the complexity of the particulars in all of their details. Through perception, we discern the morally salient features of a case. Without first discerning what is morally salient, we cannot proceed any further with ethical reflection. Perception therefore necessarily precedes the application of general rules because we cannot know which rules might apply until we fully appreciate the particularity that lies before us. Neither Nussbaum nor Sherman denies the importance of general rules for the moral life, but they do suggest that rules are not sufficient for making us virtuous or for achieving the good. We must first be able to offer correct, complex, detailed, and rich descriptions of the particulars to know what rules, if any, are relevant. In Sherman's words, starting with general rules rather than particular perceptions "begins too far down the line"[82] of ethical discernment.

Perception underlies our ability to be equitable, according to Nussbaum and Sherman. Two of the primary characteristics of equity, according to Nussbaum, are "its attentiveness to particularity and its capacity for sympathetic understanding."[83] Both of these characteristics entail accurate perception of the case at hand. Nussbaum states further that, "*Epieikeia* [equity] is a gentle art of particular perception, a temper of mind that refuses to demand

---

[79] Ibid., 77.

[80] Ibid., 84.

[81] Sherman (1989), 29.

[82] Ibid., 26. For another illuminating discussion of the role of perception in ethical discernment, see Aristotelian virtue ethicist Lawrence A. Blum, *Moral Perception and Particularity* (Baltimore: Johns Hopkins University Press, 1994).

[83] Nussbaum (1999), 168.

retribution without understanding the whole story."[84]   Through perception we are able to recognize whether an act is rooted in an error of judgment, misfortune, or criminality; we are able to see others for who they are rather than merely what they did. We are able to describe a particular act in full detail, appreciating the whole story in which the act fits as well as the intentions of the actor. Perception also allows us to attend to the whole story that brought about particular laws and the intentions of the legislators who wrote them. This faculty, then, enables us to be equitable, to see where strict legal justice is limited, and to seek its correction or supplementation in light of the particular cases before us. Perception, in short, is fundamental to equity, and thus, to the realization of justice in its fullest form.

Nussbaum and Sherman respectively also find in Aristotle's philosophy a relationship among the faculties of perception, emotion, and imagination, and consequently they conclude that development of the latter two faculties is also necessary for ethical discernment and for being equitable.   Regarding connections between emotion and perception, Sherman observes that Aristotle understands the emotions as informing our attention to the particulars. Agreeing with him, she writes,

> Often we see not dispassionately, but because of and through the emotions....   We notice through feeling what might otherwise go unheeded by a cool and detached intellect. To see dispassionately without engaging the emotions is often to be at peril of missing what is relevant.[85]

Whereas we discern the morally salient features of a case through perception, emotion directs our attention to these features so we can perceive them accurately. Nussbaum similarly argues that the emotions influence our perceptions and that they must be trained to provide us

---

[84] Ibid., 159. Cf. Sherman (1989), 13-22.
[85] Ibid., 45.

with appropriate responses to various situations.[86] Without the right emotions, we cannot possibly come to correct descriptions of what lies before us because our vision will be clouded by inappropriate passions. Emotion is a primary faculty enabling our ethical discernment in particular situations because it informs our perceptions and accordingly our understanding of what is relevant for our judgment. Equitable persons then must possess not only a keen faculty for perception but also the capacity for right feelings about the cases before them. Nussbaum writes, "[T]he truly good person will not only act well but also feel the appropriate emotions about what he or she chooses."[87]

Perception also relates to imagination. Both Sherman and Nussbaum base their descriptions of imagination on their interpretations of Aristotle's concept of *phantasia*.[88] Sherman does not

---

[86] Nussbaum's most thorough discussion of the role of emotions in shaping reason, perception, and imagination can be found in *Upheavals of Thought* (2001). Also, see Nussbaum (1990), 77-84.

[87] Nussbaum (1990), 78.

[88] The role and meaning of *phantasia* for Aristotle is disputed, as is the translation of *phantasia* as imagination in modern English. For varying assessments of *phantasia*, see Joyce Engmann, "Imagination and Truth in Aristotle," *The Journal of the History of Philosophy* 14 (1976): 259-265; Deborah Modrak, *Aristotle: The Power of Perception* (Chicago: University of Chicago Press, 1987), 81-110; Michael V. Wedin, *Mind and Imagination in Aristotle* (New Haven: Yale University Press, 1988); Malcolm Schofield, "Aristotle on the Imagination," in *Essays on Aristotle's De Anima*, ed. Martha Nussbaum and Amélie Rorty (Oxford: Clarendon Press, 1992): 249-277; Dorothea Frede, "The Cognitive Role of *Phantasia* in Aristotle," in *Essays on Aristotle's De Anima*, ed. Martha Nussbaum and Amélie Rorty (Oxford: Clarendon Press, 1992): 279-295; and Victor Caston, "Why Aristotle Needs Imagination," *Phronesis* 41.1 (1996): 20-55. Martha Nussbaum's fifth essay in *Aristotle's De Motu Animalium* (Princeton: Princeton University Press, 1978), 221-270 provides an exhaustive discussion of *phantasia* in Aristotle that informs much of her later work on imagination as well as Sherman's interpretations of this faculty. For the purposes of my argument here, disputes about the role and meaning of *phantasia* and its translation are less relevant

discuss *phantasia* extensively, instead deferring to Nussbaum's assessment of this faculty.[89] Nussbaum summarizes her interpretation of *phantasia*:

> Aristotle does not have a single concept that corresponds exactly to our "imagination." His *phantasia*, usually so translated, is a more inclusive human and animal capability, that of focusing on some concrete particular, either present or absent, in such a way as to see (or otherwise perceive) it *as* something, picking out its salient features, discerning its content. In this function it is the active and selective aspect of perception.... [*Phantasia*] can do much of the work of our imagination, though it should be stressed that Aristotle's emphasis is upon its selective and discriminatory character rather than upon its capability for free fantasy. Its job is more to focus on reality than to create unreality.[90]

Like emotion, *phantasia* directs our attention to particular features of experience so that we perceive them appropriately. Drawing on Nussbaum, Sherman writes that *phantasia* is "the way an object of desire 'appears to' a subject" so as to inspire a sense of its desirability.[91] Through *phantasia*, we recognize certain aspects of an object as beneficial or detrimental to a specific end. A glass of cool, clear water, for example, appears to us *as* a means for slackening our thirst, and we therefore desire it when thirsty. The most salient feature of the water is not its temperature or clearness (though these features may become more relevant if the water is stagnant), but its thirst-quenching power. *Phantasia* focuses our attention on this feature, thus

---

than how Nussbaum and Sherman adopt this concept in their understanding of imagination.

[89] See Sherman (1989), 32, n. 35.

[90] Nussbaum (1990), 77.

[91] Sherman (1989), 32, n. 35.

focusing our desire for the glass of water. So also in ethical discernment, *phantasia* enables us to perceive the morally relevant aspects of a particular situation as beneficial or detrimental, as contributing to or undermining our conceptions of the good and the right.

Based upon their interpretations of Aristotle's *phantasia*, Sherman and Nussbaum each elaborate upon the role and meaning of imagination in ethical discernment generally and being equitable specifically. For Sherman, imagination is "the capacity to re-enact the agent's point of view and to consider what it is like for that agent to do that action in that context."[92] Imagination focuses our attention on the perspective of a moral actor, empowering us to see the salient features of his or her experience. It enables us to enter the narratives of others' lives and so to perceive their possible intentions and to fit particular actions within their whole stories. Nussbaum makes a similar claim to Sherman's when she repeatedly contends that reading literature can train our imaginations in the practice of picking out the salient features of others' stories, making us more morally perceptive.[93] But she goes further than Sherman when she argues that imagination helps us to see relationships among the particulars that may not be obvious, "to link several imaginings or perceptions together, 'making a unity from many.'"[94] This characteristic of imagination allows us to find connections in our experiences and to uncover morally relevant aspects that cross various situations. In sum, according to Nussbaum and Sherman, imagination like emotion shapes our perception of particular cases by highlighting morally relevant aspects and focusing our attention upon certain details of various situations. It does so by locating those cases within broader narratives; drawing connections

---

[92] Sherman (1989), 36.

[93] This theme is common in a large number of Nussbaum's writings. See especially Nussbaum (1990), Chapters Two, Five, and Six; (1997), Chapter Three; and (1995), Chapter One.

[94] Nussbaum (1990), 77.

among various cases that may not seem related *prima facie*; and in some cases, giving our perceptions more complexity, detail, and richness. Since, in Nussbaum's and Sherman's consideration, imagination is necessary for ethical discernment, it is also necessary for our efforts to realize justice as equity.

Sherman and Nussbaum make a strong case for the roles of perception, emotion, and imagination in processes of ethical discernment based on Aristotle's discussion of justice as equity. Despite these contributions, I find that their descriptions of moral imagination are limited because they depend too much upon their interpretations of Aristotle's *phantasia* in developing their understanding of this faculty. Note that Nussbaum allows in the extended quotation above that *phantasia* ought not to be correlated directly with imagination and that imagination in modern usage entails more than *phantasia*. Yet she does not discuss those aspects of imagination that fall outside of *phantasia*. In her most explicit discussion of the relationship among perception, emotion, and imagination,[95] she does not expand her understanding of imagination beyond *phantasia*. Although Nussbaum seems to use "fancy" often interchangeably with "imagination" in this discussion, she also seems to contrast *phantasia* with fancy, or at least, "free fantasy," leaving some confusion about the connection between *phantasia* and imagination.[96] Sherman, because she defers to Nussbaum on these

---

[95] See Nussbaum (1990), 75-82.

[96] The confusion between "imagination" and "fantasy" is largely a modern development. See Engell (1981), McFarland (1985), Tilmouth (2007) for historical discussions of this confusion particularly as it developed during the Romantic period of the 19th century. The roots of this confusion could be traced in part to Kant's conclusion that imagination cannot help us to discern the moral, but it can help us to discern the beautiful. As discussed above, Kant found that imagination is too tainted with the empirical for it to contribute to pure reason. Iris Murdoch describes Kant's assessment of imagination and notes that one consequence of his confinement of imagination to discerning beauty is that this faculty is then associated with "invention" and "genius" in

points, likewise presents an understanding of imagination narrowly based on Aristotle's *phantasia*. As a consequence, Nussbaum and Sherman give accounts of imagination only as a faculty that aids in our perception of reality, not as one that can also enable us to "create unreality." That is, imagination in their view predominantly gives us images of the world as it is, not of the world's possibilities as well. Modern usage of the term imagination in contrast typically incorporates both of these senses and includes the activity of creating images of what the world could become.[97]

---

art; imagination then invents its own rules. In contrast, pure reason cannot invent rules because morality is "a harmonious *obedience* to universal rational law." See Murdoch (1992), 315. The association of imagination, invention, and genius then develops after Kant into the confounding of imagination and fantasy, resulting in a negative assessment of imagination's connections to reason, especially with respect to moral questions. Many recent philosophers, best exemplified by Murdoch, have contested the confusion between imagination and fantasy, arguing that imagination differs from fantasy in that the former is creative, but still draws from the perception of experience. Drawing on Plato, Murdoch concludes that fantasy is dangerous to the moral life. She describes it as "a selfish dream life," "egoistic illusion associated with a lack of moral sense with an inability to reflect" (317). In contrast, imagination is "a power working at a barrier of darkness, recovering verities which we somehow know of, but have in our egoistic fantasy life 'forgotten'" (320). The difference between fantasy and imagination, for Murdoch, is that the latter is grounded in attention to reality in its creativity, rather than spinning off into unreality. For a view contrary to Murdoch's, see Kekes (2002), 30-32.

[97] Seyla Benhabib also discusses the role of "moral imagination" in processes of ethical discernment, but she calls these processes "moral judgment." Although her interpretation of moral imagination is not rooted in Aristotle's *phantasia*, it suffers from similar difficulties as Nussbaum's and Sherman's, that is, her use of moral imagination concerns its contribution to perception of the world as it is, and not necessarily consideration of what the world could become as well. For Benhabib, moral imagination is one aspect of "enlarged thinking," a concept that she develops from Hannah Arendt's neo-Kantian and neo-Aristotelian interpretation of moral and political judgment. Benhabib

Imagining the world's possibilities, I suggest, is a necessary component of ethical discernment. When we imagine what the world could become, we work at envisioning the good, and our visions of the good shape our moral assessments of particular situations. Nussbaum and Sherman are right that imagination helps us to attend to the world as it is—that is, to enter the narratives of others' lives, to appreciate their perspectives, and to draw connections across particular cases. But imagination also empowers us to see possibilities, and these visions shape our processes of ethical discernment generally and our efforts to realize justice as equity specifically. Nussbaum might refer to the function of imagination in envisioning possibilities as "fancy," "free fantasy," or "creating unreality." While these terms may deride, or at least, downplay the capacity of imagination to envision alternatives to our world as it is, our visions of what the world could become also

---

"thinks with Arendt against Arendt" about this concept in order to generate a model of interactive rationality in discursive theory. Enlarged thinking involves "taking the standpoint of the other" so that one can come to see as many perspectives as might bear upon our understanding of a situation. One stage in enlarged thinking is moral imagination, in which one considers different ways in which one's actions might be described from the perspectives of others. That is, through moral imagination, we consider the manner in which others might construe our actions from their standpoints. While I agree with Benhabib that moral imagining does involve this activity—which I summarize in terms of "entering into others' stories and appreciating their perspectives"— the next section will demonstrate that I think moral imagining also involves other activities, particularly considering possibilities for what the world could become. Nevertheless, Benhabib's reflections on the connection between the moral and the political, and the need for political institutions that support the ability of enlarged thought in moral judgment may serve as helpful guides in thinking about the need to create structures in our criminal and juvenile justice systems that enable sentencing practices where vivid and expansive moral imagining is fostered in processes of ethical discernment. See Seyla Benhabib, *Situating the Self: Gender, Community, and Postmodernism in Contemporary Ethics* (New York: Routledge, 1992), especially chapter 4.

inform our perceptions of particular cases as well as our emotional responses and processes of reasoning.

In recent years, many authors have discussed moral imagination as the capacity to create images both of the world as it is and of its possibilities in order to move beyond the limitations of the principles and procedures (that is, "laws" of another sort) of their fields. Understanding their interpretations of this faculty in their fields may help us to understand more fully the need for moral imagination in ethical discernment as well as in realizing justice as equity. Their discussions of moral imagination may also help us to move beyond the limitations of strict legal justice and related practices such as constraining judicial discretion through sentencing guidelines, and to recognize the need to foster vivid and expansive moral imagining in our criminal and juvenile justice systems. Works by moral imagination authors may thus clarify a broader role for moral imagination in processes of ethical discernment and in being equitable than that recognized by Nussbaum and Sherman.

THE SIGNIFICANCE AND MEANING OF MORAL IMAGINATION

Several authors in a wide variety of fields have recently called for greater appreciation of the significance of "moral imagination" in the theories and practices of their disciplines. Although most of these authors are not ethicists and are not primarily concerned with issues of justice, they could provide some insight into the role of moral imagination in ethical discernment generally and efforts to realize justice as equity specifically in light of the work of Aristotelian virtue ethicists.

The range of academic literature employing the concept of moral imagination has greatly expanded in the last five decades.[98] It includes work in anthropology,[99] literary studies,[100] professional ethics[101]

---

[98] Steven Fesmire notes that in the 1960s, only six books and articles in philosophy touched on moral imagination. This figure increased ten-fold in the 1990s, when over sixty books and articles addressed this topic. See *John Dewey and Moral Imagination: Pragmatism in Ethics* (Bloomington: University of Indiana Press, 2003), 2. If one were to survey fields other than philosophy, as the remainder of this paragraph shows, the number of such texts would far exceed sixty.

[99] See T.O. Beidelman, *Moral Imagination in Kaguru Modes of Thought* (Washington, DC: Smithsonian Institution Press, 1993); James W. Fernandez and Mary Taylor Huber, eds., *Irony in Action: Anthropology, Practice, and the Moral Imagination* (Chicago: University of Chicago Press, 2001); and Charles Stewart, *Demons and the Devil: Moral Imagination in Modern Greek Culture* (Princeton, NJ: Princeton University Press, 1991).

[100] See, for example, Gertrude Himmelfarb (1991, 2006). Also, Christopher Clausen, *The Moral Imagination: Essays on Literature and Ethics* (Iowa City: University of Iowa Press, 1986); Robert Coles, *The Call of Stories: Teaching and the Moral Imagination* (Boston: Houghton Mifflin Company, 1989); Vigen Guroian, *Tending the Heart of Virtue: How Classic Stories Awaken a Child's Moral Imagination* (New York: Oxford University Press, 1998); John Kekes (1989, 2006); Russell Kirk, *Eliot and His Age: T.S. Eliot's Moral Imagination in the Twentieth Century* (Peru, IL: Sugden, 1988); John Klause, *The Unfortunate Fall: Theodicy and the Moral Imagination of Andrew Marvell* (Hamden, CT: Archon Books, 1983); Martin Price, *Forms of Life: Character and Moral Imagination in the Novel* (New Haven, CT: Yale University Press, 1983); and Lionel Trilling, *The Liberal Imagination: Essays on Literature and Society* (New York: The Viking Press, 1950).

[101] Other authors within the disciplines of theological and philosophical ethics have also highlighted the importance of moral imagination. Theological ethicists interested in moral imagination include Keane (1984); Daniel C. Maguire, *The Moral Choice* (Garden City, NY: Doubleday, 1978); Thomas R. McFaul, *Transformation Ethics: Developing the Christian Moral Imagination* (Lanham, MD: University Press of America, 2003); and Philip Rossi, *Together Toward Hope: A Journey to Moral Theology* (Notre Dame: University of Notre

(including fields such as peace-building,[102] business,[103] public policy,[104] medicine,[105] architecture,[106] and education[107]), biblical studies,[108]

Dame Press, 1983). Philosophical ethicists include Susan E. Babbitt, *Impossible Dreams: Rationality, Integrity, and Moral Imagination* (Boulder: Westview, 1996) and *Artless Integrity: Moral Imagination, Agency, and Stories* (Lanham, MD: Rowman & Littlefield Publishers, 2001); Steven Fesmire (2003); John Kekes, *Moral Tradition and Individuality* (Princeton: Princeton University Press, 1989) and *The Enlargement of Life: Moral Imagination at Work* (Ithaca, NY: Cornell University Press, 2006); Charles Larmore, *Patterns of Moral Complexity* (Cambridge: Cambridge University Press, 1987); Iris Murdoch, *Metaphysics as a Guide to Morals* (New York: Penguin Books, 1992); Paul Ricoeur (1994); Edward Stevens, *Developing Moral Imagination: Case Studies in Practical Morality* (New York: Sheed and Ward, 1998); and Edward Tivnan, *The Moral Imagination: Confronting the Ethical Issues of Our Day* (New York: Simon and Schuster, 1995).

[102] Lederach (2005).

[103] See Patricia H. Werhane, *Moral Imagination and Management Decision-Making* (New York: Oxford University Press, 1999) and Oliver Williams, ed., *The Moral Imagination: How Literature and Films Can Stimulate Ethical Reflection in the Business World* (Notre Dame: University of Notre Dame Press, 1998).

[104] Thomas McCollough, *The Moral Imagination and Public Life: Raising the Ethical Question* (Chatham, NJ: Chatham House Publishers, 1991).

[105] See Coles (1989).

[106] Yi-Fu Tuan, *Morality and Imagination: Paradoxes of Progress* (Madison, WI: University of Wisconsin Press, 1989).

[107] See Coles (1989) as well as William Walsh, *The Use of Imagination: Educational Thought and the Literary Mind* (London: Chatto and Windus, 1959).

[108] For example, Dale Allison, *The Sermon on the Mount: Inspiring Moral Imagination* (New York: Herder and Herder, 1999) and William P. Brown, *The Ethos of the Cosmos: The Genesis of Moral Imagination in the Bible* (Grand Rapids, MI: Eerdmans, 1999). Also, Walter Brueggemann, *Hopeful Imagination: Prophetic Voices in Exile* (Philadelphia: Fortress Press, 1986); *Texts under Negotiation: The Bible and Postmodern Imagination* (Minneapolis: Fortress Press, 1993); *The Prophetic Imagination*, 2nd edition (Minneapolis:

history,[109] and cognitive sciences.[110] The quality of the development of the concept of moral imagination in these fields and among these authors varies immensely. Some authors merely mention moral imagination in their titles, introductions, or conclusions, often failing to offer even a cursory definition of the term.[111] In contrast, other authors have expended a great deal of energy trying to understand moral imagination and its relevance to their fields. In this section, I use their discussions of moral imagination as a basis for my own definition and description of this faculty and its role in ethical discernment.

It may be helpful to begin by noting a common theme among Aristotelian virtue ethicists and moral imagination authors. Although the many moral imagination authors write out of a variety of disciplines, their common interest in this topic is remarkable because it is rooted in similar frustrations with the theories and practices of their fields, frustrations that mirror Aristotelian critiques of a legalistic interpretation of justice. Regardless of academic discipline, most of these authors are dissatisfied with what they view as their disciplines' lack of attention to the particulars of human life, which cannot be summarized by simple rules of conduct or decision-making procedures.

Fortress Press, 2001); and *An Introduction to the Old Testament: The Canon and Christian Imagination* (Westminster John Knox Press, 2003). Further, Carol Newsom, *The Book of Job: A Contest of Moral Imagination* (New York: Oxford University Press, 2003); and Philip Rossi, "Moral Imagination and the Narrative Modes of Moral Discourse," *Renascence* 31.3 (1979): 131-141.

[109] See Engell (1981), Himmelfarb (1991, 2006), Ishiguro (1966), Keane (1984), McFarland (1985), Strawson (1970), Tilmouth (2007), Warnock (1976), and White (1990).

[110] See Mark Johnson, *Moral Imagination: Implications of Cognitive Science for Ethics* (Chicago: University of Chicago Press, 1993) and Nathan L. Tierney, *Imagination and Ethical Ideals: Prospects for a Unified Philosophical and Psychological Understanding* (Albany: SUNY Press, 1994).

[111] A short list of these authors includes Allison (1999), Himmelfarb (1991, 2006), Kirk (1988), Klause (1983), Stevens (1998), Trilling (1950), and Walsh (1959).

They frequently observe that their disciplines emphasize either deontological or utilitarian modes of discernment, which overstate the role of reason and often employ principles and procedures that cannot fully encapsulate all particular cases. Because of the infinite number of possibilities presented by human life, new situations will always arise, and the principles and procedures of these various disciplines will require supplementation and correction. Yet too much dependence upon principles and procedures enfeebles the faculties necessary to supplement and correct them and to respond appropriately to new situations. The coherence of this body of literature then lies in that its authors call for the development of moral imagination to help theorists and practitioners in their disciplines assert independence from overly confining principles and procedures.

Some examples of arguments by moral imagination authors may clarify the substance of their frustrations as well as illuminate their resemblance to Aristotelian arguments against a legalistic interpretation of justice.[112] I described in chapter one the use of moral imagination by John Paul Lederach.[113] Drawing on decades of practical experience as a peace-builder, he recalls several situations in which he followed the principles and procedures of his profession, but still found the groups of people with which he worked locked in violent opposition to each other. The chains of conflict were broken only when someone had the moral imagination to break out of the conflict and try a new, creative way of relating to the other. Among his many examples, Lederach includes the story of the women of Wajir, a district in northern Kenya that lies near the Ethiopian and Somali borders.[114] Trapped by feuding

---

[112] With the following examples, I do not necessarily espouse these authors' assessments of their disciplines or areas of critique. Rather I present them in order to highlight a certain trend in the argumentation of moral imagination authors.

[113] Lederach (2005).

[114] For this story, see Lederach (2005), 10-13. Lederach also includes three other examples in his first chapter, including the transformation of an ethnic

clans and conflicts spilling over from war-torn Somalia in the early 1990s, these women created a system of monitoring local markets so that women from any clan could safely procure needed goods for their families. The decision to work together to secure the markets was the imaginative catalyst that eventually stopped the violent battles within Wajir. This situation and others like it led Lederach to encourage peace-builders to attend to the complexities of conflict transformation. He argues for the necessity of a strong foundation in professional guidelines and techniques, the basis for a well-developed practice of conflict transformation. But Lederach also contends that moral imagination, which cannot be fully encapsulated within guidelines and techniques, must arise from disciplined practice in order to "serendipitously"[115] transcend human discord.

In the field of public policy, Thomas E. McCollough likewise exemplifies the trend toward moral imagination. In *Moral Imagination and Public Life*,[116] he bemoans the ascendance of a view of political life over the last fifty or so years in which "a democratic elite employing professional experts"[117] makes all major public-policy decisions. This view of political life, McCollough argues, results in a sort of technocracy that limits the abilities of ordinary citizens to shape their communities and societies. Public-policy makers then make decisions based upon the principles and procedures of professional experts rather than the will of the people who have tested preferred courses of action through reasonable conversation and debate about valued practices, beliefs, and attitudes. Breaking away from this view of political life and creating truly shared communal and social lives

---

conflict in Ghana, an incident in which peasants in Colombia were able to transcend the violent demands of both guerilla and government military forces, and a case in Tajikistan in which a philosopher convinced a warlord to participate in peace talks by asking the warlord to put his life at stake only when he too was willing to put his own life at stake for the sake of peace.

[115] Ibid.

[116] McCollough (1991).

[117] Ibid., 5.

requires moral imagination, which McCollough defines as "the capacity to empathize with others and to discern creative possibilities for ethical action."[118] He turns to moral imagination because he believes that only through this faculty can we fully recognize the complexity of building public policy in a democracy, a task that cannot be reduced to the principles and procedures of technocrats.

Robert Coles, in *The Call of Stories: Teaching and the Moral Imagination*,[119] similarly argues that the methods of teaching and training professionals have become preoccupied "with matters of technique, of knowledge"[120] instead of the creation of moral agents capable of responding to the particular issues of the people who turn to them for assistance. Concentrating on relationships between doctors and patients, Coles maintains that the institutional structures in which doctors work place limits on the ways that they can imagine their patients' lives and thereby diminish the quality of treatment even if doctors possess the right knowledge and techniques. Doctors lack the capability of applying their knowledge and techniques appropriately in particular situations. Only by entering into others' stories can professionals open their imaginations beyond the institutional structures that limit their capacities to respond fully to people who seek their services. For Coles, breaking out of these limitations and trying to imagine the lives of others is a moral imperative for professionals: "Listening adequately to the stories of others is *to do justice* by them."[121] The sort of justice he advocates here cannot be achieved by rigorously following professional principles and procedures alone; it requires moral imagination.

Like Lederach and McCollough, Coles illustrates a common disappointment among authors writing about moral imagination: they find that their disciplines' principles and procedures cannot account

---

[118] Ibid., 16.
[119] Coles (1989).
[120] Ibid., 118.
[121] Ibid., 28.

adequately for the complexities of human life.[122] Whether in peace-building, policy-making, medicine, or a variety of other fields, these principles and procedures cannot attend to the possibilities of all particular cases. With these frustrations, the arguments of moral imagination authors mirror Aristotelian arguments about the limitations of the law. However, also like Aristotle, who recognizes the necessity of law even with its limitations, these authors *do not* argue that principles and procedures are unimportant in the theories and practices of their disciplines.[123] Peace-builders ought to understand general features of conflict, public-policy makers need to be aware of the insights of professional experts, and doctors surely must know medical techniques. But principles and procedures are not enough to make good peace-builders, policy makers, or doctors, let alone good people. Success in these fields requires more than good reasoning and the application of principles and procedures. It demands that people engaged in the practices of these disciplines build upon their principles and procedures with moral imagination. These authors thus agree with Aristotelian virtue ethicists that successful response to particulars also demands other faculties. Unlike Nussbaum and Sherman, though, they emphasize the role of moral imagination both in expanding our understanding of what the world is *and* in envisioning what it could become.

---

[122] Other authors who arguably express this frustration and then turn to moral imagination to address them include Beidelman (1993), Brown (1999), Clausen (1986), Fernandez and Huber (2001), Fesmire (2003), Johnson (1993), Keane (1984), Kekes (1989, 2006), McFaul (2003), Price (1983), Rossi (1979, 1983), Tierney (1994), Walsh (1959), Werhane (1999), and Williams (1998).

[123] For example, see Coles (1989), 118-122; McCollough (1991), 20; and any of Lederach's classic handbooks on peace-building, including *Building Peace: Sustainable Reconciliation in Divided Societies* (Washington, D.C.: U.S. Institute of Peace Press, 1998); *The Journey Toward Reconciliation* (Scottdale, PA: Herald Press, 1999); and *The Little Book of Conflict Transformation* (Intercourse, PA: Good Books, 2003).

Despite the similarities between the arguments of moral imagination authors and Aristotelian virtue ethicists, a compelling gap also lies between them. On the one hand, the latter group recognizes the need for equity to correct and supplement strict legal justice in order to realize a more perfect form of justice that can better respond to the particulars of human life. Furthermore, Nussbaum and Sherman draw on Aristotle to show that justice as equity requires developing the faculties of perception, emotion, and imagination in addition to reason. They give a limited role to imagination compared to other faculties, suggesting that this faculty predominantly feeds our images of the world as it is. On the other hand, moral imagination authors have suggested that this faculty also gives us images of the world as it could become, and that it is necessary to correct and supplement the principles and procedures of their disciplines. I have not, however, found any recent author who has explored the implications of moral imagination so understood in the disciplines of law or criminal justice. The gap then between the arguments of these two bodies of theoretical literature lies at the intersection of moral imagination, as discussed by recent authors, and of justice as equity, as discussed by Aristotelian virtue ethicists. In the remainder of this section, I will begin to bridge this gap by constructing a definition of moral imagination that is informed by the former group. The next section will complete the bridge by relating this definition back to my previous discussion of justice as equity based on Aristotelian virtue ethics.

With regard to the first task, moral imagination authors do not all agree to a single definition of this faculty or are even aware of other authors' discussions. They do not write in common disciplines, and so for the most part, do not seem to have constructed their various definitions in conversation with each other. Nevertheless, because they are responding to common frustrations within their respective disciplines, these authors have a shared sense of the role and meaning of moral imagination in overcoming these frustrations. Peace-builder John Paul Lederach, for example, describes moral imagination as "the capacity to imagine something rooted in the challenges of the real world yet capable of giving birth to that which does not yet exist."[124] Similarly, anthropologist T.O. Beidelman writes that moral imagination is both "the ways that people construct images of the world in which they live" and "the ways in which people picture a world different from that which they actually experience…a means by which people extend their vision of what may be possible."[125] Likewise theologian Philip Rossi argues that moral imagination refers to human efforts to represent "the world as it is" as well as possibilities for "the world as it ought to be."[126] Drawing on these various descriptions, I propose a preliminary definition of moral imagination as *the cognitive faculty that gives us the power to create images of our world and its possibilities.*

Before discussing the positive content of this definition, it may be helpful to clarify what moral imagination *is not* in comparison with other faculties.   Cognitive scientist Nathan Tierney distinguishes between imagination and the faculties of perception, memory, belief, and reason.[127] His distinctions clarify the scope and role of imagining in encountering our world, although even with these distinctions, many of these faculties often overlap and at times entail each other—an issue to which I return below. First, imagination differs from perception in that "the imagined object is, at least in part, generated internally rather than produced by external stimuli."[128] That is, when we imagine, we can generate visions of things beyond those things directly present to us, while perception is limited more to realities in our midst. Perception concerns the world as it is; imagination concerns both the world as it is and as it could become. Unlike memory, imagination

---

[124] Lederach (2005), ix.

[125] Beidelman (1993), 1-2.

[126] Rossi (1983), 42-45. Other authors present similar definitions of moral imagination. See Brown (1999), 20; Fesmire (2003), 65-67; Johnson (1993), 206; Keane (1984), 73-75, 81-83; Kekes (2006), 19-24, 34; Larmore (1987), 12; Maguire (1979), 189; McFaul (2003), xi; Newsom (2003), 262; Ricoeur (1994), 123-126; Tierney (1994), 50-60; and White (1990), 184-192.

[127] Tierney (1994), 43-44.

[128] Ibid.

involves more than recollection of past experiences; it primarily involves envisioning our present and future. Tierney argues that imagination differs from belief in that we do not necessarily judge the truth of our images. We can imagine flying pigs without believing in them. But we can also imagine what heaven will be like and believe that these images are true and will come to pass. Imagination is not reason in that it does not involve a method or procedure, such as induction or deduction. We can imagine at our whim; our imaginations do not need to follow rules of logic. Finally, although Tierney does not draw this distinction, imagination differs from emotion in that it does not necessarily entail the passions. Although our images of the world and its possibilities can inspire desire or repulsion, we can also imagine idly, without stirring strong feelings.

Given these distinctions, one question that arises regarding the consensus among moral imagination authors is what precisely the power to create images of the world and its possibilities has to do with morality. These authors, largely because most of them are not ethicists, are less clear about the meaning of morality. I suggested in chapter one that "moral situations" are situations in which questions about self, other, and our relationships arise, usually because of some ambiguity, conflict, or disturbance. "Morality," then, is reflection and action concerning self-identity, perceptions of the other, and relationships between self and other. How we imagine our world and its possibilities situates our particular understanding of self, others, and our relationships, and so imagining our world and what it could become has moral implications. Moral imagination is never a purely individualistic affair. These images are always informed by embodied relationships with others amidst cultural interactions, social arrangements, and institutional structures. We create them as we participate in practices, through which we interact with one another, generate meaning, and organize experience.

Two overlapping categories of images comprise the substance of our moral imaginations: our images of the world as it is and our images of the world's possibilities. The first category composes what both

Beidelman and biblical scholar William P. Brown call our "cosmologies," which provide frameworks or mental maps that help us to navigate within our communities and societies. We draw these maps as we test the terrain of our cultural interactions, social arrangements, and institutional structures through embodied relationships within the world. They tell us about the paths offered by the roles and expectations of our practices so that we may gain better understanding of our relationships with others as we engage in shared activities with them. They provide meaning and orient us toward the world, guiding our actions in our relationships and practices.

Because most people are formed within multiple overlapping communities, because we are aware of the diversity of cultures, societies, and institutions across the world, and because we are aware of historical changes, the construction of our cosmologies is always a piecemeal and multivalent affair. In Beidelman's words, our cosmologies are "always myriad, contradictory, and loaded with conflicting and ambivalently charged elements,"[129] but these characteristics are part of the strength of these mental maps of the world because they represent accurately the diversity and complexity of human life. The multiple representations of the world among members of the same communities and societies will tend to resemble each other since we draw them within common relationships and practices. These images will, however, retain their individual particularity because each person has unique experiences, which also influence his images of the world, that do not always coincide with collective experiences.

The second category of images generated by moral imagination is those that portray possibilities of what the world could become. These images, unless they are pure flights of fancy, always relate back to the first category. That is, our images of the possible typically draw upon our images of the real. We gain a sense of the possible in our embodied relationships with the world when we engage in the practices embedded in our cultural interactions, social arrangements, and

---

[129] Beidelman (1993), 4-5.

institutional structures. Our images of the world, therefore, in some ways bound our ability to imagine possibilities. If this second category of images exists, however, it cannot be entirely confined to images of the world as it is and it cannot be determined entirely by practical, cultural, social, and institutional constraints. Human beings—and our imaginations—are shaped, but not determined, by our locations in communal structures. We have the freedom to imagine multiple possibilities for what the world could become because of our formation in multiple communities, our awareness of different communities both around the world and throughout history, and disjunctions between individual and collective experiences. The diversity and complexity of experience permits the imagination of other possible worlds because our images of the world as it is are always piecemeal and multivalent.

The relationship between the first and second categories that compose moral imagination, however, is not one-way; our images of the world as it could possibly become also affect our images of the world as it is, and therefore, our moral judgments of the world. Suppose that a person could not imagine alternative possibilities. She would perceive the world as it is as a consequence of the natural order of things, unchangeable and eternal. If, in contrast, she could imagine a different way of being in the world, then she might perceive the world as it is perhaps as less then what it could be. The imagination of possibilities of what the world could become may be a basis for moral agents to re-examine their images of the world as it is, to critique the cultural, social, or institutional order before them, and perhaps to suggest actions for transformation of those aspects of the world that they see as falling short of their images of goodness and rightness. Recognition of other possibilities, however, need not have these results. Moral agents may imagine a wide range of possibilities for what the world could become and still believe that the world as it is now is the best of all possible worlds. Nevertheless, the more significant point here is that without the second category of images, transformation of the world as it is—for better or worse—cannot occur.

This discussion suggests that our moral imaginations, by creating images of the world as it is and its possibilities, are central to the organization of our experience. Any human being with a certain level of cognitive functioning has the power to create these images, and so, is morally imaginative.[130] Images of the world as it is offer mental maps or frameworks or cosmologies that help us to understand ourselves in relationships with others in our cultures, societies, and institutions as we participate in various practices. Where these images cannot adequately account for the diversity and complexity of human life, images of the possibilities of the world provide options for changing our relationships and practices and for finding different ways of organizing our experience. Nathan Tierney describes the organizational role of imagination as the creation of "schema" through which human beings draw connections across our experiences in order make them meaningful to us.[131] We employ certain tools to draw these connections. Narratives, metaphors, and symbols in particular provide the content of types of moral imagination and serve as the lines on our mental maps connecting the nodes of our experience.[132] When we

---

[130] On this point, I differ with some moral imagination authors (for example, John Paul Lederach) who indicate that only certain images of the world and its possibilities are moral, that is, good, and therefore only the people who draw upon those particular images are morally imaginative. I believe that drawing upon different types of moral imagination is fundamental to organizing and making meaning of our experience. Some types of moral imagination, however, are better than others, as the ensuing discussion reveals.

[131] Tierney (1994), chapter 4.

[132] I do not use "narrative," "metaphor," or "symbol" in a literary sense. Rather I understand narratives, metaphors, and symbols as tools for drawing the connections across our experiences in different ways. Narratives, for instance, imply causality: "First, A happened, then B." They also suggest anticipation: "Given that A happened, previous experience tells me that B should happen next." Metaphors draw connections by indicating resemblance, but not identity, among experiences: "A is like B, but A is not B." Both similarities and differences between two experiences bear meaning. Symbols, in contrast,

attend to how we use these tools in particular moral situations, we may gain better understanding of how we organize and make meaning of those situations within our images of the world and its possibilities.

As individuals are formed and sustained within certain cultural, social, and institutional locations and as they participate in various practices, they use the narratives, metaphors, and symbols around them to create images of the world as it is and of what it could become. Although these images are always piecemeal and multivalent because of the diversity and complexity of our experience, they also retain some level of consistency and coherence because of their schematic nature. The content of the moral imaginations of individuals can then be described in terms of the narratives, metaphors, and symbols that they use most frequently to organize and make meaning of their experience. Because individuals who are similarly located culturally, socially, and institutionally or who engage in the same practices will organize similar experiences using similar narratives, metaphors, and symbols, the moral imaginations they draw upon will tend to resemble each other, although differences between them will remain because each person has unique experiences. Different types of moral imagination that share common narratives, metaphors, and symbols could be compared based on the adequacy of their images of the world as it is in reflecting reality as well as their capacity to provide possibilities for resolving ambiguity, conflict, and disturbance within experience.

---

are concrete representations of something else, usually something invisible and intangible: "A is B, but B is not contained in A." These tools therefore specify different kinds of relationships among our experiences. A certain type of moral imagination can be analyzed in terms of how the people who use them employ specific narratives, metaphors, and symbols. But these mental maps can also be examined in terms of their underlying interpretations of a particular experience causing, resembling, or representing another experience, which may not involve the explicit use of narratives, metaphors, and symbols. In the analysis in chapter four, I attend to both explicit use of these tools by participants in restorative justice and their underlying interpretations of experiences rooted in these tools.

Thus far, I have used "moral imagination" as a noun, as the cognitive faculty that empowers us to create images in two categories: our world as it is and our world as it could become. Moral imagination, however, also possesses an active component. "To imagine morally" is to use these images in our interpretations of the world and our organization of experience. Moral imagining involves several activities. Nussbaum and Sherman provide descriptions of a few of these activities, including entering into others' stories, appreciating their perspectives, and making connections across particular cases. While I agree that we do these things when we imagine morally, moral imagination entails more than Aristotle's *phantasia*. It also involves the creation of images of what the world could become, the consideration of possibilities for the future.

One's capacities to imagine morally are more or less vivid and expansive depending on her facility with these specific activities. People capable of vivid and expansive moral imagining can create a wide range of images of the world and what it could become. They can readily enter into the narratives of others' lives and appreciate their perspectives. They are easily able to draw connections across particular cases, seeing the similarities and differences throughout the diversity and complexity of experience. Their mental maps or frameworks or cosmologies are multi-dimensional. They can envision myriad possibilities for the world and are not confined to their perceptions of the state of the world as it is now. Such people imagine in ways that may be described as "subtle and high rather than simple and coarse; precise rather than gross; richly colored rather than monochromatic; exuberant rather than reluctant; generous rather than stingy; suffused with loving emotion rather than mired in depression."[133]

Types of moral imagination and activities of moral imagining are related reciprocally (figure 1). On the one hand, different types of moral imagination may either foster or restrict vivid and expansive

---

[133] Nussbaum (1990), 152.

Figure 1. Interconnection of Moral Imagination and Activities of Moral Imagining

Characteristics of Moral Imagination

- The cognitive faculty that enables us to create images of the world as it is and as it could become.
- Draws upon narratives, metaphors, and symbols to organize and interpret experience.
- Describe types of moral imagination in terms of narrative, metaphorical, and symbolic schemes.
- Types of moral imagination formed within cultural, social, and institutional contexts.

Activities of Moral Imagining

- Entering into others' stories.
- Appreciating others' perspectives.
- Drawing connections and seeing relationships across experiences.
- Considering myriad possibilities for the future.

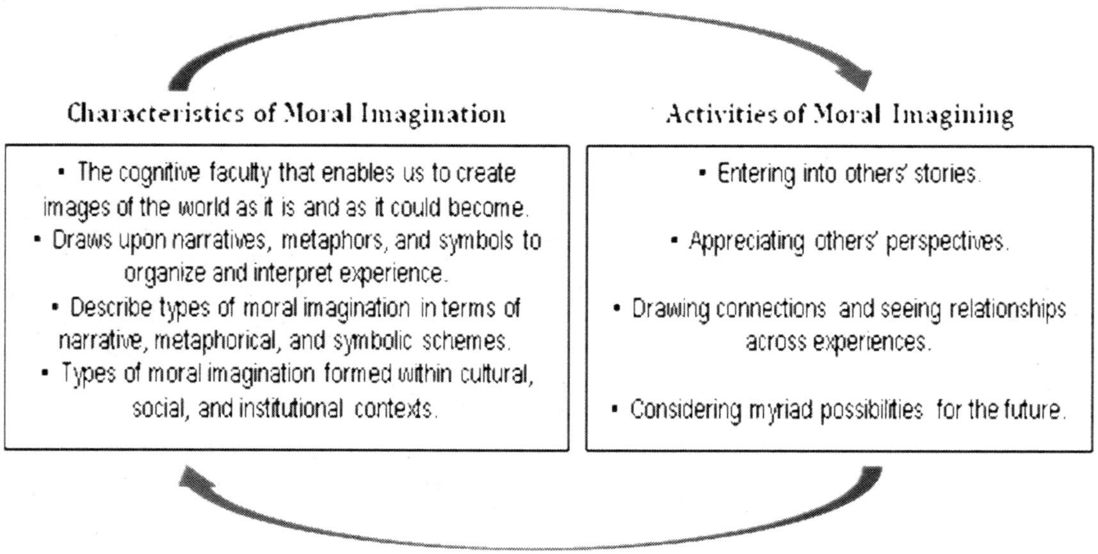

moral imagining. A xenophobic type of moral imagination, for example, that portrays certain groups of human beings, such as people with different racial or ethnic backgrounds, as animal-like or less than human or somehow threatening would probably result in deadened and narrowed moral imagining with respect to these others. People operating with such a moral imagination would not be likely to see certain others' perspectives or stories as worth entering or to acknowledge any connections between their experiences and those of others they deemed less than themselves. In contrast, people who use the metaphor of human beings as brothers and sisters regardless of racial and ethnic differences would be more likely to engage in vivid and expansive moral imagining with others. On the other hand, vivid and expansive moral imagining can transform narratives, metaphors, and symbols that we draw upon in our images of the world and its possibilities. For instance, if a xenophobe were to enter the story of someone he had not previously seen as fully human, then he might come to recognize that his previous images of her were inadequate and so adopt new images that acknowledge her humanity. Our activities of moral imagining and the types of moral imagination that we draw upon in interpreting our world are thus woven tightly together. Based on figure 1, chapter three examines whether restorative moral imagination as described by advocates should in theory inspire among participants in restorative justice practices activities of vivid and expansive moral imagining.

For the most part, the vividness and expansiveness of our moral imagining is shaped by our formation within particular cultural, social, and institutional locations as well as by our exposure to a multitude narratives, metaphors, and symbols within the practices in which we participate. If we have few of these tools available to us and if we rarely use them, then our moral imagining will tend to be deadened and narrowed. The world will seem to be as given and its possibilities will seem to be few. If we exercise these activities, however, and are exposed to different sorts of narratives, metaphors, and symbols, our moral imagining may become more vivid and expansive. The character of our moral imagining may change in the course of our lives as we become members within multiple, overlapping communities and as we gain awareness of different communities both throughout history and around the world. It may also change as we engage in different practices or as we become more grounded in certain practices. Our moral imagining may also become more vivid and expansive by listening carefully to others' stories, by looking for similarities and differences across experiences, by searching for meaning within our own experiences, and by envisioning ways in which the world could change. The development of our moral imagining through these means enables us to attend better to the diversity and complexity of experience and so to create more nuanced and vibrant images of the world and its possibilities.

In light of this interpretation of moral imagination, we ought to reconsider how this faculty relates to emotion, perception, and reason. Regarding the relationship between imagination and emotion, it may be helpful to recall Sherman's observation about the relationship between perception and emotion: "Often we see not dispassionately but because of and through the emotions."[134] The relationship between imagination and emotion is analogous in that often the images that we create are shaped by our emotional responses to aspects of the world as well as to ways in which the world can change. For example, our love of another person and the pain of losing him may make us resist imagining a world without him, or our empathy with disadvantaged people may drive us to imagine a movement for social change. Our inclination and capacity for creating images of the world and its possibilities is influenced by our desire for or aversion to the changes envisioned and their effects upon us. But imagination may also conversely influence our emotional responses to the situations immediately before us. Imagining the loss of our loved one may lead us to feel our love more poignantly while he is still around, and imagining social justice may cause us to feel more hope in the work for change. Imagination and

---

[134] Sherman (1984), 45.

emotion are entwined in providing the motivation for both working toward or resisting the possibilities presented by imagination.[135]

Like emotion and imagination, perception and imagination also mutually shape each other. On the one hand, our images of the world as it is are primarily composed of the accumulation of innumerable perceptions of particular situations. We create our mental maps or frameworks or cosmologies in the course of specific interactions with others within our cultural, social, and institutional locations. Perception of these interactions provides the raw material from which we form images of the world as it is. Furthermore, our images of the possibilities of the world result from perception, which indicates what could become of the world as it is. Perception helps us to distinguish the possible from the impossible and so determines the boundary between imagination and fantasy. As we perceive new cases that do not fit within previous imaginings, we must revise our images to provide better accounts for our experiences.

On the other hand, our capacity for imagination influences our perceptions of particular situations. Returning to the examples above, imagining the possibility of a world without our loved one could inspire us to attend more carefully to him in the present, to appreciate the richness and concreteness of his being in the world now. Or imagining the possibility of a world in which all people are free and equal may lead us to attend to ways in which particular policies inhibit the creation of this sort of world. These examples suggest that imagination of possibilities for the world may cause us to look again at what lies before us in order to understand how these particulars relate to our visions of what could be. As philosopher Mary Warnock writes, "Imagination is our means of interpreting the world, and it is *also* our means of forming images in the mind. The images themselves are not separate from our interpretations of the world.... It seems to me both plausible and convenient to give the name 'imagination' to what allows

---

[135] For more on the connections between imagination and emotion, see Beidelman (1993), Introduction.

us to go beyond the barely sensory into the intellectual or thought-imbued territory of perception."[136]

The question of the relationship of moral imagination to reason brings us back to the frustrations of recent authors writing about this faculty. These authors turned to moral imagination because they found that their disciplines depend too much upon following principles and procedures according to reason. In their appeals to imagination, these authors would agree with Sherman that while reason as well as principles and procedures are indispensable, depending on reason alone in our processes of ethical discernment begins too far down the line.[137] Our every effort to reason about the appropriate principles and procedures in a particular situation is always preceded and accompanied by an effort to imagine that situation in the context of our world and its possibilities. Philosopher and novelist Iris Murdoch writes,

> When we settle down to be "thoroughly rational" about a situation, we have already, reflectively or unreflectively, imagined it in a certain way. Our deepest imaginings which structure the world in which "moral judgments" occur are already evaluations.[138]

---

[136] Warnock (1976), 194-195.

[137] Cf. Sherman (1989), 26.

[138] Murdoch (1992), 314-315. For Murdoch, the moral life cannot be reduced to the moment of decision or the examination of rational will. Rather the moral life depends in large part on the quality of thought of the agent. Attention and imagination thus play a large part in her moral philosophy because they shape our motives and beliefs, particularly with respect to our understanding of ourselves, others, and our relationships. According to Murdoch, "at crucial moments of choice most of the business of choosing is already over." See *The Sovereignty of Good* (New York: Schocken Books, 1970), 37. The ways that we imagine situations and the images that we draw upon in interpreting ourselves, others, and our relationships, therefore, fundamentally shape our decisions and actions. To understand the moral life, then, we must not only

To improve our responses to moral situations, we must not only refine our reasoning about the application of principles or procedures. We must also hone our capacities to imagine the world and its possibilities and to situate particulars within these images. We must attend to how the types of moral imagination we draw upon portray ourselves, others, and our relationships. We must also be aware of how our location within cultures, societies, and institutions influences the content of our moral imaginations as well as how the narratives, metaphors, and symbols that we employ may shape our conclusions about what might be reasonable. Furthermore, in moments of ambiguity, conflict, and disturbance, we must try to appreciate the ways in which other people might imagine the world and its possibilities and how their different images may result in different conclusions about what might be reasonable. Recent authors who have written about moral imagination appeal to this faculty because it enables us to grasp the richness and complexity of particular situations that is often excluded by reasoning about principles and procedures alone.

To be clear, I do not wish to suggest that greater appreciation of the significance of imagination alone is sufficient for understanding processes of ethical discernment. Such an argument could quickly be defeated by warnings against the dangers of fantasy in the moral life. Rather I maintain that we must be aware of the role imagination plays in the moral life alongside the other faculties of emotion, perception, and reason (not to mention memory and belief). Vivid and expansive moral imagining is a necessary, but not sufficient, component of ethical discernment. Those other faculties also play important roles in our moral lives, including acting as checks upon our ways of imagining the world and its possibilities. Nevertheless, although imagination is not sufficient for being moral, we cannot understand fully the nature of morality without understanding imagination and its relationships with emotion, perception, and reason.

---

understand processes of reasoning, but also our habits of imagination and the interconnections between reason and imagination.

In summary, I have offered in this section a definition of moral imagination as the cognitive faculty that enables us to create images of the world and its possibilities. This definition is rooted in my reading of moral imagination authors who have appealed to this faculty in order to overcome their common frustrations with an overdependence on principles and procedures in their fields. These authors share with Aristotelian virtue ethicists a recognition of the limits of principles and procedures as similar to the limits of law. But the former give a larger part to moral imagination in overcoming these limitations. A broader definition of moral imagination than that offered by Sherman and Nussbaum reveals that our moral questions about self-identity, perceptions of the other, and the relationships between self and other are always answered in view of our images of the world as it is and of its possibilities. These images help to organize and give meaning to our experience using the tools of narrative, metaphor, and symbolism that we find amidst the cultural interactions, social arrangements, and institutional structures in which we are located. We can describe different types of moral imagination by highlighting their use of narrative, metaphorical, and symbolic schemes. Furthermore, types of moral imagination can foster or hinder activities of moral imagining, such as entering into others' stories, appreciating their perspectives, drawing connections among various experiences, and considering myriad possibilities for the world. In turn, vivid and expansive moral imagining can transform our images of the world and its possibilities. Awareness of the types of moral imagination we draw upon and our activities of moral imagining may help us to understand processes of ethical discernment because imagination both precedes and accompanies perception, emotion, and reason as we try to make sense of moral situations. Without understanding our images of the world and its possibilities, we cannot understand ourselves, others, or our relationships.

MORAL IMAGINATION AND JUSTICE AS EQUITY

What difference then does vivid and expansive moral imagining make for efforts to realize justice as equity? Consider first the images of the world and its possibilities presupposed by a legalistic interpretation of justice. In a parenthetical statement above, I remarked that even with strict legal justice, moral imagination would play its part, although it would seem that vividness and expansiveness would actually hinder the realization of justice here. This interpretation of justice depends upon images of the world as governed by laws that comprehensively, universally, and accurately account for all types of wrongdoing. According to these images, law reflects the balance of the moral order of good against evil and right against wrong. The only possibility in response to a crime according to this sort of moral imagination is the return of punishment against offenders in order to reinstate the moral balance upheld by law. The content of the sort of moral imagination presupposed by a legalistic interpretation of justice may be summarized in one of its central symbols: Lady Justice. Standing with sword and scale, she represents the force of law backed by the violence of punishment as well as the balance of the cosmic order (she is a goddess). Her image typically appears in front of courts of law, which assume the symbolic power of Lady Justice in their efforts to uphold the law. When we settle down to apply laws to particular situations according to the mandates of reason, as a legalistic interpretation dictates, we have already imagined the world as one in which Lady Justice reigns. This interpretation of justice, therefore, assumes a particular type of moral imagination because it draws on certain images of the world and its possibilities in which this interpretation can be meaningful.

A legalistic interpretation of justice does not necessarily require, or even encourage, vivid and expansive moral imagining. Lady Justice does wear a blindfold after all. Her inability, or unwillingness, to see symbolizes the requirement that justice apply the law strictly, without consideration of the particular characteristics of the offense, offender, victims, or communities in which the crime took place. Undeniably, her blindness often serves justice because all too frequently the consideration of certain characteristics of stakeholders in a crime, such as their racial or ethnic backgrounds, have resulted in unequal treatment under the law—hence, the advent of sentencing guidelines in the 1980s as a reform of our criminal and juvenile justice systems. Nevertheless, blindness also inhibits her ability to recognize when the law might be mistaken or biased or overly harsh in particular circumstances. Justice cannot deviate from the law, cannot ponder responses to crime that have not been enumerated by a legislator, and cannot recognize situations in which the law has nothing to say or would seem to get it wrong. A legalistic interpretation of justice discourages expansive and vivid moral imagining because it assumes that the only procedure or principle necessary for judgment is the balancing of the scales, which were presumed to be balanced at the outset. We ought not to contemplate the narratives of the lives of victims, offenders, and community members because their stories are irrelevant to this procedure. We ought not try to make connections between the crime and other aspects of our experience, such as possible connections between theft and economic plight. Nor ought we attempt to enliven our images of the case in order to understand it more fully; to understand it, we need only the facts that we can plug into a chart or logarithm. And we ought not to consider possibilities other than sentences enumerated in the law. A legalistic interpretation of justice therefore narrows and deadens moral imagining.

To be fair, our current criminal and juvenile justice systems do not fully embody a legalistic interpretation of justice in practice. Some aspects of our courts of law rather defy the ideal represented by Lady Justice. In the last few decades, for example, the use of victims' impact statements, which situate particular offenses within the contexts of victims' lives, has become more prevalent. Also, in determining mitigating and aggravating factors in sentencing phases of particular offenses, especially capital offenses, the life stories of offenders have been told in court in an effort to reveal the effects of bad education, physical and mental abuse, or poverty on criminal behavior. Moreover, many judges bristle against the restrictions placed upon them by sentencing guidelines precisely because they find that these restrictions inhibit them from responding to the particulars of specific cases where the law might fail for various reasons. These practices and efforts help to lift the blindfold, to allow the people who participate in our criminal and juvenile justice systems to enter into others' narratives, to appreciate their perspectives, to draw connections among cases, and to contemplate possibilities outside of mandatory or routine sentences— and so to consider the demands of justice as equity as well as the demands of the law.

But these aspects moral imagining ought not to be overemphasized; the practices of our current criminal and juvenile justice systems still give little room for this faculty. The vast majority of cases are dispensed with through plea bargaining, in which no one gets to tell any story. Moreover, plea bargaining has become increasingly a practice of applying the same short-hand sentence to similar types of crime for the sake of expedience, without respect to the particulars of each offense, offender, victim, or community.[139] Those cases that are not pled out meander through largely adversarial procedures that only permit moral imagining in the final moment—at sentencing. Even then, the judgment is typically left to the judge alone, and her discernment process is restricted evermore by the requirements of sentencing guidelines designed by legislators. This system would seem to deaden and narrow moral imagining, to limit images of the world as it is and its possibilities available to the people who participate in it. Reflection and action concerning self-identity, perceptions of the other, and relationships between self and other are confined by the dictates of law, and the resolution of the ambiguities, conflicts, and disturbances raised by crime only comes through reference to legal

---

[139] For an overview of sentencing practices in the United States, see Brian Forst, "Prosecution and Sentencing," in *Crime*, ed. James Q. Wilson and Joan Petersilia (San Francisco: ICS Press, 1995), 363-386.

Table 1. Characteristics of Strict Legal Justice versus Justice as Equity.

Strict Legal Justice	Justice as Equity
Judgment follows only from statement of law.	Law is important in judgment, but not the only source of moral knowledge.
Law is comprehensive, universal, and accurate, reflecting a balanced moral order.	Law is inherently limited because of its necessary generality. The moral order is not necessarily balanced already; it may reflect various injustices, which may be reified in law.
Only judges make decisions.	People other than judges can make decision (for example, arbitrators).
Particulars of specific cases are irrelevant to the application of the law.	Particulars of specific cases require attention; we cannot know how the law applies without first attending to the particulars.
Intent of law and context of legislators is irrelevant to application of the law.	Being equitable requires considering intent of law and context of legislators in writing the law.
Actions are the primary data for judgment; the context of actions, the intentions and characters of actors, and aspects of ongoing relationships among stakeholders are irrelevant.	Actions are important, but not the only relevant factors in judgment. Context, intention, character, and relationship must also be considered.
Justice requires punishment in order to right the balance of the moral order; amount of appropriate punishment is enumerated in the law.	A higher form of justice allows for forgiveness, grace, and mercy.
Litigation and force are used to reach and implement judgment.	Negotiation and arbitration may be used to reach judgment.
Reason is the most important faculty used in processes of ethical discernment generally and efforts to realize justice specifically.	Other faculties, such as emotion, imagination, and perception, in addition to reason are necessary for processes of ethical discernment generally and efforts to realize justice specifically.

codes. Of course, the principles and procedures of our legal system offer important protections for everyone involved in crime that ought not to be undervalued, but many of the practices of our current criminal and juvenile justice systems also tend to limit our faculties of moral imagination and our capacities to be equitable.

An equitable interpretation of justice in contrast presupposes images of the world and its possibilities that are much more diverse and complex than those of a legalistic interpretation. Martha Nussbaum summarizes this picture of the world well: "The world of...equity...is a world of imperfect human efforts and complex obstacles to doing well."[140]   An equitable interpretation of justice supposes a world in which law is limited because the world contains multitudes of possibilities that cannot be summarized comprehensively, universally, and accurately. Law is undeniably necessary for the good ordering of communal life, and in some ways, it does uphold a moral order. But a view of the world from a position of equitable justice sees ways in which the law can also be incomplete and incorrect, sometimes resulting in mistakes or excessive harshness. Human beings make the law to fit their needs; it is not handed down from above by God or Lady Justice or Zeus. We cannot know beforehand the circumstances of all crimes, and so we must allow some room for discerning what ought to be done when the law in its generality fails us, which it inevitably will. The scales of justice are always in flux as we stumble through this world, and sometimes the precisely equal return demanded by corrective justice ought to be mitigated or qualified by a touch of grace and mercy. This way of imagining the world is more piecemeal and multivalent, admitting more of the ambiguity, complexity, and disturbance of human experience, than the type of moral imagination associated with strict legal justice (table 1).

The layers of images of the world and its possibilities associated with an equitable interpretation of justice imply the need for more expansive and vivid moral imagining.   The realization of justice as

---

[140] Nussbaum (1999), 159.

equity within such a diverse and complex world requires certain habits of character that are not necessary or encouraged within a legalistic interpretation of justice. Aristotle describes several of these habits associated with the virtue of equity: being merciful to the weakness of human nature, weighing the intentions of legislators in addition to the words of legal codes, recognizing the limitations of the law and considering other possibilities when the law fails, bearing in mind the entire life stories of offenders when examining their actions, and allowing for negotiation and arbitration rather than insisting upon force and litigation. These habits entail activities associated with vivid and expansive moral imagining such as entering into others' stories; appreciating their perspectives; drawing connections across multiple, complex experiences; and considering possibilities for the future outside of sentences enumerated in the law.

Weighing the intentions of legislators, for example, involves entering imaginatively into their narratives in order to appreciate their images of the world and its possibilities. By attending to their narratives, we gain a more thorough sense of their cosmologies or frameworks or mental maps and how particular laws fit within them. We also begin to perceive the cultural interactions, social arrangements, or institutional structures that they wished either to change or to uphold through legislation. Equity, therefore, requires that we weigh the intentions of legislators underlying particular laws, but this habit of character demands certain capacities of vivid and expansive moral imagining that can move beyond the often simple and coarse, gross, and monochromatic images of the world and its possibilities presented by legal codes. The other habits of character associated with equity likewise demand the capacities of vivid and expansive moral imagining. To supplement and correct the law adequately we must be able to create images of the world and its possibilities that are subtle and high, precise, and richly colored.

In short, the realization of justice as equity requires expansive and vivid moral imagining. The relationship between being equitable and activities of moral imagining are summarized in table 2; exploring this relationship in processes of ethical discernment among participants in restorative justice practices will be the focus of chapter four.

Table 2. Being Equitable in Comparison with Activities of Moral Imagining.

Being Equitable	Activities of Moral Imagining
• Attending to particulars of specific cases.	
• Looking at intentions of legislators in context in which laws were written.	• Appreciating others' stories and perspectives.
• Understanding actions within the context of an entire story and an entire life. Considering intentions underlying actions.	• Drawing connections and seeing relationships across experiences.
• Giving weight to positive aspects of relationships.	• Enlivening perceptions of particular circumstances.
• Allowing for negotiation and arbitration. Finding responses outside of the strict demands of the law.	• Considering myriad possibilities for the future.

If our current criminal and juvenile justice systems tend to deaden and narrow moral imagining, then in order to serve justice better, we must explore what sorts of cultural interactions, social arrangements, and institutional structures would foster the vivid and expansive moral imagining necessary for equitable responses to crime. The practices associated with these interactions, arrangements, and structures would presumably help the people who participate in them to create a wide range of images of the world and its possibilities. Ideally they would facilitate our capacity to enter into others' life stories and to appreciate their worldviews. These practices would aid participants in making connections across particular cases and considering multiple possibilities for the futures of stakeholders in crime. The types of moral imagination fostered within these interactions, arrangements, and structures would allow for the diversity and complexity of experience, generating images of the world and its possibilities that are vibrant and nuanced. The narratives, metaphors, and symbols cultivated by these practices would leave room for ambiguity, conflict, and disturbance in order to address the particulars of the concrete cases before us. Any criminal or juvenile justice system that encourages this sort of vividness and expansiveness in moral imagining would differ dramatically from the status quo.

CONCLUSION

I began this chapter with a warning to the reader that the bulk of Western moral philosophy would deny the significance of moral imagination in processes of ethical discernment generally and in efforts to justice specifically. In a world in which we would often prefer clear answers to moral questions, especially questions of justice, imagination as a cognitive faculty would seem to introduce too much ambiguity, conflict, and disturbance into the organization of our experience. Reason trumps imagination, as well as the related faculties of perception and emotion, because it seems to simplify the diversity and complexity of the world brought to light when we attend closely to the particulars. It provides straight-forward conclusions about right and wrong, good and evil. The view that reason should be the ultimate guide of our processes of ethical discernment and efforts to realize justice is closely allied with a legalistic interpretation of justice, which supposes that justice is served through the strict application of the law.

In the course of this chapter, however, I have introduced alternative streams of thought that both recognize the limitations of a legalistic interpretation of justice and value imagination, emotion, and perception alongside reason. The headwaters of one of these streams lie in the thought of Aristotle, who maintained that equity must supplement and correct strict legal justice in order to attain a higher form of justice. Being equitable entails engagement in certain activities such as attending to the particulars of specific cases, considering the intentions of legislators and the contexts in which they wrote laws, understanding actions within the narrative arc of an entire life, contemplating the contexts in which a person committed an action, giving weight to the positive aspects of relationships, and allowing for some flexibility in formulating responses to others' actions. Nancy Sherman and Martha Nussbaum, in their interpretations of Aristotle, have drawn upon his discussions of justice as equity to demonstrate the need for faculties other than reason when we embody this virtue. They have focused especially on perception and emotion, although they have given imagination some credit for the achievement of justice as equity. The second stream begins in the common frustrations of moral imagination authors who have found that their disciplines depend too much upon principles and procedures in their discernment processes. These authors have found relief for their frustrations in the concept of moral imagination. Their work suggests that this faculty may help practitioners in their various fields to overcome the limitations of a strictly procedural and principled understanding of their practices.

The confluence of these streams brings together moral imagination and the realization of justice as equity. I have defined moral imagination, drawing on the latter stream, as the cognitive faculty that enables human beings to create images of the world and what it could become. The activities of moral imagining include entering into others' stories, appreciating their perspectives, making connections across particular cases, and considering myriad possibilities for the future. This faculty is moral because our images of the world and what it could become situate our reflections and actions concerning self-identity, perceptions of the other, and relationships between self and other. We generate these images as we engage in practices located within the contexts of cultural interactions, social arrangements, and institutional structures. The narratives, metaphors, and symbols that fill our imaginations arise from these contexts, and we organize our experiences schematically by drawing upon these tools. While imagination in itself is not sufficient for being moral and it must be accompanied by reason, emotion, and perception, this discussion has suggested that understanding ethical discernment generally, and efforts to realize justice as equity specifically, necessitates understanding the part that moral imagination plays.

Although imagination plays a role in the moral lives of all human beings with a certain level of cognitive functioning, I have suggested here that some people sometimes imagine in response to moral situations more vividly and expansively than others. The extent to which our moral imagining is vivid and expansive depends greatly upon our cultural, social, and institutional locations. Certain locations tend to deaden and narrow our moral imagining while others expose us to diverse narratives, metaphors, and symbols. I maintain that a legalistic interpretation of justice entails a set of images of the world and its possibilities that is constrained by the limits of the law, and so the cultures, societies, and institutions associated with this interpretation contribute to the deadening and narrowing of moral imagining.

But if we believe with Aristotle that this interpretation of justice needs correction and supplementation by equity, then we will begin to see that higher forms of justice both foster and demand vivid and expansive moral imagining. We must move beyond the mechanical application of the law according to the mandates of reason—for example, through sentencing guidelines—toward practices in which we enter the stories of others' lives, appreciate their perspectives, draw connections across our experiences, and consider myriad possibilities for changing the world. Our imaginations must engender layers of images of the world and its possibilities. By cultivating these practices, our efforts to realize justice may more readily respond to the diversity and complexity of human experience, especially as revealed in incidents of crime. Vivid and expansive moral imagining is necessary for realizing justice as equity. With this premise established, the following two chapters explore the type of moral imagination assumed by restorative justice advocates and whether it fosters vivid and expansive moral imagining among participants in restorative justice practices, thereby enabling them to respond equitably to particular cases.

CHAPTER 3

Restorative Moral Imagination

I n his classic text on restorative justice, *Changing Lenses*,[141] Howard Zehr argues that our current criminal justice systems fail to respond to the realities faced by offenders, victims, and communities in the aftermath of crime. Based on rehabilitative and retributive philosophies of punishment, our institutional responses to crime "mythologize and mystify"[142] the human dramas of those people most directly affected by crime. As crime becomes defined as an offense against the state rather than real harm caused to specific people, victims are marginalized from the legal process, unless they are useful as state witnesses. Offenders must disappear behind their lawyers because the adversarial legal process and the threat of severe punishment discourages their honesty about whether and why they violated the law. Communities become conflated with the state and have no voice other than the prosecutor's in a courtroom proceeding. As a result, Zehr argues, we are blind to the real harm done to people by crime. Because our current criminal justice systems dominated by the lenses of

---

[141] Howard Zehr, *Changing Lenses: A New Focus for Crime and Justice* (Scottdale, PA: Herald Press, 1990).
[142] Ibid., 18.

retribution and rehabilitation occlude our vision, the harm cannot be adequately repaired and our current systems fail to address the needs of victims, offenders, and communities.

According to Zehr, these failures signal the need to look at crime in a new way, to shift the paradigm by which we understand the essence of legal offenses. He proposes a "restorative" lens that allows us to see more clearly the causes and effects of crime. This proposal has now become one of the guiding metaphors of discussions about restorative justice. Almost without exception, restorative justice advocates cite Zehr's call for changing lenses and likewise appeal to their readers to transform criminal and juvenile justice systems to respond to crime in a restorative manner. They juxtapose restorative justice against the dominant practices of criminal justice shaped by theories of retribution and rehabilitation. Like Zehr, other proponents of restorative justice suggest that we must think about crime in new ways and that our new ways of thinking will result in practices that will more adequately respond to the experiences of victims, offenders, and communities.

Restorative justice advocates' petition to transform our conceptions of crime is often linked to a request that we transform our moral imaginations from a retributive or rehabilitative type to a restorative type. They would like us to imagine those who commit crimes, their victims, and the communities in which they live in ways that "repair the harm" of crime rather than ways that punish or treat the offender. This chapter explores the narratives, metaphors, and symbols of a restorative type of moral imagination as presented by leading advocates of restorative justice. I conclude that the images of a restorative moral imagination ought to encourage participants to enter into others' stories, to appreciate their perspectives, to draw connections across several cases, and to consider myriad possibilities for what can arise from the moral situations precipitated by crime. That is, adopting a restorative lens on the world and its possibilities should in theory cultivate activities of vivid and expansive moral imagining among participants in these practices. Doing so should also thereby enable them be more equitable in their processes of ethical discernment than if they drew on rehabilitative or retributive moral imaginations.

DEFINING "RESTORATIVE JUSTICE"

Before describing restorative moral imagination, we must establish a definition of "restorative justice" that places appropriate boundaries on this concept and its associated practices. Although some advocates contest the need for a definition of restorative justice and often conversations among advocates about definitions resemble what one observer calls "a weird inter-faith squabble in an obscure religious sect,"[143] the definition used here may be a useful hermeneutical tool for filtering out models and programs that do not meet restorative justice ideals.

Three particularly thorny problems arise when defining restorative justice. First, the term is used by a broad array of programs that on the surface seem to have little in common. Although advocates argue that restorative justice recalls ancient justice practices of indigenous peoples around the world,[144] the concept has developed in the modern Western

---

[143] Quoted in Gordon Bazemore and Mara Schiff, "Paradigm Muddle or Paradigm Paralysis? The Wide and Narrow Roads to Restorative Justice Reform (Or, a Little Confusion May Be a Good Thing)," *Contemporary Justice Review* 7, no. 1 (2004), 51. Howard Zehr discusses the difficulties of defining restorative justice and the reasons for defining it despite these difficulties in his seminal text, *The Little Book of Restorative Justice* (Intercourse, PA: Good Books, 2002). This book is frequently used by programs as a brief introduction to restorative justice theories and practices for volunteers, community members, and facilitators. While interviewing program directors, every director made sure that I had a copy of my own.

[144] This claim is quite common throughout restorative justice literature; an exhaustive citation of everyone who makes it is impossible. For some examples, see Denise Breton and Stephen Lehman, *The Mystic Heart of Justice: Restoring Wholeness in a Broken World* (West Chester, PA: Chrysalis

world only within the last four decades to describe programs such as victim-offender mediation and dialogue, truth-and-reconciliation commissions, family-group conferencing, citizen- and neighborhood-accountability boards, and community conferencing. While the actual practices of these programs differ significantly, they tend to share "a wide array of face-to-face non-adversarial decision-making dialogue encounters between victim, offender, and community members in response to specific crime and/or incidents of harm."[145] These programs most frequently involve juvenile offenders, their victims, and their communities, but they are not limited to juvenile justice systems. The South African Truth and Reconciliation Commission, for example, worked with a broad swath of the population of that country from young adults to the elderly. Restorative justice programs have much in common, but they also differ in significant ways, making definition of restorative justice a complex matter.

Another difficulty with defining restorative justice is that while this concept has been widely used, it has also been widely abused. This problem is particularly evident in the United States where most restorative justice programs are small, local operations that may not have much contact with peers around the country and the world.[146]

Books, 2001); Daniel W. Van Ness and Karen Heetderks Strong, *Restoring Justice*, 2nd edition (Cincinnati: Anderson Publishing Company, 2002); Gordon Bazemore and Mara Schiff, *Juvenile Justice Reform and Restorative Justice: Building Theory and Policy from Practice* (Portland, OR: Willan Publishing, 2005); Elmar Weitekamp, "The History of Restorative Justice," in *Restorative Juvenile Justice: Repairing the Harm of Youth Crime*, ed. Gordon Bazemore and Lode Walgrave (Monsey, NY: Criminal Justice Press, 1999); and Howard Zehr (1990). See also Zehr's *The Little Book of Restorative Justice* (Intercourse, PA: Good Books, 2002).

[145] Bazemore and Schiff (2005), 35.

[146] Bazemore and Schiff (2005) discuss this difficulty as a product of "the historical absence of any national juvenile justice legislation" in the United States (6). Their text provides a helpful account of the prevalence of types of restorative justice programs throughout the U.S. and their faithfulness to

Facilitators of some restorative justice programs could look at other programs that claim to be restorative and see little or nothing restorative about them. One reason for this difficulty is that restorative justice programs have arisen in the United States at the same time that criminal and juvenile justice systems have become more punitive by transferring young offenders to criminal courts and restricting judicial discretion through various forms of sentencing guidelines, including mandatory-minimum, determinate, and blended sentencing mandates. Criminologists Gordon Bazemore and Mara Schiff observe that,

> Interestingly, and somewhat ironically, during roughly this same period [since the 1970s], some twenty states also adopted restorative justice language into their juvenile court purpose clauses, while another fifteen added restorative justice to state juvenile justice administrative codes or similar policy documents…. Indeed, restorative justice language in some states…was passed as a part of the same juvenile justice legislation that contained more punitive provisions mandating expanded transfer to criminal court.[147]

The simultaneous rise of punitive justice systems and restorative justice has resulted in confusion about the meaning of restorative justice. A cynical interpretation of these events would suppose that legislators included the language of restorative justice in order to soften the blow of punitive measures that have circumscribed the social welfare powers of the juvenile court. A slightly less cynical interpretation would suppose that legislators just did not know what restorative justice entails, but included the term because of its catchiness or political

---

restorative principles. Other nations, including New Zealand, Australia, and Great Britain, have been able to create mandates for restorative justice in their juvenile justice systems, contributing to consistency and accountability in their programs because of guidance on a national level.

[147] Ibid., 6.

correctness.   Of course, more hopeful interpretations are possible. However, the lack of support for implementing restorative justice programs in most (though admittedly not *all*) states militates against them.[148]

A third challenge in defining restorative justice is that it is one among many competing alternative conceptions of justice that have arisen over recent years, including community and transformative justice.[149] "Community justice" advocates, for example, often include restorative justice among their ideal concepts and practices, but restorative justice is also merely one component in a broader program

---

[148] Minnesota, for example, is one notable exception. As will become apparent in Chapter Four, Colorado also has the potential to be an exception, although the jury is still out in this case. On March 31, 2008, Governor Bill Ritter signed into law House Bill 08-1117, which gives judges the authority to offer accused juvenile offenders the legal option to participate in restorative justice processes voluntarily. While the law opens the door to restorative justice, it does not provide funding for the programs necessary to implement it. See Joshua Wachtel, "Colorado Children's Code Authorizes Restorative Justice Conferences for Adjudicated Youth (Parts 1 & 2)," *Restorative Practices eForum*, International Institute of Restorative Practices, posted May 21 and July 17, 2008, www. iirp.org.

[149] The March 2004 issue of *Contemporary Justice Review* (7, no. 1) provides a useful collection of articles by leaders in these movements debating the relationships among community, transformative, and restorative justice. For a good introduction to community justice see David R. Karp and Todd R. Clear, "Community Justice: A Conceptual Framework," in *Criminal Justice 2000*, vol. 2 in *Boundary Changes in Criminal Justice Organizations* (Washington, D.C.: National Institute of Justice, 2000): 323-368.   Available at http://www.ncjrs.gov/criminal_justice2000/vol_2/02i2.pdf.   Also, David R. Karp and Todd R. Clear, eds., *What is Community Justice? Case Studies of Restorative Justice and Community Supervision* (Thousand Oaks, CA: Sage Publications, 2002). For an overview of transformative justice, see M. Kay Harris, "Transformative Justice: The Transformation of Restorative Justice," in *Handbook of Restorative Justice: A Global Perspective*, ed. Dennis Sullivan and Larry Tifft (New York: Routledge Press, 2006): 555-566.

that also includes community policing and corrections. Determining where restorative justice stops and community justice starts is difficult. Likewise, drawing the line (if there is one) between restorative justice and "transformative justice" presents problems. Viewing transformative justice as a corrective of underlying inequalities throughout society, various advocates have argued that transformative and restorative justice are identical, overlapping, *and* diametrically opposed.

Together these challenges suggest that any definition of restorative justice must describe existing programs while both offering normative guidance as to what counts as restoration and remaining open to innovation in restorative justice in the future. It must also address both the processes and the outcomes of restorative justice. These requirements, therefore, disqualify the definition offered by Paul McCold and Ted Wachtel, who claim that restorative justice is "a collaborative process involving those most directly affected by a crime, called the 'primary stakeholders,' in determining how best to repair the harm caused by the offense."[150] The main problem with this definition is that it focuses on the processes of restorative justice without delimiting the outcomes. Any outcome of these processes would be considered restorative, even if the primary stakeholders collaborated to repair the harm in a retributive or rehabilitative manner. Howard Zehr's definition—"a process to involve, to the extent possible, those who have a stake in a specific offense and to collectively identify and address harms, needs, and obligations, in order to heal and put things as right as possible"—does little better.[151] By emphasizing process and excluding consideration of outcomes, he also seems to suggest that any outcome of a restorative justice process is *de facto* restorative.

---

[150] Paul McCold and Ted Wachtel, *In Pursuit of Paradigm: A Theory of Restorative Justice*, paper presented at the XIII World Congress of Criminology, 10-15 August 2003, Rio de Janeiro, 1. Retrieved at http://fp.enter.net/restorativepractices/paradigm.pdf.

[151] Howard Zehr (2002), 37.

Problems with these definitions are evident in a case described by John Braithwaite.[152] The participants in a restorative justice process in Canberra, Australia agreed that a 12-year-old boy who had shoplifted should wear a t-shirt emblazoned with the words "I am a Thief" in front of the store from which he stole. During this conference, all the major stakeholders in the offense participated to identify and repair the harms that the young boy caused, and they all felt that they had put things right.   Yet the outcome of the process was a humiliating and demoralizing experience for the offender, who was not reintegrated into the community after fulfilling his obligations arising from his offense. Controversy followed this decision because some advocates argued that any outcome from a restorative justice process is restorative while others found that this outcome did more to shame and stigmatize the boy than to repair the harm caused by his crime.   Critics called for restrictions on conference agreements in order to avoid degrading or humiliating outcomes and suggested that restorative principles should prohibit any such outcomes in the future.

To address these issues, Gordon Bazemore and Lode Walgrave have created a "goal-focused" definition of restorative justice: "every action that is primarily oriented to doing justice by repairing the harm that has been caused by a crime."[153] For the purposes of this text, this definition provides the most appropriate boundary to delineate restorative justice; it will serve as a hermeneutical filter for models and programs that meet restorative ideals.   It describes a wide-range of programs from New Zealand family-group conferencing to the South African Truth and Reconciliation Commission, and it may include a variety of actions that fall outside of existing restorative justice

---

[152] John Braithwaite, *Restorative Justice and Responsive Regulation* (New York: Oxford University Press, 2002).

[153] Gordon Bazemore and Lode Walgrave, "Restorative Juvenile Justice: In Search of Fundamentals and an Outline for Systemic Reform," in *Restorative Juvenile Justice: Repairing the Harm of Youth Crime*, ed. Gordon Bazemore and Lode Walgrave (Monsey, NY: Criminal Justice Press, 1999b), 48.

programs, allowing for future innovation in the field of restorative justice. This definition also includes a normative requirement: an action must seek to "repair harm" to be restorative. The outcome of the Canberra conference, for instance, would be rejected as restorative justice because it aimed not at repairing the harm associated with the crime, but at causing harm to the boy, punishing him for the sake of punishment and inflicting more harm that would then need to be repaired as well. Another advantage of this definition is that it includes processes and outcomes since both are actions that satisfy the normative requirement of repairing harm.

Each of the components of this definition requires greater elaboration.[154] First, like most restorative justice advocates, Bazemore and Walgrave reject a definition of "crime" as a violation of the law or an offense against the state. Instead, they maintain that crime is first and foremost harm done by offenders against other people. The harm that offenders cause through the commission of crime may include "material losses, physical injuries, psychological consequences, relational problems, and social dysfunctions."[155] This alternative definition of crime emphasizes the relational aspects of restorative justice and stresses that the central conflict caused by crime is not between offenders and the state, but between offenders and their victims.

Second, victims are primarily defined as the individuals most directly hurt by crime, but also secondarily as the community in which

---

[154] In an article highly critical of this definition, Paul McCold claims that what he calls Bazemore and Walgrave's "maximalist model" allows court-ordered community services and other retributive sanctions to count as restorative. However, McCold's criticisms are based on several mischaracterizations of Bazemore and Walgrave's argument. In particular, McCold does not seem to acknowledge Bazemore and Walgrave's elaboration of the components of their definition. See Paul McCold, "Toward a Holistic Vision of Restorative Juvenile Justice: A Reply to the Maximalist Model," *Contemporary Justice Review* 3.4 (2000): 357-414.

[155] Bazemore and Walgrave (1999b), 49.

a crime occurred because it also has undergone material, physical, psychological, relational, and social harms. Bazemore and Walgrave waffle as to whether society or the state should also be considered a victim, but seem to suggest that the government has a role, albeit a supporting role, in repairing the harm caused by crime.

Finally, Bazemore and Walgrave offer a three-tiered interpretation of "doing justice." They maintain, first, that doing justice entails legal protection of the procedural rights of all participants as citizens of a particular jurisdiction. Here Bazemore and Walgrave suggest that the state has a supporting role in restorative justice insofar as it can provide certain safeguards through measures such as legal review of restorative justice processes and outcomes that protect against violation of the rights of victims and offenders.

Second, doing justice means attaining "*satisfaction* of all parties with a stake in the offense."[156] Bazemore and Walgrave describe what satisfaction might mean for victims, offenders, and communities. For victims, satisfaction requires the opportunity to express anger and fear; the feeling that they have been heard, supported, and taken seriously; and reparation or compensation for their losses. Offenders should be informed that they have harmed others through their crime. They also need to have the opportunity to repair the damage caused by their wrongdoing. The satisfaction of communities requires the re-establishment of social efficacy and cohesion with the reintegration of both victims and offenders in a safe and secure environment.

Lastly, doing justice requires establishing "a feeling of *equity*, of being treated in a similar way as others in similar circumstances."[157] Note that for Bazemore and Walgrave "doing justice" corresponds better with an Aristotelian interpretation of justice as equity than with a legalistic interpretation of justice, although they do not develop their understanding of equity any more than this brief description, thereby limiting comparison of this interpretation with Aristotle's.

---

[156] Ibid. Emphasis in original.
[157] Ibid., 53. Emphasis in original.

Nonetheless, for Bazemore and Walgrave, the justice of a case is primarily determined not by strict application of the law, but by like treatment for like cases. They do not discuss any further what is required to realize like treatment for like cases. However, understanding equity as like treatment seems to imply that doing justice requires consideration of the particulars of every case on its own terms, allowing for thorough consideration of how cases differ or are alike.

In sum, Bazemore and Walgrave define "restorative justice" as every action that is primarily oriented to achieving fairness and satisfaction for all parties affected by a crime—victims, offenders, and communities—while protecting their legal rights, often with the assistance of the state. Fairness and satisfaction are achieved by repairing the material, physical, psychological, relational, and social harms caused by a crime, defined as the infliction of harm by an offender upon other people. This interpretation of restorative justice includes both the processes of reaching consensus among victims, offenders, and communities about how to repair the harm of a crime and the outcomes of these processes, thereby avoiding the difficulties with McCold and Wachtel's and Zehr's definitions. Furthermore, this definition accounts for a broad array of programs and models that abide by restorative ideals, and it allows for innovation in the field. It also has a normative component with its insistence that actions must repair the harm caused by crime, thereby filtering out retributive and rehabilitative programs and models that instead follow the normative guides of balancing the scales of justice or treating the illness of offenders. Because of these strengths, Bazemore and Walgrave's definition will serve within this study as the measure of which models and programs count as restorative.

Building upon the foundation of this definition, Bazemore and Walgrave suggest delineating principles that define the goals of their "goal-focused" definition.[158] The literature on restorative justice

---

[158] Bazemore and Schiff (2005) employ a similar strategy when defining restorative justice. I use the term "principle" here because it is the most

provides many options for what these principles could be. Bazemore and Walgrave draw upon Daniel Van Ness and Karen Heetderks Strong's three principles of restorative justice, which are among the most commonly cited principles in the literature:

(1) Justice requires that we work to restore those who have been injured: victims, communities, and even offenders;

(2) Those most directly involved and affected by crime—victims, offenders, and community—should have the opportunity to participate as fully in the response as they wish; and

(3) While the government is responsible for preserving a just public order, the community's role in establishing and maintaining a just peace must be given special significance.[159]

---

common term within restorative justice literature. For now, I will use these principles in my definition of restorative justice, although I dispute the model of the moral life that this definition presupposes. That is, this definition assumes that principles are central to the moral life rather than summaries of moral experience. While principles are important as guidelines and they may support an environment that fosters certain virtues, most people do not behave in a certain way because they are applying a principle to a given situation. Rather they have been formed in an environment that supports certain principles and that formation leads them to behave in a particular manner as new situations arise. My use of these principles is meant to delineate what types of programs might be restorative. Programs that facilitate the participation of all stakeholders, draw on their participation to delineate the harm and appropriate measures to repair it, and empower communities to preserve public order fall within this definition.

[159] Van Ness and Strong (2002), 38-43. Several advocates of restorative justice as well as their professional guilds have offered comprehensive accounts of the principles of restorative justice. Among the most influential is *The Declaration of Leuven on the Advisability of Promoting the Restorative Approach to Juvenile Crime*, from the first International Conference on "Restorative Justice for Juveniles: Potentialities, Risks, and Problems for Research," 12-14 May 1997, Leuven, Belgium. Another international document describing a general

These principles represent both what many restorative justice programs actually do as well as what they aspire to do, and they are commonly recognized by restorative justice practitioners as restorative.[160] They describe and prescribe "repairing the harm" as including the outcome of "healing" injuries caused by crime as well as the injuries that may have contributed to crime (for example, systemic injuries incurred by offenders such as poverty); empowerment of lay stakeholders through participation in processes to respond to crime; and transformation of relationships of the government to communities in which crimes occur, leading to the de-professionalization and informalization of legal proceedings regarding crime. With the goal-focused definition, these principles help to distinguish restorative justice programs and literature; to summarize the moral knowledge of practitioners, theorists, and advocates; and to evaluate the extent to which programs achieve "restorativeness." The models and programs considered in this chapter and the next will satisfy the goal-focused definition.

MORAL IMAGINATION AMONG RESTORATIVE JUSTICE ADVOCATES

While this definition of restorative justice helps to delimit the literature and programs pertinent to a discussion of restorative moral

---

consensus on restorative justice principles is *Basic Principles on the Use of Restorative Justice Programmes in Criminal Matters*, United Nations, 2000. Other authors that have delineated restorative justice principles include Zehr (2002), especially chapter two.

[160] Bazemore and Schiff (2005) performed a qualitative study of restorative justice programs to verify the extent to which facilitators recognize these principles as restorative and succeed in implementing them. Their text offers unique insight into some of the challenges of operating programs according to principles that are difficult to put into practice and that often come into conflict.

imagination, it does not fully reveal what restorative moral imagination might be. As defined in previous chapters, moral imagination is the cognitive faculty that empowers human beings to create images of the world and its possibilities. These images inform our understanding of ourselves, others, and our relationships with one another through the schematic use of narratives, metaphors, and symbols. Because of the schematic character of moral imagination, we can describe different types of moral imagination in terms of the narratives, metaphors, and symbols that they use. Some types of moral imagination are better suited to fostering the activities of vivid and expansive moral imagining. This section explores "restorative moral imagination" as presented by advocates, especially as they contrast restorative justice with rehabilitation and retribution. I conclude that narratives, metaphors, and symbols of restorative moral imagination would seem to promote activities of vivid and expansive moral imagining in the processes of ethical discernment among participants in these practices, and so better enable them to realize justice as equity in their responses to crime.

"Restorative moral imagination" is my term, not a term indigenous to restorative justice advocates. However, following Howard Zehr, most advocates agree that the success of restorative justice depends not only on transforming criminal and juvenile justice systems, but also upon transforming how we envision the world and its possibilities, that is, our moral imaginations, particularly our images of crime and justice. Thus, while restorative justice advocates do not use the term "moral imagination" as I have defined it, they do draw upon the concepts encapsulated within it. They often argue that restorative justice requires a whole new worldview in order to achieve the goals and abide by the principles detailed in defining restorative justice. Mark Umbreit, for example, writes,

> At a time when the public debate around issues of crime and punishment is driven largely by political leaders embracing the conservative or liberal solutions of the past, restorative

justice offers a *fundamentally different framework* for understanding and responding to crime and victimization in society.[161]

He continues, "Restorative justice provides an *entirely different way of thinking* about crime and victimization."[162] For Umbreit, restorative justice completely breaks with other models of criminal and juvenile justice by emphasizing the need to repair the harm of crime. This emphasis entails a new way of envisioning offenders, victims, communities, and their relationships, a new type of imagination relative to the moral situation precipitated by crime.

In an argument similar to Umbreit's, Daniel Van Ness and Karen Heetderks Strong conclude their seminal text on restorative justice with an invitation to change our criminal and juvenile justice systems first by changing our visions of ourselves, others, and our relationships with each other. They write that restorative justice

...begins with transformation of ourselves, for we too have recompense to pay, reconciliation to seek, forgiveness to ask, and healing to receive. We look not only for justice "out there," but must turn the lens on ourselves as well—on our daily patterns of life and on our treatment of and attitudes toward others. Restorative justice is an invitation to renewal in communities and individuals as well as procedures and programs. Transformation of the world begins with transformation of ourselves.[163]

Van Ness and Strong maintain that restorative justice compels us to look again at how we envision ourselves within the world and to

---

[161] Mark S. Umbreit, *The Handbook of Victim-Offender Mediation* (San Francisco: Jossey-Bass, 2001), xxv, emphasis mine.

[162] Ibid., xxvii, emphasis mine.

[163] Van Ness and Strong (2002), 249.

reconsider what both could become. The changes promised by restorative justice cannot come about without self-transformation, including transformation of our moral imaginations.

Dennis Sullivan and Larry Tifft likewise call for an entirely different way of thinking with restorative justice, although they argue for even more extensive changes of our moral imaginations than most advocates. They write that restorative justice requires a "process of transformation, of examining and dislodging the justifications for treating others as less than one's self."[164] This process of transformation, Sullivan and Tifft argue, leads us to reject power in response to the needs of others. In turn, "the process of stripping ourselves of power *works on the imagination*."[165] For Sullivan and Tifft, this process is mystical, moral, political, and economic, changing one's entire way of being in the world:

> Through the selfless presence that the unveiling process fosters, the aspirant's imagination projects the more whole self into the life circumstances of others so as to experience on a feeling level how those others live, and then to incorporate the concerns of these others into one's own life. The boundaries between self and other disintegrate.[166]

The disintegration of boundaries between self and other, especially between victims and offenders, indicates a radical change in moral imagination for restorative justice compared to retributive and rehabilitative models, according to Sullivan and Tifft. Retribution and rehabilitation require the separation of ourselves from others, usually resulting in relationships based on power instead of responding to each

---

[164] Dennis Sullivan and Larry Tifft, *Restorative Justice: Healing the Foundations of Our Everyday Lives* (Monsey, NY: Willow Tree Press, 2001), 168.

[165] Ibid., 173, emphasis mine.

[166] Ibid., 173-174.

other's needs. The call of Sullivan and Tifft to selflessly strip ourselves of power and to give ourselves over to the needs of others, to the point where we cannot differentiate between their needs and our own, is a call to transform our moral imaginations based on their model of restorative justice. They believe that without this transformation, the political and economic transformations promised by restorative justice are impossible.

Similar rhetoric about transforming moral imagination fills restorative justice literature.[167] Although restorative justice advocates do not use the term "moral imagination" in their appeals for transformation, they frequently refer to the concepts contained within this term. For most advocates, the full realization of restorative justice

---

[167] Other examples of restorative justice advocates using rhetoric of "transformation" and "change" with respect to moral imagination can be found in Gordon Bazemore and Mara Schiff, "What and Why Now: Understanding Restorative Justice," in *Restorative Community Justice: Repairing Harm and Transforming Communities*, ed. Gordon Bazemore and Mara Schiff (Cincinnati, OH: Anderson, 2001): 21-46; John Braithwaite, "Restorative Justice and a Better Future," *Dalhousie Review* 76.1 (1996): 9-32; Braithwaite (2002); Breton and Lehman (2001); John R. Gehm, "The Function of Forgiveness in the Criminal Justice System," in *Restorative Justice on Trial: Pitfalls and Potentials of Victim-Offender Mediation—International Perspectives*, ed. Heinz Messmer and Hans-Uwe Otto (Dordrecht, the Netherlands: Kluwer, 1992): 541-550; Joe Hudson and Burt Galaway, "Introduction," in *Restorative Justice: International Perspectives*, ed. Joe Hudson and Burt Galaway (Monsey, NY: Criminal Justice Press, 1996): 1-14; Virginia Mackey, *Restorative Justice: Toward Nonviolence* (Louisville, KY: Presbyterian Criminal Justice Program, 1997); McCold (2000); Lode Walgrave, "Beyond Retribution and Rehabilitation: Restoration as the Dominant Paradigm in Judicial Intervention Against Juvenile Crime," paper presented at the International Congress on Criminology, Budapest, Hungary, 1993; Weitekamp (1999); and Evelyn Zellerer and Joanna B. Cannon, "Restorative Justice, Reparation, and the Southside Project," in *What is Community Justice: Case Studies of Restorative Justice and Community Supervision*, ed. David R. Karp and Todd R. Clear (Thousand Oaks, CA: Sage Publications, 2002): 89-107.

comes about only when we fundamentally rethink the ways we imagine ourselves, others, and our relationships. The arguments of Umbreit, Sullivan and Tifft, and Van Ness and Strong among others exemplify this appeal to adopt new images of the world and its possibilities in response to the problems of crime and victimization.

In addition to agreeing that we must transform our moral imaginations, most advocates of restorative justice would agree that retributive and rehabilitative moral imaginations currently dominate societal responses to crime. The narratives, images, and metaphors that members of our society and culture most frequently draw upon in the wake of crime call for either the treatment of offenders or their punishment for the sake of inflicting pain for wrongdoing. Transformation requires rejection of retributive or rehabilitative moral imaginations and replacement by restorative moral imagination. Examining these other types of moral imagination as presented by restorative justice advocates clarifies the content of restorative moral imagination by contrast. I do not suppose that the descriptions of retributivism and rehabilitationism by restorative justice advocates necessarily reflect the ideas of these two models of criminal justice; in many ways, their descriptions are caricatures of these models and idealizations of restorative justice.[168] I offer their descriptions in order

---

[168] For readers interested in how advocates of rehabilitative and retributive schemes would represent themselves and their ideas, Andrew von Hirsch and Andrew Ashworth have collected source texts from various models of criminal justice in *Principled Sentencing: Readings on Theory and Policy*, 2nd edition (Oxford: Hart Publishing, 1998). Advocates of retributive justice, or what advocates would generally describe as justice based on "desert," include Michael Moore in "The Moral Worth of Retribution," in *Responsibility, Character, and the Emotions: New Essays in Moral Psychology*, ed. Ferdinand Schoeman (Cambridge: Cambridge University Press, 1987): 179-219; Andrew von Hirsch in *Doing Justice: The Choice of Punishments* (New York: Hill and Wang, 1976), among other texts; R.A. Duff in "Desert and Penance," in *Principled Sentencing: Readings on Theory and Policy*, 2nd edition (Oxford: Hart Publishing, 1998): 161-167; H.L.A. Hart in *Punishment and*

to highlight the contrast that advocates see between restorative justice and retributive and rehabilitative responses to crime, and so to better reveal the distinctive narratives, metaphors, and symbols of restorative justice.[169]

Responsibility: Essays in the Philosophy of Law, 2nd edition (New York: Oxford University Press, 2008); and Norval Morris in *Punishment, Desert, and Rehabilitation* (Washington, DC: U.S. Government Printing Office, 1976). Michael Tonry in "Proportionality, Parsimony, and Interchangeability of Punishments," in *Penal Theory and Penal Practice*, ed. R.A. Duff et al. (Manchester: Manchester University Press, 1992) and Barbara Hudson in "Beyond Proportionate Punishment: Difficult Cases and the 1991 Criminal Justice Act," *Crime, Law, and Social Change* 22 (1995): 59-78 also advocate hybrid models of retributivism, in which principles of desert are mitigated by the concerns of other models of criminal justice. *The Model Penal Code* by the American Law Institute (Philadelpia: American Law Institute, 1962) is a classic of rehabilitation theory. Advocates of rehabilitation include Francis T. Cullen and Karen E. Gilbert in *Reaffirming Rehabilitation* (Cincinnati: Anderson Publishing Co., 1982) and Sue Rex in "A New Form of Rehabilitation?" in *Principled Sentencing: Readings on Theory and Policy*, 2nd edition (Oxford: Hart Publishing, 1998): 34-41.

[169] Not all restorative justice advocates would agree with strict distinctions among restorative justice and retributive and rehabilitative models of criminal justice. Kathleen Daly, for example, argues persuasively that in practice all justice models tend to overlap and sharp lines drawn between them tend to obscure what the concepts of restoration, rehabilitation, and retribution actually do. While I agree with Daly that these lines should not be drawn too sharply, most advocates still draw these lines, and how they draw them reveals how they understand restorative moral imagination versus retribution and rehabilitation. See Kathleen Daly, "Restorative Justice: Moving Past the Caricatures," paper presented to the Seminar on Restorative Justice, Institute of Criminology, University of Sydney Law School, April 1998a, available at http://www.gj.edu.au/school/ccj/kdaly.html, accessed January 2006; "Revisiting the Relationship between Retributive and Restorative Justice," in *Restorative Justice: Philosophy to Practice*, ed. Heather Strang and John Braithwaite (Aldershot: Ashgate/Dartmouth, 2000): 33-54; and "Restorative Justice: The Real Story," *Punishment and Society* 4.1 (2002): 55-79.

Table 3. Features of Restorative, Retributive, and Rehabilitative Moral Imaginations.

		Restorative	Retributive	Rehabilitative
Crime		• an offense committed by one person against another person that injures specific victims and communities as well as offenders themselves: "disconnection and disengagement," "tears," "damages," "injuries," "a wound in the community, a tear in the web of relationships" • an opportunity to address the underlying conflicts that disrupt our relationships	Willful violation of the law, disruption of a just social order, injury to the state	Symptom of a more serious underlying disorder, whether mental, emotional, social, spiritual, or physical
Offenders		Holistic vision of persons and human beings; members of community and relational web; primary perpetrator of the harm caused by crime, but also suffering from harms	Free moral agents responsible for their wrongdoing; "bad"; not affected by environmental factors and thus having entirely free will	Patients in need of appropriate treatment; sick, pathological, or ill; not "bad"; products of their environment and thus lacking free will
Victims		Holistic vision of persons and human beings; members of community and relational web; primary focus of the harm caused by the crime	Inconsequential because the real victim is the state	Inconsequential because cannot contribute to treatment of offenders
Community		Relational web; requires reintegration of all members in order to preserve the integrity of the web; also harmed by crime and damage to relationships	Inconsequential because the real victim is the state	Inconsequential because cannot contribute to treatment of offenders
State		Republican: Freedom as Non-Dominance	Liberal Individualist: Freedom as Non-Intervention	Social Welfare

Table 3. Features of Restorative, Retributive, and Rehabilitative Moral Imaginations, continued.

	Restorative	Retributive	Rehabilitative
Type of Sentencing	Indeterminate; tailored to offense, offender, victim, and community through consensus decision-making process	Determinate; just deserts determined by the nature of the crime, not the criminal; length of sentence determined by judges and attorneys	Indeterminate; tailored to the criminal instead of the crime; length of sentence determined by treatment professionals
Purpose of Sanctions	Repair the harm, foster healing of relationships, reintegrate and empower all members of community, satisfy needs of all stakeholders, mutual accountability	Punish in proportion to severity of offense	Treat cause of offense, achieve rehabilitation

The distinctions among retributive, rehabilitative, and restorative moral imaginations become apparent beginning with metaphors for crime attributed to each by restorative justice advocates. Once crime in each type of imagination is described, other components of its schematic worldview follow logically (table 3). So rehabilitative models of criminal justice, according to restorative justice advocates, envision crime as merely a symptom of some sort of systemic ailment or disturbance—whether emotional, mental, social, spiritual, or physical—of people who violate the law.[170] Imagining crime as a

---

[170] This depiction of rehabilitative moral imagination follows its portrayal in various restorative justice texts, including Gordon Bazemore, "Three Paradigms for Juvenile Justice," in *Restorative Justice: International Perspectives*, ed. Burt Galaway and Joe Hudson (Monsey, NY: Criminal Justice Press, 1996): 37-67; Gordon Bazemore, "After Shaming, Whither Reintegration: Restorative Justice and Relational Rehabilitation," in *Restorative Juvenile Justice: Repairing the Harm of Youth Crime*, ed. Gordon Bazemore and Lode Walgrave (Monsey, NY: Criminal Justice Press, 1999): 155-194; Gordon Bazemore and Mark Umbreit, "Rethinking the Sanctioning Function in

symptom of a more serious disease suggests the remaining aspects of rehabilitative moral imagination. Offenders are viewed as ill, or as patients needing treatment, and therefore they are not responsible for their crime because their behavior is determined by their particular ailment. They lack free will, and their personalities are plastic and malleable, permitting the possibility of a cure. Since a particular crime is only a symptom of an offender's illness, victims are inconsequential to the response to crime because they cannot heal the offender. The important relationship is between offenders and the state, built on a social welfare model. Criminal and juvenile justice systems determine the proper treatment for each individual offender based on his or her "best interests." The state employs highly trained professionals to treat the various types of illness, and the treatment by the state stops only when the offender is deemed rehabilitated, often resulting in long

---

Juvenile Court: Retributive or Restorative Responses to Youth Crime," *Crime and Delinquency* 41.3 (1995): 296-316; Gordon Bazemore and Lode Walgrave, "Introduction: Restorative Justice and the International Juvenile Justice Crisis," in *Restorative Juvenile Justice: Repairing the Harm of Youth Crime,* ed. Gordon Bazemore and Lode Walgrave (Monsey, NY: Criminal Justice Press, 1999a): 1-14; Wesley Cragg, *The Practice of Punishment: Towards a Theory of Restorative Justice* (New York: Routledge, 1992); Barry C. Feld, "Rehabilitation, Retribution, and Restorative Justice: Alternative Conceptions of Juvenile Justice," in *Restorative Juvenile Justice: Repairing the Harm of Youth Crime,* ed. Gordon Bazemore and Lode Walgrave (Monsey, NY: Criminal Justice Press, 1999): 17-44; Dean E. Peachey, "Restitution, Reconciliation, Retribution: Identifying the Forms of Justice People Desire," in *Restorative Justice on Trial: Pitfalls and Potentials of Victim-Offender Mediation—International Perspectives,* ed. Heinz Messmer and Hans-Uwe Otto (Dordrecht, the Netherlands: Kluwer, 1992): 551-558; Sullivan and Tifft (2001); Van Ness and Strong (2002); Andrew Von Hirsch, et al., eds., *Restorative Justice and Criminal Justice: Competing or Reconcilable Paradigms?* (Portland, OR: Hart Publishing, 2003); Ted Wachtel and Paul McCold, "Restorative Justice in Everyday Life," in *Restorative Justice and Civil Society,* ed. Heather Strang and John Braithwaite (Cambridge: Cambridge University Press, 2001): 114-129; and Zehr (1990).

indeterminate sentences. Rehabilitative moral imagination primarily uses medical metaphors for describing the world and the possible cure of its ailments.

Late nineteenth-century reformatories in the United States created primarily by Christian reformers of early penitentiaries are one example of the practices and institutions that both follow from and support rehabilitative moral imagination.[171] Zebulon Brockway, the first warden of Elmira Reformatory founded in New York in 1876, envisioned offenders as at least partly inflicted with a spiritual ailment. As a result, he prescribed Bibles and mandatory attendance of religious services for their cure. Reformatory prisoners could expect time trimmed off their sentence for responding well to their treatment.[172] Juvenile justice systems founded by early twentieth-century Progressives are another example of the outcome of rehabilitative moral imagination. Progressives viewed juvenile delinquency as a symptom of social illnesses rooted in "bad" (read, "minority, immigrant, and impoverished") neighborhoods and families. Successful treatment required removing juveniles suffering from these social illnesses from their families and offering them services to socialize them "properly" (read, "in accordance with white, Anglo-Saxon, middle-class standards").[173]

Restorative justice advocates note several ways in which rehabilitative moral imagination provides faulty visions of the world and its possibilities and thus fails to respond to the realities of people

---

[171] That imagery influences penal practices and institutions has been argued by David Garland, *Punishment and Modern Society* (Chicago: University of Chicago Press, 1990). By invoking the power of images here, I do not intend to imply that other forces do not also influence penal practices and institutions, particularly political and economic factors. Nonetheless, imagery derived from cultural, social, and institutional forces also plays a role, however contested.

[172] See Britton (2003), Brockway (1912), and Friedman (1993).

[173] See Mary E. Odem, *Delinquent Daughters: Protecting and Policing Adolescent Female Sexuality in the United States, 1885-1920* (Chapel Hill, NC: University of North Carolina Press, 1995). Also, Feld (1999).

dealing with crime. First, the rehabilitative scheme focuses solely on offenders, ignoring the needs of victims and communities. While offering services for the "cure" of offenders, this model does not require anything of them in return except to get better—small consolation for those people who may have been hurt as a result of offenders' illnesses. Also, rehabilitative moral imagination does not provide images of a different world for anyone other than the offender.

Second, restorative justice advocates maintain that the treatment of offenders rarely addresses the crime itself. The nature and seriousness of the offense are irrelevant to the diagnosis of offenders since the real problem is understood to be the underlying ailment, not the offense, which is a mere symptom. The response of the state is tailored to the criminal instead of to the crime.   Within rehabilitative moral imagination, focusing on the crime rather than the mental, social, spiritual, or physical disturbance of offenders would be akin to giving someone aspirin for a headache when he or she actually suffers from a brain tumor. However, pain management is an important part of any medical treatment, even if only relieving a symptom of a more systemic problem, and condemning specific criminal behavior as a violation of another person and of community norms ought to be part of any response to crime, even if offenders have bigger problems that have contributed to their wrongdoing. Gordon Bazemore notes,

> There is little in the message of the treatment response that attempts to communicate to an offender that he or she has harmed someone, should take action to repair damages or make amends, and must receive a consequence that is linked to the harm caused by the offense.[174]

Once again, by focusing on offenders, victims and communities are absent from rehabilitative images of the world and its possibilities.

---

[174] Bazemore (1996), 42.

Finally, restorative justice advocates argue that since a rehabilitative scheme never sends the message that specific criminal behavior is wrong, this model fails to send the message that certain community norms ought not to be violated and other persons ought not to be harmed. The moral guidance provided by the sanctioning of wrongdoing is lost, suggesting that people are not responsible for what they do because if they commit crime, they are sick, not bad. Rehabilitative moral imagination suggests that people are the products of their environments, not actors with free will, and so their environments ought to be condemned, not the people. While this view of human beings is somewhat hopeful—we can after all change with the right treatment—it ultimately crashes on the reef of determinism, which leaves human beings at the mercy of fate or luck as far as their moral character is concerned. Rehabilitative moral imagination cannot account for the intermingling of free will and environmental factors in the creation of moral character. By attending only to environmental factors, it ignores the choices that people make to commit crime and fails to condemn those choices as a violation of other persons and community norms. As a result, restorative justice advocates would find that rehabilitative moral imagination gives only partial images of the world and what it possibly could become with respect to crime, and thus, risks devolving into mere fantasy because of its lack of correspondence to reality.

In contrast to rehabilitative models of criminal justice, retributive moral imagination envisions crime as a willful violation of the law, a disruption of a just social order. Just as imagining crime as a symptom of some broader illness shapes the other narratives, metaphors, and symbols of rehabilitative moral imagination, imagining crime as injury to the state shapes retributive moral imagination. Offenders, as individual members of society, are free moral agents who have defied the law of their own volition and who are therefore responsible to the state for their wrongdoing.[175] They are not ill; they are bad. Offenders' crimes are understood as signs of their disrespect for the rule of law and the balance of justice. Victims are unimportant because the real violation is against the state; the harm caused to victims merely reveals offenders' disregard of law and order. The only appropriate response to offenders is to deliver their "just deserts" to them, punishing them in proportion to the advantage they took of a just and equal society by breaking the law. The state is obligated to punish offenders in order to rebalance the scales of justice, and the severity and nature of the offense determines the appropriate sentence. The community context of crime is legally irrelevant because offenders are individually responsible for their actions and societies are presumed to provide freedom, justice, and equality to all of their members regardless of where they come from. The state within retributive moral imagination is typically envisioned as liberal individualist, where freedom is understood as non-intervention. The justice of a conviction and sentence depends upon whether the state respected the procedural rights of the offender and whether the punishment is proportional to the offense. Too little and too much punishment are equally unjust.

---

[175] This depiction of retributive moral imagination follows its portrayal in various restorative justice texts, including Bazemore (1996); Bazemore and Umbreit (1995); Bazemore and Walgrave (1999a); John Braithwaite and Christine Parker, "Restorative Justice is Republican Justice," in *Restorative Juvenile Justice: Repairing the Harm of Youth Crime*, ed. Gordon Bazemore and Lode Walgrave (Monsey, NY: Criminal Justice Press, 1999): 103-126; John Braithwaite and Peter Pettit, *Not Just Deserts: A Republican Theory of Criminal Justice* (Oxford: Oxford University Press, 1990); Cragg (1992); Feld (1999); Peachey (1992); Peter Pettit and John Braithwaite, "Not Just Deserts, Even in Sentencing," *Journal of the Institute of Criminology* 4.3 (1993): 225-239; Sullivan and Tifft (2001); Umbreit (2001); Van Ness and Strong (2002); Von Hirsch, et al. (2003); Wachtel and McCold (2001); Weitekamp (1999); and Zehr (1990). For an example of an appeal to retribution in opposition to restorative justice, see Skotnicki (2006).

Some of the changes in criminal and juvenile justice systems in the United States since the 1960s and 1970s illustrate the institutional and practical consequences of retributive moral imagination. These changes include the use of sentencing guidelines to make sure punishment fits each particular crime (that is, the concern is no longer that the treatment fits each particular criminal, as with rehabilitative moral imagination). Also, greater protection of procedural rights, for example, through the reading of Miranda rights to arrestees and more access to legal defense for juvenile offenders, mark a shift from viewing offenders as patients to viewing them as full members of society, despite their alleged wrongdoing.[176]

Just as restorative justice advocates find the vision of rehabilitative moral imagination myopic, they similarly fault retributive moral imagination. First, while retributivism assumes the free will of offenders, it fails to allow offenders an active role in responding to the harm they have caused to their victims and communities. Charts and logarithms that match the nature and severity of an offense to a proportional punishment determine offenders' fates.[177] By looking at a grid or performing a calculation, judges can easily match a third-time offender who has committed a class A violent felony with a punishment of at least twenty-five, but no more than fifty, years in prison, for example. In this process, offenders never take responsibility for what they have done by recognizing the harm they have caused or trying to repair damages or make amends; they are passive recipients of punishment. Furthermore, the severity of punishment encourages offenders to avoid taking responsibility, instead hiding behind professional lawyers who act as their advocates. Restorative justice advocates find that this disempowerment of offenders in repairing the harm of their crimes hides the particulars of individual cases and obscures responsibility.

---

[176] Feld (1999).

[177] I discuss such charts and graphs in chapter two, under Section II: "Justice as Equity."

An additional problem with retributive moral imagination, according to advocates of restorative justice, is that retribution dictates punishment that lacks meaning. Judges reading charts to determine a proportional punishment may come up with the same sentence for someone who has committed rape as someone who has committed armed robbery, extortion, or embezzlement. The nature and severity of the harm caused by these crimes, however, is vastly different. By determining responses to crime through abstract equations, the actual harm caused by any one offense is obfuscated. This abstraction hides the nature and severity of the pain inflicted on real people because it determines the nature and severity of a crime by the extent to which it deviates from the law. Retributive moral imagination fails to attend to the experiences of victims and communities and so presents a deficient picture of a world affected by crime. While restorative justice advocates would not recommend a policy based upon "an eye for an eye" (the horror of proportionally returning rape for rape and the impossibility of returning armed robbery for armed robbery, for example, militates against this policy), they do suggest that sanctions for crimes can relate more meaningfully to what offenders actually did to their victims and communities.

Restorative justice advocates also argue that retributive moral imagination is as guilty as the rehabilitative model of failing to attend to victims and communities. Since crime is a violation of the state, victims and communities have no claim upon offenders. Punishment inflicts pain upon offenders, which may satisfy a retributive streak in many victims and communities,[178] but it does not tend to alleviate the

---

[178] Many studies suggest that this retributive streak is less virulent than people often assume. See John Doble Research Associates, Inc., *Crime and Corrections: The Views of the People of Vermont* (Waterbury, VT: Report to the Vermont Department of Corrections, 1994); Peachey (1992); and Martin Wright, "What the Public Wants," in *Mediation and Criminal Justice: Victims, Offenders, and Community*, ed. Martin Wright and Burt Galaway (London: Sage Publications, 1989): 264-268.

alienation, grief, and anger of victims. Moreover, punishment does not address the disorder of communities plagued by crime and may actually increase the sense of chaos and injustice within these communities as offenders return home at the end of their sentences having done little but sit in prison cells. As with the rehabilitative approach, retributive moral imagination provides only partial images of the world and its possibilities, and so restorative justice advocates argue that we need a different way of framing or mapping our experiences of crime.

By rejecting rehabilitative and retributive moral imaginations, advocates of restorative justice seek an alternative that would transform how we imagine the world and its possibilities in the aftermath of crime. John Braithwaite argues,

> Restorative justice is most commonly defined by what it is an alternative to. Juvenile justice, for example, is seen as seesawing back and forth during the century between a justice and a welfare model, between retribution and rehabilitation. Restorative justice is touted as a long-overdue third model or a new "lens," a way of hopping off the seesaw, of heading more consistently in a new direction while enrolling both liberal politicians who support the welfare model and conservatives who support the justice model.[179]

To get off the seesaw between retribution and rehabilitation, a new "paradigm" or "lens" must show us how to respond to crime in ways other than punishment or treatment. According to restorative justice advocates, the reform of our criminal and juvenile justice systems comes with transforming our images of the world and its possibilities and adopting a new type of moral imagination.

As with rehabilitative and retributive moral imaginations, once crime is defined within a restorative justice framework, other components of this schematic worldview follow logically. Like

---

[179] Braithwaite (2002), 10.

Bazemore and Walgrave, most advocates agree that we ought to understand crime primarily as an offense committed by one person against another person that injures specific victims and communities as well as offenders themselves. Crime is not simply a violation of the state or a symptom of an offender's disorder; it is first and foremost harm done by an offender to a victim that results in broken relationships throughout communities. Advocates tend to use a variety of metaphors to describe this harm: "disconnection and disengagement,"[180] "wounds,"[181] "tears,"[182] "damages,"[183] or "injuries."[184] These metaphors indicate that crime is personal, that it affects real people in a visceral way. They might also, however, suggest some agreement with the rehabilitative moral imagination as to the nature of crime. Disconnection and disengagement, wounding, tearing, damaging, and injuring as metaphors for crime bear resemblance to the rehabilitative use of disorder and illness. Nevertheless, within the usage of restorative justice advocates, the restorative metaphors refer to all people who may be affected by a crime—victims, offenders, and communities—while the rehabilitative metaphors refer only to offenders. Michael L. Hadley summarizes this difference well: "Restorative justice differs from conventional justice by viewing criminal acts more comprehensively and by involving more interest groups in dealing with the issues."[185] Restorative moral imagination envisions crime more holistically than retributive or rehabilitative schema when it sees crime as "a wound in the community, a tear in the web of relationships."[186]

---

[180] Dennis Sullivan and Larry Tifft, eds., *Handbook of Restorative Justice: A Global Perspective* (New York: Routledge, 2006).

[181] Zehr (1990).

[182] Ibid.

[183] Ibid.

[184] Van Ness and Strong (2002).

[185] Hadley (2006), 185.

[186] Zehr (2002), 20.

Restorative justice advocates have a secondary interpretation of crime as well: crime as an opportunity to address the underlying conflicts that disrupt our relationships. Zehr argues, "Crime then is at its core a violation of a person by another person, a person who himself or herself may be wounded. It is a violation of the just relationship that should exist between individuals."[187] Crime presents an opportunity to establish that just relationship among victims, offenders, and communities. The metaphor of crime as opportunity arose early in the restorative justice movement in an influential article by Nils Christie, "Conflict as Property,"[188] in which he argues that the conflicts that surround criminal acts could be used by the people who are most directly affected by them to become more direct participants in their society, to clarify norms, and to build more just relationships. Most other advocates of restorative justice have followed Christie in viewing crime as an opportunity to begin to respond to each other more justly. John Braithwaite, for example, echoes Christie when he writes,

> [P]reventing crime is an impoverished way of conceiving [the mission of criminologists]. Crime is an opportunity to prevent greater evils, to confront crime with a grace that transforms human lives to paths of love and giving.[189]

Braithwaite goes beyond Christie by suggesting that crime presents an opportunity for more loving and giving relationships, not only more just relationships. However, Braithwaite's assessment of the opportunity offered by crime has become common among restorative justice advocates, who generally agree that crime opens the door to transform human lives through certain acts of grace.

---

[187] Zehr (1990), 182.

[188] Nils Christie, "Conflict as Property," *The British Journal of Criminology* 17 (1977): 1-14.

[189] Braithwaite (2002), 3.

Again, the metaphor of crime as opportunity within restorative moral imagination bears resemblance to rehabilitative interpretations of crime. As a symptom of illness or disorder, crime could present an opportunity to provide adequate treatment and to remove offenders from circumstances that have allowed the problem to fester. The holistic usage of the metaphor of opportunity within restorative moral imagination nevertheless undermines this comparison between rehabilitation and restoration. Whereas with rehabilitative moral imagination crime represents an opportunity for treatment of the offender alone, with restorative moral imagination crime represents an opportunity for victims, offenders, and communities to resolve a conflict and build better relationships. Denise Breton and Stephen Lehman argue, "Instead of being reactive to events, this model uses events as opportunities for everyone to feel heard, to share hurts from injustices, to rebuild trust in ourselves and each other, and thereby to restore relationships."[190] According to restorative justice advocates, rehabilitationism would not permit such a positive assessment of crime as an opportunity, instead maintaining that crime at its best is merely a symptom of bigger problems.

Interpreting crime as harm caused by one person against another person and as an opportunity to address ruptured relationships requires new ways of imagining both offenders and victims. Rather than reducing victims and offenders to their experiences of crime, restorative justice advocates envision victims and offenders as persons and as human beings. The rehabilitative vision of offenders as ill and the retributive vision of offenders as bad tend to discourage rebuilding relationships by masking the humanity and personhood of offenders by either pathologizing or demonizing them. The humanity and personhood of victims are hidden by naming the state as the victim of crime, thereby ignoring the harm that crime inflicts upon real people. Restorative justice advocates counter rehabilitative and retributive moral imaginations by insisting first that offenders and victims be seen

---

[190] Breton and Lehman (2001), 13.

as human beings, persons that deserve recognition by virtue of their personhood alone. Howard Zehr argues that offenders and victims must be viewed holistically as people with multiple dimensions to their lives other than their criminal behavior or victimization.[191]

Seeing offenders as persons seems much more difficult than seeing victims as persons. Nevertheless, Daniel Van Ness and Karen Heetderks Strong warn of the dangers of stereotyping offenders based upon their crime:

> Crime and injustice are moral problems at their root. A criminal act's nature as wrongdoing is important to the participants and to their communities.... A danger, however, in recognizing that crime has moral roots is that it can lead us into hypocrisy. "Crime has moral roots; therefore criminals are immoral. I am not a criminal; therefore...." Our glib assertions lead us into another "us/them" dichotomy and intensify, often without our realizing it, the existing state of war against criminals.[192]

Reducing people who commit crime to their offense, Van Ness and Strong argue, masks our common human frailty and the tendency of even "good" people for moral failure, particularly "hypocrisy, injustice, and indifference."[193] Mark Umbreit and Robert Coates suggest that restorative justice practices "humanize" offenders by allowing the stories of their crimes to be contextualized within a whole life:

> [Offenders] are given the opportunity to become known as a person and even to express remorse in a very personal fashion. Through open discussion of their feelings, both victim and offender have the opportunity to deal with each other as

---

[191] Zehr (1990).

[192] Van Ness and Strong (2002), 247.

[193] Ibid., 248.

people, oftentimes from the same neighborhood, rather than as stereotypes.[194]

When we break out of pathologizing or demonizing images of offenders, we can find some common ground as people who have similar needs, hopes, and desires. Restorative justice advocates hold that common ground militates against retributive or rehabilitative responses to offenders that "sanction, control, and survey."[195]

Restorative justice advocates maintain that victims of crime are also often dehumanized and depersonalized. They note that our current criminal and juvenile justice systems allow victims to tell their stories only to the extent that doing so bolsters the state's evidence against offenders. By hiding the real victim behind the state, the victim's humanity is also hidden. Dennis Sullivan and Larry Tifft argue that hiding victims' stories contributes to blame or pity for victims, but not the true empathy that they deserve as human beings. Our failures to empathize contribute to an inability to respond to victims as anything other than "agency cases or clients to be processed."[196] Depersonalizing victims in this way allows those around them to ignore their needs:

> Their identities are to be known by the roles they play in the drama of the state's retributive, adjudicative process. We somehow assert that their stories have nothing to tell us about how we live and what structural changes we need to make in our own families, schools, workplaces, and neighborhoods.[197]

---

[194] Mark S. Umbreit and Robert B. Coates, "Cross-Site Analysis of Victim-Offender Mediation in Four States," *Crime and Delinquency* 39 (1993), 572.
[195] Sullivan and Tifft (2001), 82.
[196] Ibid., 39.
[197] Ibid., 82.

The harm caused by crime cannot be repaired until we recognize the humanity of all people affected by a crime—especially that of victims. Mark Umbreit avers, "Little healing of the emotional wound is likely to occur without an opening of the heart through genuine dialogue, empowerment, and a recognition of each other's humanity despite the conflict."[198]

In addition to seeing offenders and victims as persons and as human beings, restorative justice advocates draw on the metaphor of a "relational web" to emphasize the common ties that hold all people together. Howard Zehr notes that underlying the understanding of crime as "a violation of people and of interpersonal relationships...is an assumption about society: we are all interconnected.... All things are connected to each other in a web of relationships."[199] He relates this notion of interconnectedness to the biblical concept of *shalom*, which Zehr describes as a condition in which all people are joined in a state of "all rightness" with God and one another.[200] John Braithwaite similarly introduces the South African concept of *ubuntu*, which he defines as "the idea that our humanity is relationally tied to the humanity of those we live with,"[201] to articulate his sense that our common humanity implies our interconnectedness. For Braithwaite, our existence in a relational web intimates that offenders cannot be simply written off as sick or bad and victims cannot be ignored. Our well-being depends on their well-being and vice versa. Similarly, Denise Breton and Stephen Lehman hold that,

> [Restorative justice] considers the whole person in webs of relationships that go back generations. When relationships break down, this model considers everyone involved, what's

---

[198] Umbreit (2001), 3-4.

[199] Zehr (2002), 19-20.

[200] Ibid., 130-132.

[201] Braithwaite (2002), 5.

going on inside each of them, and what experiences led each to think, feel, and act as he or she did.[202]

The relationality of human beings suggests a positive moral obligation to improve the well-being of others when and where we can, even if those others have committed or are victims of crime.

Other advocates also use the metaphor of a relational web to argue that offenders cannot be purged from society. Dennis Sullivan and Larry Tifft, for example, draw upon Navajo interpretations of a person who harms another as "act[ing] as if he [*sic*] has no relatives."[203] The proper response to this alienation is to "talk things out" so offenders can reconnect to the relational web of humanity, what Sullivan and Tifft call "a one-world body of relatives."[204] The practice of talking things out, according to Sullivan and Tifft, depends upon a worldview in which,

> People saw their lives "bound up together in…one common life. The members of one kindred looked on themselves as one living whole, a single animated mass of blood, flesh, and bones, of which no member could be touched without all the members suffering." In other words, when one person suffers a harm, all suffer from the harm to one degree or other. And all are responsible for making things right in such situations because all are in some way responsible for that harm occurring in the first place.[205]

The relational web that brings human beings together implies that while offenders may bear the brunt of responsibility for the harm they have caused, all people with whom they are connected also share the

---

[202] Breton and Lehman (2001), 12.

[203] Sullivan and Tifft (2006), 1.

[204] Ibid.

[205] Ibid.

responsibility. Because we share responsibility, severing offenders from the relational web intrinsically damages the integrity of the ties that bind human beings together. Furthermore, denigrating them as pathological or demonic threatens the humanity of the web as a whole. In contrast especially to retributive moral imagination, which depends upon an liberal-individualist conception of the self, restorative moral imagination envisions every person, but particularly offenders, as inherently bound to all other people.

Another metaphor that restorative justice advocates apply to offenders and victims is that they are members of a community.[206] This metaphor is similar to that of the relational web except that it draws the web closer to identify specific groups of people bound to offenders and victims. Daniel Van Ness and Karen Heetderks Strong highlight a difficulty that victims and offenders share with respect to their communities:

> Restorative justice places a high value on taking the steps needed to help both victims and offenders reenter their communities as whole, productive, contributing members.... Victims and offenders often share one common problem: the community treats each as an outcast; each is stigmatized.[207]

The communities in which offenders and victims live include family members, friends, neighbors, and other associates. When one person harms another person, each person often seems ruined: the offender as malicious, the victim as weak. But as members of their communities, the challenge raised by restorative justice is to reintegrate both victims and communities for their own good but also for the good of the

---

[206] The definition of "community" in restorative justice literature is hotly disputed, especially among authors trying to distance restorative justice from community justice. See *Contemporary Justice Review* 7.1 (March 2004) for alternative perspectives.

[207] Van Ness and Strong (2002), 101.

community united by a tightly-knit relational web. As members of these communities, offenders bear certain obligations by virtue of their relationships. When they commit a crime, they also acquire additional responsibilities to victims and other community members to repair the harm they have caused.[208]   In addition, communities hold responsibilities for victims to ensure their safety and to assure them of their full membership despite their degradation at the hands of the offender. Just as the relational web binding offenders and victims to all other people implies that they cannot be cut away or ignored, the health of the community holding offenders accountable and seeking the restoration of victims requires that offenders and victims be reintegrated to become full members again.

The vision of crime within restorative moral imagination as harm caused by one person against another person and as an opportunity to address ruptured relationships further suggests particular responses to crime that differ from retributive or rehabilitative models. Punishment and treatment cannot adequately respond to crime, restorative justice advocates argue, because these methods ignore victims, fail to repair relationships, and disregard the community contexts of crime. Advocates avow that only those measures that deal with the harm caused to persons and that seize the opportunity to rebuild relationships will be just responses to crime.

The metaphor of justice as "healing" predominates these arguments about appropriate responses to crime. Howard Zehr, for example, suggests imagining justice as "healing a wound,"[209] arguing that justice requires the healing of those most directly involved in crime—victims, but also offenders and communities.[210]   John Braithwaite similarly avers that justice requires "healing the hurts caused by the failure to fulfill our obligations."[211]   Likewise Mark

---

[208] Zehr (1990).

[209] Zehr (1990), 189.

[210] Zehr (2002), 20.

[211] Braithwaite (2002), x.

Umbreit maintains that justice is more like "healing broken relationships, not solving problems."[212] Denise Breton and Stephen Lehman write, "More than restoring even, healing justice uses instances of hurt to enhance bonds between people and to build communities."[213] Van Ness and Strong also appeal to this metaphor in the opening pages of their influential introduction to restorative justice. They call for criminal justice practitioners to see themselves as "healers of the wounds caused by crime."[214] While Van Ness and Strong's argument may resemble rehabilitative imperatives to heal the disorders of offenders, they carefully distinguish their use of the metaphor of healing from that within rehabilitative models. They maintain that rehabilitation only addresses those injuries that led offenders to commit crimes. Restorative justice, in contrast, also tends to the harms that follow crime and that affect victims and communities. Van Ness and Strong contend that the most appropriate responses to crime are akin to the holistic healing of the harms associated with crime, particularly the damages inflicted on the relationships among victims, offenders, and communities.

Deciding when healing has occurred, and thus when justice has been served, however, presents a particular problem for restorative justice advocates. Rehabilitative models determine healing of offenders according to when appropriate professionals have deemed them cured. Retributive models determine when justice has been served according to when offenders have completed a sentence proportional to their offense dictated by law. The "healing of broken relationships" is vague relative to these other standards. To specify this standard, restorative justice advocates generally agree that the appropriate measure of healing is whether the needs of all stakeholders of a crime have been met. What these needs might be remains open for dispute. John Braithwaite argues that the needs of victims, offenders,

---

[212] Umbreit (2001), 8.

[213] Breton and Lehman (2001), 13.

[214] Van Ness and Strong (2002), 3.

and communities depend upon whatever matters to them; their needs cannot be determined *a priori*.[215] Dennis Sullivan and Larry Tifft seem to agree with Braithwaite on this point by suggesting that healing occurs when the needs of all are met, "but met as they are defined by each person."[216] For these authors, determining when healing has occurred and justice has been served varies with each situation as participants in restorative justice determine their own needs.

Other restorative justice advocates, however, suggest that a general sense of the needs of victims, offenders, and communities can be compiled and used as a measure of the healing that occurs. David Gil, for example, maintains that people are not always the best judges of their own needs. Rather than relying on individual assessments of human needs, Gil recommends enumerating needs based on the requirements of human survival, development, and health.[217] Many restorative justice advocates now provide general lists of needs of each stakeholder in a crime as guides to the requirements of healing. Howard Zehr's list is often cited.[218] This list begins with needs of victims, which include the need for the truth about what happened to them and why the offender harmed them; a need to tell their own stories and express their feelings of anger and sadness; a need for vindication of their pain and denunciation of the wrongdoing; a need for proportional restitution or compensation of their losses; a need for empowerment and participation in the process to address the crime; a need for safety and support within their communities; and a need to reintegrate into their communities with the possibility of forgiveness and reconciliation with offenders. By responding to these needs, the

---

[215] Braithwaite (2002), 11.

[216] Sullivan and Tifft (2001), 113.

[217] David G. Gil, "Toward a 'Radical' Paradigm of Restorative Justice," in *Handbook of Restorative Justice: A Global Perspective*, ed. Dennis Sullivan and Larry Tifft (New York: Routledge, 2006), 499-500.

[218] Zehr (1990), 191-201.

spiritual, social, material, physical, and psychological wounds of victims might be healed.

After the needs of victims are addressed, the needs of communities must also be assessed. Zehr describes the needs of communities as requiring condemnation of wrongdoing, assurance that something is being done about it, and confidence that steps have been taken to prevent its recurrence. When these needs have been addressed, Zehr avers, community members may find that justice has been realized and that the harms associated with a particular crime have been healed.

Beyond the needs of victims and communities, Zehr insists that offenders also have needs that must be met for complete healing. Offenders primarily need to be held accountable:

> Genuine accountability...includes an opportunity to understand the human consequences of one's acts, to face up to what one has done, and to whom one has done it. But real accountability involves more. Accountability also involves taking responsibility for the results of one's behavior. Offenders must be allowed and encouraged to help decide what will make things right, then to take steps to repair the damage.[219]

The healing of offenders begins with their assumption of responsibility for the harms they have caused. But since restorative justice envisions particular crimes within the context of an offender's whole life as a person, a member of a community, and a tie within the relational web, healing also requires addressing the offender's needs that may have contributed to their criminal behavior in the first place. At this point, restorative justice most resembles a rehabilitative model because it examines conditions within communities that may have harmed offenders. As Zehr writes, "If we are to address harms and causes [of crime], we must explore the harms that offenders themselves have

---

[219] Ibid., 42.

experienced."[220] Appealing to the web of relationality, Sullivan and Tifft concur with Zehr:

> As relatives we will want to attend to the wounds of our brothers and sisters (restoratively) and we will want to hold accountable those responsible for causing those wounds (restoratively), but we will want as well to correct the conditions and social situations so that such pain and suffering are less likely to appear in our lives. This is...restorative justice in its most transformative dimension.[221]

Within restorative moral imagination, healing requires that all members of communities assume responsibility for others within the relational web and that offenders participate actively in the process. Ted Wachtel and Paul McCold argue, "Restorative practices demonstrate mutual accountability—the collective responsibility of citizens to care about and take care of one another."[222] Because restorative moral imagination interprets crime as harm done to persons that results in broken relationships, healing those relationships requires healing every person affected by crime—including offenders—as well as healing the web that binds all people together. This healing can occur only when offenders are accountable for their actions and when members of communities take mutual accountability for their actions. According to restorative justice advocates, only when this healing has occurred in response to the opportunity presented by crime will justice be realized.

Imagining crime as harm caused by one person against another person impacts how restorative justice advocates envision justice practices. Advocates argue that retributive and rehabilitative moral imaginations conjure practices that exclude victims, demonize or pathologize offenders, and confuse the state with the community

---

[220] Zehr (2002), 30.

[221] Sullivan and Tifft (2006), 13.

[222] Wachtel and McCold (2001), 114.

context of crime. These problems result in the exclusion and disempowerment of victims, offenders, and communities from the processes that respond to crime. Since advocates imagine crime primarily as harm caused by one person against another person, the practices that respond to crime must begin with the people who have a direct stake in the crime: victims and offenders. Daniel Van Ness and Karen Heetderks Strong conclude that if victims and offenders wish, they should be included in the process of addressing the injuries caused by crime at the earliest time and to the fullest extent possible.[223] They ought to be allowed to tell their stories, express their feelings, and enter into a dialogue with each other about how to repair the harm. Mark Umbreit characterizes this process as one of "dialogue and mutual aid" that humanizes the participants for each other and reveals their personal interconnectedness.[224] The practices of restorative justice differ from those of rehabilitative and retributive models because they are non-adversarial and encourage victims and offenders to engage one another directly and assume power over their own healing.

The second metaphor of crime with restorative moral imagination—that it represents an opportunity to establish just relationships among victims, offenders, and communities—likewise shapes restorative justice practices. Drawing on Christie's argument that the state has "stolen" the conflicts of communities and deprived them of the opportunities that conflicts present, advocates maintain that governments should give the opportunities raised by crime back to communities.[225] John Braithwaite, for example, appeals to the traditional Roman Catholic principle of subsidiarity to suggest that responses to crime should be based within their community contexts unless these responses exceed the skills and resources of communities in particular cases.[226] Van Ness and Strong similarly argue that the

---

[223] Van Ness and Strong (2002), 37ff.

[224] Umbreit (2001), 39. See also Umbreit and Coates (1993).

[225] Christie (1977).

[226] Braithwaite (2002).

government ought not to have a monopoly over society's responses to crime. They hold that the government may be responsible for preserving a just public order, but communities have special responsibilities for establishing and maintaining a just peace. This responsibility requires the participation of community members in responding to crime. Without community members, the relational web broken by crime cannot be fully repaired and the needs of victims and offenders cannot be fully satisfied. The healing offered by restorative justice will be incomplete.

This vision of the role of community in restorative justice practices departs from rehabilitative and retributive practices in which the community is confounded with the state based on either a welfare-state or liberal-individualist model of government. Rather the community assumes particular importance relative to the government, which in restorative moral imagination is based on a republican model where freedom is understood as non-domination, not non-interference.[227] Advocates hold that this model is more democratic because it includes the voices of victims, offenders, and communities. Wachtel and McCold, for example, maintain that,

> By involving all of those affected by a specific offense, conferences and circles enhance democratic processes by moving responsibility for decision-making away from judges and lawyers and giving it to those citizens with a direct interest at stake.[228]

The opportunity to make decisions empowers communities to create more just relationships and more democratic societies in which each member has the chance to build communities of dialogue and mutual accountability.

---

[227] Braithwaite and Parker (1999), Braithwaite and Pettit (1990), and Pettit and Braithwaite (1993).

[228] Wachtel and McCold (2001), 12.

Restorative moral imagination thus differs from rehabilitative and retributive types of moral imagination beginning with its images of crime. Rather than describing crime as a symptom of offenders' disorders or as a violation of the state, restorative justice advocates define crime as harm caused by one person to another person resulting in broken relationships among victims, offenders, and communities. They also suggest that crime represents an opportunity to address the underlying conflicts that disrupt our relationships and to find ways to live together most justly and peacefully. Crime is both harm and opportunity—images that shape how advocates imagine victims, offenders, communities, and restorative justice practices. Victims and offenders must first and foremost be seen as human beings with full personhood; they ought not to be ignored, demonized, or pathologized. They are also ties in a relational web that binds the well being of all people together. Moreover, restorative justice advocates argue that we must recognize victims and offenders as members of our communities, the more tightly wound webs of relationship based on closer association. Responses to victims and offenders must seek justice through the healing of their wounds. Healing occurs when the needs of victims and offenders along with communities have been met. To meet these needs, justice practices must allow the inclusion and empowerment of all stakeholders in a crime. In these processes, the state, understood as the government of a non-domineering republican society, takes a back seat to the driving forces of citizens who have seized the opportunity to respond to crime in a democratic manner.

In light of this description of restorative moral imagination, restorative justice as presented by advocates would seem hypothetically to foster activities of vivid and expansive moral imagining, and so would be well-disposed to enabling its participants to realize justice as equity in their processes of ethical discernment.[229] Imagining offenders

---

[229] On the relationship between types of moral imagination and activities of moral imagining, refer to figure 1; on the relationship between activities of moral imagining and being equitable, see table 2.

as persons and as human beings rather than demonizing or pathologizing them, for example, could lead participants in restorative justice to try to situate particular crimes within the life stories of offenders, which include multiple dimensions other than their criminal behavior.   Seeing offenders as whole persons requires appreciating their perspectives even if we disagree with them or find them flawed. We might avoid the dangers of demonizing and pathologizing, which tend to reduce a person's life story to his bad acts or state of disorder. In seeing the offender as a person or as a human being, we see him as someone who shares at least some part of our natures, and so we might be better prepared to empathize with him.   Imagining offenders as persons and as human beings also entails making connections between their crimes and other aspects of their lives that may have contributed to their actions.   Furthermore, envisioning others as persons, as human beings implies that the others have not only a past through which we understand the present, but also future possibilities as they continue their lives after this encounter.   The metaphors of offender as human being, as person thus may encourage participants in restorative justice to enter into the stories of offenders, to appreciate their perspectives, to draw connections across different experiences, and to consider possibilities of what offenders might become given certain circumstances.   Similarly viewing victims as human beings and as persons could draw restorative justice participants to empathize with their stories, perspectives, and possibilities as well.

Imagining all parties affected by crime as bound together in relational webs and as united in community would also seem to cultivate activities associated with vivid and expansive moral imagining. These metaphors may encourage participants in restorative justice to try to understand how our ties with one another take shape in particular cases, to see how a crime affects not only victims and offenders, but also everyone connected to them, however tangentially. Finding these connections requires participants to enter into others' narratives more deeply to discover how their stories intermingle and overlap.   But exploring the ties that bind participants in restorative justice together may also reveal important differences among one another because each member stands in a different location in the community. Recognizing these differences even while finding areas of commonality could encourage restorative justice participants to hear the others' stories in full, to try to understand their perspectives, and to avoid reducing another's experiences to one's own. Further, the metaphors of a relational web and a community may foster a tendency to consider the future of others in these relationships. Since everyone's well-being depends on everyone else's, the possibilities of all restorative justice participants demands consideration; no one can be purged from the circle of relationship without damaging all of the members of that circle. The imagery of relational web and of community then involves more complex assessments of our relationships to other participants in restorative justice, our connections with one another, and the possibilities of our relationships with each other in the future. By holding this imagery, participants could be drawn to delve more deeply into the moral situations precipitated by crime and perhaps to imagine the particulars of those situations more vividly and expansively.

The imagery of healing, of opportunity to repair broken relationships harmed by crime, of responding to the needs of participants would seem likewise to foster within restorative justice participants activities of entering into others' stories and appreciating their perspectives, of drawing connections across particular cases, of envisioning myriad possibilities of what could become of any given case. Understanding the harms and wounds that need healing and repair requires, first, listening to the story of the crime from the perspectives of all stakeholders. Restorative justice participants must be able to locate the crime and its causes and effects in the narratives of each stakeholder's life in order to grasp how they have been hurt and what they need to address the harm. With victims, assessing the harm may require restorative justice participants to connect this incident to previous experiences of victimization that may inform one's responses to the crime. With offenders, participants may need to link the offense to underlying problems that may have contributed to the wrongdoing. Furthermore, healing and repair require consideration of possibilities for transforming relationships and creating new ways for each stakeholder to interact in the world. These metaphors suggest that the way the world is now is harmful, damaged, or unhealthy. Restorative justice thus asks its participants to envision what the world could become if relationships were no longer broken, if the needs of stakeholders were met, and if all people could engage in healthy interactions—as well as to create concrete plans for realizing these visions. Participants in restorative justice practices therefore may engage in activities of vivid and expansive moral imagining in order to find ways to bring about healing, whole relationships, and the satisfaction of stakeholders' needs.

These examples indicate that the narratives, metaphors, and symbols of restorative moral imagination may hypothetically vivify and expand moral imagining of participants in restorative justice in their processes of ethical discernment. Restorative justice practices should result in fuller, more nuanced accounts of the ambiguity, diversity, and complexity of experiences of crime. They should generate greater awareness of when the law does not address adequately the particulars of a case and so requires correction and supplementation. In doing so, restorative moral imagination, because it supports activities of vivid and expansive moral imagining, should in theory better equip participants in restorative justice practices in their efforts to realize justice as equity.

EVALUATION OF RESTORATIVE JUSTICE

Whether participants in restorative justice practices actually use restorative moral imagination in their processes of ethical discernment has not been a concern in the restorative justice evaluative literature. Neither has determining if the use of the type of moral imagination described by restorative justice advocates contributes to vivid and expansive moral imagining among participants, and therefore to more equitable responses in restorative justice practices. Because most evaluations focus of "what works" in terms of reducing recidivism and satisfying stakeholders, qualitative questions such as these have not received much scrutiny.

While policy makers may be particularly interested in whether restorative justice "works," advocates maintain that effective restorative justice programs do much more than reduce recidivism and satisfy stakeholders, although these are important goals as well. As the definition of restorative justice alone indicates, restorative justice tries to accomplish many different goals: achieving fairness and satisfaction for all parties affected by a crime; protecting participants' legal rights; repairing the material, physical, psychological, relational, and social harms caused by crime; including victims, offenders, and communities in responding to crime; providing a forum for victims to express anger and fear and to be heard, supported, and taken seriously; re-establishing the social efficacy and cohesion of communities; and finally, reintegrating both victims and offenders in a safe and secure environment.

Beyond these goals, the writing of advocates suggests that restorative justice might also transform the moral imaginations of participants. Restorative justice practices may lead people to interpret crime as a violation of persons and a rupture of relationships as well as an opportunity to repair the harm. By participating in these practices, people could come to see victims and offenders as human beings, persons deserving of respect as persons. They may also come to see all people as bound in a relational web and as members of communities. Advocates also argue that restorative justice could foster a vision of justice as healing and encourage people to attend to each other's needs. In addition to asking whether restorative justice works at reducing recidivism and whether it achieves the goals delineated in Bazemore and Walgrave's definition, evaluation of restorative justice should address whether and how it transforms participants' moral imaginations or effects their capacities for being equitable.

Over the last decade, restorative justice advocates have sought to evaluate the extent to which restorative justice effectively achieves its various goals. However, while the trend toward evaluation may be part of the second generation of restorative justice literature, efforts at evaluation are still somewhat nascent. In an excellent summary of evaluation research until 2003, Leena Kurki delineates some of the limitations of this research.[230] One difficulty is that most researchers have focused on short-term effects on participants, thereby neglecting long-term effects that restorative justice may have on victims, offenders, communities, and society at large. Differences in the lives of participants six months, one year, or two years after involvement in a restorative justice program remain largely unknown.

Another difficulty is that the results of evaluation data may often reflect self-selection bias more than effects of participation in restorative justice programs because few evaluations use truly experimental methods with control groups and random sampling. Mark Umbreit, Robert Coates, and Betty Vos, for instance, have found that in most victim-offender mediation programs, participation is a highly self-selective process often affected by the dynamics of race and class as well as by the seriousness of the offense and the institutional role of victims (for example, school principals are more likely to participate in victim-offender mediation than someone without an official institutional affiliation).[231] This bias may limit the generalizability of evaluation literature to date.

A further challenge with this literature is that it may include evaluations of improperly implemented programs, and thus fail to evaluate restorative justice at all. If a program calls itself restorative

---

[230] Leena Kurki, "Evaluating Restorative Justice Practices," in *Restorative Justice and Criminal Justice: Competing or Reconcilable Paradigms?*, ed. Andrew Von Hirsch et al. (Portland, OR: Hart Publishing, 2003): 293-314.

[231] Mark S. Umbreit, Robert B. Coates, and Betty Vos, "The Impact of Victim-Offender Mediation: Two Decades of Research," *Federal Probation* 65.3 (2001): 29-35.

yet fails to implement restorative ideals in practice, then its failure or success tells us little about the effectiveness of restorative justice. Evaluations must therefore attend to both processes and outcomes to determine effectiveness. Furthermore, each aspect of a restorative process may not be equally important. Some studies have found that expressions of remorse by offenders and reaching agreements by consensus in family-group conferences may lower recidivism rates while other restorative aspects such as the presence of victims and the expression of emotion had no measurable effects on re-offending.[232] More research is needed on each component of restorative justice processes and outcomes as well as on programs as a whole in order to understand better what exactly contributes to specific effects. Also, different types of programs employ these components differently: citizen- and neighborhood-accountability boards approach reaching agreements by consensus differently than family-group conferences, for instance. Evaluations of certain types of programs may not therefore reflect on other types.

Given these caveats about the quality of evaluations of restorative justice to date, we can still draw some conclusions about the effectiveness of certain processes and outcomes. Participants in victim-offender mediation and dialogue and family-group conferences generally report high levels of satisfaction relative to their counterparts in other criminal or juvenile justice processes or to those who were

---

[232] See Kathleen Daly, *South Australia Juvenile Justice (SAJJ) Research on Conferencing: Technical Report No. 1: Project Overview and Research Instruments* (Brisbane, Australia: School of Criminology and Criminal Justice, 1998b); and *South Australia Juvenile Justice (SAJJ) Research on Conferencing: Technical Report No. 2: Research Instruments in Year 2 (1999) and Background Notes* (Brisbane, Australia: School of Criminology and Criminal Justice, 2001). Retrieved on July 18, 2007 at http://www.griffith.edu.au/school/ccj/kdaly.html. Also, Hennessey Hayes and Kathleen Daly, "Youth Justice Conferencing and Reoffending," *Justice Quarterly* 20.4 (2003): 725-764.

referred to mediation but did not participate.[233]   Victims, however, report slightly lower levels of satisfaction than other participants, although their satisfaction is still higher than that of victims who

---

[233] For summary, see Braithwaite (2002) and Kurki (2003). Also, Robert B. Coates and John Gehm, *Victim Meets Offender: An Evaluation of Victim-Offender Reconciliation Programs* (Valparaiso, IN: PACT Institute of Justice, 1985), and "An Empirical Assessment," in *Mediation and Criminal Justice: Victims, Offenders, and Community*, ed. Martin Wright and Burt Galaway (London: Sage Publications, 1989): 251-263; Gabrielle M. Maxwell and Allison Morris, "Research on Family Group Conferences with Young Offenders in New Zealand," in *Family Group Conferences: Perspectives on Policy and Practice*, ed. Joe Hudson, et al. (Monsey, NY: Criminal Justice Press, 1996): 88-110; Paul McCold and Benjamin Wachtel, *Restorative Policing Experiment: the Bethlehem Pennsylvania Police Family Group Conferencing Project* (Pipersville, PA: Community Service Foundation, 1998); Paul McCold and Ted Wachtel, *Restorative Justice Theory Validation*, paper presented at the Fourth International Conference on Restorative Justice for Juveniles, 2000, Tübingen, Germany; Edmund McGarrell, et al., *Returning Justice to the Community: The Indianapolis Juvenile Restorative Justice Experiment* (Indianapolis: Hudson Institute, 2000); David B. Moore with L. Forsythe, *A New Approach to Juvenile Justice: An Evaluation of Family Conferencing in Wagga Wagga* (Wagga Wagga: Charles Sturt University, 1995); Heather Strang, *Victim Participation in a Restorative Justice Process* (Oxford: Oxford University Press, 2001); Mark S. Umbreit, "Mediating Victim-Offender Conflict: From Single-Site to Multi-Site Analysis in the U.S.," in *Restorative Justice on Trial: Pitfalls and Potentials of Victim-Offender Mediation—International Perspectives*, ed. Heinz Messmer and Hans-Uwe Otto (Dordrecht, the Netherlands: Kluwer, 1992): 431-444; Mark S. Umbreit, *Victim Meets Offender: The Impact of Restorative Justice and Mediation* (Monsey, NY: Criminal Justice Press, 1994); Mark S. Umbreit, *Mediation of Criminal Conflict: An Assessment of Programs in Four Canadian Provinces* (St. Paul, MN: The Center for Restorative Justice and Mediation, University of Minnesota, 1995); Mark S. Umbreit and Ann Warner Roberts, *Mediation of Criminal Conflict in England: An Assessment of Services in Coventry and Leeds* (St. Paul, MN: The Center for Restorative Justice and Mediation, University of Minnesota, 1996); and Umbreit, Coates, and Vos (2001).

experienced more common criminal or juvenile justice processes.[234] In a meta-analysis of studies that addressed participant satisfaction in restorative justice programs using a variety of practices, James Bonta and his colleagues found that on average about 88% of offenders expressed satisfaction with their experience; about 82% of victims likewise expressed satisfaction.[235] Nancy Burrell and her colleagues found in a similar meta-analysis that offenders reported an 89% satisfaction rate with victim-offender mediation and dialogue, and victims reported an 85% satisfaction rate. Furthermore, victims participating in victim-offender mediation and dialogue were 94% more satisfied than victims who did not participate in these programs, and offenders participating in victim-offender mediation and dialogue were 56% more satisfied that offenders who did not participate in these programs—a less outstanding number in comparison with victims, but still a significant finding.[236] Victim-offender mediation and dialogue has also been found to reduce victims' anger, anxiety, fear of re-victimization by the same offender, and fear of crime in general.[237] Both victims and offenders find the processes and outcomes associated with victim-offender mediation and dialogue to be fair, and at least nine out of ten participants would recommend victim-offender mediation

---

[234] For summary, see Braithwaite (2002) and Kurki (2003). Also, Strang (2001); Umbreit and Coates (1993); Umbreit and Roberts (1996); and Umbreit, Coates, and Vos (2001).

[235] James Bonta, et al., "Restorative Justice and Recidivism: Promises Made, Promises Kept?," in *Handbook of Restorative Justice: A Global Perspective,* ed. Dennis Sullivan and Larry Tifft (New York: Routledge, 2006), 114.

[236] Nancy Burrell, et al., "Victim-Offender Mediation: A Meta-Analysis," paper presented at the annual meeting of the NCA 95th Annual Convention, Chicago, IL, November 11, 2009.

[237] Umbreit and Coates (1993). See also Strang (2001); Heather Strang and Lawrence W. Sherman, *The Victim's Perspective: RISE Working Paper 2* (Canberra: Law Program, RSSS, Australian National University, 1997); Umbreit (1992); and Umbreit and Roberts (1996).

and dialogue to a friend.[238] Agreements are reached in practically all cases using victim-offender mediation and dialogue, and the vast majority of plans are completed, indicating that victims and offenders who participate in victim-offender mediation and dialogue usually experience restorative outcomes, including reparation, compensation, apology, and reintegration.[239] More extensive data regarding satisfaction are not yet available for other types of restorative justice programs such as sentencing circles, or citizen- and neighborhood-accountability boards.

---

[238] Braithwaite (2002); Umbreit and Coates (1993); Umbreit and Roberts (1996); and Umbreit, Coates, and Vos (2001).

[239] Braithwaite (2002); Burrell, et al. (2009); Burt Galaway, "The New Zealand Experience Implementing the Reparation Sentence," in *Restorative Justice on Trial: Pitfalls and Potentials of Victim-Offender Mediation—International Perspectives*, ed. Heinz Messmer and Hans-Uwe Otto (Dordrecht, the Netherlands: Kluwer, 1992): 55-80; John Haley, "Victim-Offender Mediations: Japanese and American Comparison," in *Restorative Justice on Trial: Pitfalls and Potentials of Victim-Offender Mediation—International Perspectives*, ed. Heinz Messmer and Hans-Uwe Otto (Dordrecht, the Netherlands: Kluwer, 1992): 105-130; Tony Marshall, "Restorative Justice on Trial in Britain," in *Restorative Justice on Trial: Pitfalls and Potentials of Victim-Offender Mediation—International Perspectives*, ed. Heinz Messmer and Hans-Uwe Otto (Dordrecht, the Netherlands: Kluwer, 1992): 15-28; McCold and Wachtel (1998); Edmund McGarrell, *Restorative Justice Conferences as an Early Response to Young Offenders* (Washington, D.C.: Office of Juvenile Justice and Delinquency Prevention, U.S. Department of Justice, 2001), retrieved on July 16, 2007 at http://purl.access.gpo.gov/GPO/LPS18711; Kim Pate, "Victim-Offender Restitution Programs in Canada," in *Criminal Justice, Restitution, and Reconciliation*, ed. Burt Galaway and Joe Hudson (Monsey, NY: Willow Press, 1990): 135-144; Thomas Trenzcek, "A Review and Assessment of Victim-Offender Reconciliation Programming in West Germany," in *Criminal Justice, Restitution, and Reconciliation*, ed. Burt Galaway and Joe Hudson (Monsey, NY: Willow Press, 1990): 109-124; Umbreit and Coates (1993); Umbreit and Roberts (1996); and Umbreit, Coates, and Vos (2001).

The research is mixed, but promising, as to whether restorative justice lessens re-offending compared to other interventions. Some evaluations show that victim-offender mediation significantly reduces recidivism,[240] but other studies are inconclusive.[241] Meta-analysis, however, suggests that victim-offender mediation and dialogue causes a significant decline in re-offending.[242] With family-group conferences, some studies have shown that restorative justice has no significant

---

[240] Braithwaite (2002). Jeff Latimer, Craig Dowden, and Danielle Muise, *The Effectiveness of Restorative Justice Practices: A Meta-Analysis* (Ottawa: Department of Justice, 2001), retrieved on July 18, 2007 at http://www.justice.gc.ca/en/ps/rs/rep/2001/meta.pdf; and "The Effectiveness of Restorative Justice Practices: A Meta-Analysis," *The Prison Journal* 85 (2005): 127-144. Also, William R. Nugent and Jeff B. Paddock, "The Effect of Victim-Offender Mediation on Severity of Reoffense," *Mediation Quarterly* 12 (1995): 353-367; William R. Nugent, et al., "Participation in Victim-Offender Mediation and Re-Offense: Successful Replications?," *Journal of Research on Social Work Practice* 11.1 (2001): 5-23; and Jean Wynne, "Leeds Mediation and Reparation Service: Ten Years Experience with Victim-Offender Mediation," in *Restorative Justice: International Perspectives*, ed. Burt Galaway and Joe Hudson (Monsey, NY: Criminal Justice Press, 1996): 445-462.

[241] Robert C. Davis, Martha Tichane, and Deborah Grayson, *Mediation and Arbitration as Alternatives to Prosecution in Felony Arrest Cases: An Evaluation of the Brooklyn Dispute Resolution Center* (New York: Vera Institute of Justice, 1980); David Meirs, et al., *An Exploratory Evaluation of Restorative Justice Schemes* (London: Home Office, 2001), retrieved on July 18, 2007 at http://www.homeoffice.gov.uk/rds/prgpdfs/crrs09.pdf; Mike Niemeyer and David Shichor, "A Preliminary Study of a Large Victim/Offender Reconciliation Program," *Federal Probation* 60.3 (1996): 30-34; and Sudipto Roy, "Two Types of Juvenile Restitution Programs in Two Midwestern Counties: A Comparative Study" *Federal Probation* 57.4 (1993): 48-53. Also, Umbreit (1994); Umbreit and Coates (1993); Umbreit, Coates, and Vos (2001).

[242] Burrell et al. (2009); Latimer, Dowden, and Muise (2001) and (2005); and Nugent et al. (2001).

effect on recidivism[243] while others have found significantly lower re-offending rates.[244] Some evaluations have found that the effects of family-group conferences on recidivism, however, depend on the type of offense and the age of offenders (with younger offenders more likely to avoid re-offending).[245] A recent study of a hybrid restorative justice program that uses varying practices according to the particulars of each case also revealed lower rates of recidivism for youth referred to the program compared with youth who underwent traditional juvenile court processing.   These results are especially compelling because researchers evaluated recidivism rates over a relatively long period of time: four years.[246]

Two studies provide more comprehensive investigations of the effects of all types of restorative justice on recidivism rates in light of this body of evaluative research. In their meta-analysis of evaluations of all types of restorative justice programs, Bonta and his colleagues found that while previous evidence indicates that punitive responses to

---

[243] McCold and Wachtel (1998).

[244] Edmund McGarrell, *Restorative Justice Conferences as an Early Response to Young Offenders* (Washington, D.C.: Office of Juvenile Justice and Delinquency Prevention, U.S. Department of Justice, 2001), retrieved on July 16, 2007 at http://purl.access.gpo.gov/GPO/LPS18711.   See also Edmund McGarrell and Natalie Kroovand Hipple, "Family Group Conferencing and Re-Offending Among First-Time Juvenile Offenders: The Indianapolis Experiment," *Justice Quarterly* 24.2 (2007): 221-242.

[245] Heather Strang, et al., *Experiments in Restorative Policing: A Progress Report* (Canberra: Australian National University, 1999), retrieved on September 18, 2007 at www.aic.gov.au/rjustice/rise/index.html#papers. Also, Lawrence W. Sherman, Heather Strang, and Daniel J. Woods, *Recidivism Patterns in the Canberra Reintegrative Shaming Experiments (RISE)* (Canberra: Centre for Restorative Justice, Australian National University, 2000); and McGarrell and Hipple (2007).

[246] Kathleen J. Bergseth and Jeffrey A. Bouffard, "The Long-Term Impact of Restorative Justice Programming for Juvenile Offenders," *Journal of Criminal Justice* 35 (2007): 433-451.

crime such as incarceration *increase* recidivism,[247] restorative justice interventions on average significantly *decrease* recidivism, although the effect is small—about seven percent.[248] This effect is greatest on low-risk offenders. In contrast, appropriate rehabilitative interventions[249] with high-risk offenders showed the highest rate of

---

[247] This conclusion is supported by a meta-analysis by Daniel S. Nagin, Francis T. Cullen, and Cheryl Lero Jonson, which suggests that "compared with noncustodial sanctions, incarceration has a null or mildly criminogenic effect on future criminal behavior" (115), suggesting that prisons do not have a specific deterrent effect. See "Imprisonment and Reoffending," *Crime and Justice* 38.1 (2009): 115-200. See also D.A. Andrews, et al., "Does Correctional Treatment Work? A Clinically-Relevant and Psychologically Informed Meta-analysis," *Criminology* 28.3 (1990): 369-404; Paul Gendreau, Claire Goggin, and Francis T. Cullen, *The Effects of Prison Sentences on Recidivism* (Ottawa: Solicitor General Canada, 1999); Paul Gendreau, Paula Smith, and Sheila A. French, "The Theory of Effective Correctional Intervention: Empirical Status and Future Directions," in *Taking Stock: The Status of Criminological Theory*, Advances in Criminological Theory, vol. 15, edited by Francis T. Cullen, John Paul Wright, and Kristie R. Blevins (New Brunswick, NJ: Transaction, 2006), 419-445; D.A. Andrews and James Bonta, *The Psychology of Criminal Conduct*, 4th edition (Cincinnatic: Anderson/LexisNexis, 2006); Mark W. Lipsey and Francis T. Cullen, "The Effectiveness of Correctional Rehabilitation: A Review of Systematic Reviews," *Annual Review of Law and Social Science* 3 (2007): 297-320; Doris Layton MacKenzie, *What Works in Corrections: Reducing the Criminal Activities of Offenders and Delinquents* (New York: Cambridge University Press, 2006); and Paula Smith, Paul Gendreau, and Kristin Swartz, "Validating the Principle of Effective Correctional Intervention: A Systematic Review of the Contributions of Meta-analysis in the Field of Corrections," *Victims and Offenders* 4.1 (2009): 148-169.

[248] Bonta, et al. (2006).

[249] Bonta, et al. (2006) define "appropriate rehabilitative interventions" in terms of three factors: risk, need, and responsiveness. This definition is based upon a study by D.A. Andrews, James Bonta, and R.D. Hoge, "Classification for Effective Rehabilitation: Rediscovering Psychology," *Criminal Justice and Behavior* 17 (1990): 19-52. The factor of risk indicates that "the intensity of

recidivism reduction—about twenty-six percent. If treatment was delivered in the community rather than in prison or residential settings, recidivism was reduced even more—about thirty-five percent. This meta-analysis shows that restorative justice may be the most effective response to low-risk offenders in terms of recidivism reduction, while appropriate rehabilitation is necessary to reduce recidivism among high-risk offenders. Note that the authors distinguish between high-risk offenders and offenders who commit serious crimes: "Those who have committed serious, violent crimes and those who are at high risk to re-offend…are not necessarily the same."[250]   Bonta and his colleagues argue further that if restorative justice programs work with high-risk offenders, then they should be aware of rehabilitative treatment needs and opportunities that could be drawn upon in conjunction with their practices. This study therefore indicates that restorative justice may be useful for reducing recidivism, especially compared to more punitive practices, but may need to complement (rather than replace) rehabilitation in cases of high-risk offenders if we want to decrease re-offending.[251]

---

human service intervention should be proportional to the offender's risk to re-offend…treating low-risk offenders has minimal impact on recidivism" Bonta, et al. (2006), 111.   The needs addressed by interventions should be criminogenic, such as "substance abuse, cognitions supportive of crime, and social support for crime," versus non-criminogenic needs, such as self-esteem. Finally, program should be responsive to the particular capacities and motivations of offenders. For more on developments in rehabilitation theory, see Tony Ward and Shadd Maruna, *Rehabiliation: Beyond the Risk Paradigm* (London: Routledge Press, 2007).

[250] Ibid., 116.

[251] This argument is further supported by Tony War and Robyn Langlands in their article "Repairing the Rupture: Restorative Justice and the Rehabilitation of Offenders," *Aggression and Violent Behavior* 14 (2009): 205-214. See also Gordon Bazemore and Dee Bell, "What is the Appropriate Relationship between Restorative Justice and Treatment?," in *Critical Issues in Restorative Justice*, edited by Howard Zehr and Barbara Toews (Cullompton, UK: Willan,

The second comprehensive examination of the various evaluative data collected on restorative justice and recidivism was completed by Lawrence Sherman and Heather Strang.[252] In their review of literature on the effects of face-to-face restorative justice practices on re-offending, they found that "restorative justice may work better with more serious crimes rather than with less serious crimes, contrary to the conventional wisdom."[253] They divided their analysis in terms of studies that addressed violent, property, and non-victim crimes (for example, shoplifting, drunk driving, or public disorder). Evaluations of restorative justice used in response to violent offenses report success with significantly reducing, or at least not increasing, recidivism. The effects of restorative justice on re-offending among offenders who committed property crimes were smaller and less consistent. Nevertheless, at least two tests examined by Sherman and Strang indicate that restorative justice did as well or better than incarceration in reducing recidivism with property crime, indicating that restorative justice may be an effective alternative to incarceration with many offenses. Finally, although restorative justice is most commonly accepted for addressing relatively minor, non-victim offenses, the evidence for restorative justice reducing recidivism among offenders who commit these crimes is the least convincing. The work of Sherman and Strang together with that of Bonta and his colleagues indicates that restorative justice may be most effective in reducing recidivism among low-risk offenders who commit serious, violent offenses, and to a lesser degree, among low-risk offenders who commit property crimes.

2004), 119-131; and Gordon Bazemore and Sandra O'Brien, "The Quest for a Restorative Model of Rehabilitation: Theory-for-practice and Practice-for Theory," in *Restorative Justice and the Law*, edited by Lode Walgrave (Cullompton, UK: Willan, 2002), 31-67.

[252] Lawrence Sherman and Heather Strang, *Restorative Justice: The Evidence* (London: The Smith Institute, 2007).

[253] Ibid., 69.

Evaluative research to date thus begins to answer whether restorative justice effectively provides satisfaction and a sense of fairness for its participants, generates agreements about how to repair the harm of crime, leads to the completion of these agreements, and reduces recidivism. Despite these advances in the evaluation research, much about restorative justice processes and outcomes remains unexamined. Several questions remain regarding the effectiveness of restorative justice, especially when we consider the various goals delineated in restorative justice literature. For example, how effective is restorative justice at protecting participants' legal rights? If restorative justice is effective at repairing material harms through reparation and compensation, does it also effectively repair physical, psychological, relational, and social harms? Does restorative justice effectively re-establish the social efficacy and cohesion of communities and reintegrate victims and offenders in the long term? With respect to restorative moral imagination, do participants view each other holistically after involvement in restorative justice? Do they see each other as real, living human beings, as persons deserving respect and empathy? Do they understand each other as tied together in a relational web and as members of the same community? Does restorative justice contribute to their healing? To what extent do participants use the narratives, metaphors, and symbols of restorative moral imagination? And to what degree does doing so enable them to imagine morally in a vivid and expansive manner, and thus to respond to cases with equitable processes of ethical discernment?

These questions demarcate major gaps in the evaluative research, gaps that other authors have argued thwart our knowledge of the very heart of restorative justice. When evaluative research focuses only on effects such as satisfaction and recidivism, it misses some of the most vital aspects of restorative justice. John Braithwaite argues,

> With all of these quantitative findings, one can lose sight of what most moves restorative justice advocates who have seen restorative processes work well. I am not a spiritual enough

person to capture it in words: it is about grace, shalom. [Daniel] Van Ness characterizes shalom as "peace as a result of doing justice." Trish Stewart gets near its evocation when she reports one victim who said in the closing round of a conference: "Today I have observed and taken part in justice administered with love."[254]

Braithwaite here suggests that something intangible and mysterious lies within the experience of restorative justice and that this something cannot be measured using quantitative methods of evaluation alone. The words he borrows to describe this something—peace, justice, love, shalom, grace—evoke aspects of restorative moral imagination. At the same time, they call to mind aspects of equity in Aristotle's thought, with his indication that forgiveness and mercy can be necessary components of the highest form of justice. Other authors and practitioners have described this something as "soul-purging" and a "revelation,"[255] "a radical reframing of our views of self and other, that is, of our political economy of relationship" and "growth that restores personal well-being,"[256] and "forgiveness."[257] Braithwaite continues later in his text,

A mistake criminologists could make now is to do more and more research to compare the efficacy of restorative justice, statically conceived, with traditional Western justice. Rather, we must think more dynamically about developing the restorative justice process and the values that guide it.[258]

---

[254] Braithwaite (2002), 53.

[255] Mark S. Umbreit and Jean Greenwood, *National Survey of Victim-Offender Mediation Programs in the U.S.* (Washington, D.C.: Office of Juvenile Justice and Delinquency Prevention, U.S. Department of Justice, 2000), retrieved on July 16, 2007 at http://purl.access.gpo.gov/GPO/LPS6210.

[256] Sullivan and Tifft (2001).

[257] Zehr (1990).

[258] Braithwaite (2002), 69.

The next step of evaluating and improving restorative justice requires moving beyond questions of whether it provides satisfaction for participants and reduces recidivism. These questions are undeniably important for advocating restorative justice in public policy debates; a criminal justice model that fails to satisfy its participants or to reduce recidivism is not ultimately sustainable or worthwhile. But these are not the only questions surrounding restorative justice, and for many advocates, they remain peripheral questions. Among the next questions to be answered is how participants in restorative justice practices use and negotiate elements of restorative moral imagination in contrast with rehabilitative and retributive moral imaginations, whether restorative justice practices encourage activities of vivid and expansive moral imagining, and if these practices may therefore realize justice as equity in the processes of ethical discernment among their participants. Chapter four suggests some answers.

CHAPTER 4

Moral Imagining in Restorative Justice Practices

Tyson[259] sat in a circle with a bunch of much older adults. Nineteen years old, dressed in boarder shorts, a too-large t-shirt, and beaten-up flip-flops, he was not very enthusiastic about being with this particular bunch of adults sitting in institutional chairs in a stuffy room in the county courthouse on a beautiful, sunny Colorado summer evening. Tyson's parents sat on either side of him, his mother Anne dabbing away streaking mascara from her tears and his father Jake leaning forward intensely, clearly on edge. The other adults in the circle included a probation officer, three or four community members, and two restorative justice facilitators, Patrick and Kenneth. The victim of Tyson's crime had moved out of state and could not be located for this conference. Tyson seemed nervous—slouching in his chair, staring at his toes, chewing his fingernails, bouncing his knee incessantly.

---

[259] All study participants have been given pseudonyms in order to protect their identities. In some instances, I have also changed certain details about them, such as career information or aspects of family background, so that they are not readily identifiable to other people who have participated in the same restorative justice programs.

This restorative justice conference had begun as most do at this program in Foothills County.[260] Patrick, the lead facilitator, who also happened to be facilitating his first conference, established some ground rules (no cursing, no yelling, no interrupting, etc.; that is, engage in an "adult" conversation) and asked participants in the circle to introduce themselves. He then began the conversation by instructing the offender, Tyson, to tell the group about himself. The young man's response was measured and mumbled: he works at a local fast-food franchise, he has yet to complete high school or his GED, he used to like to play baseball before he had to leave school. After some questions from the group that encouraged Tyson to share a little more (Why did you quit baseball?, Were you on the school team?, How do you like work?, Are you working on your GED?, How is it living with your parents?),[261] Patrick asked him about the offense that eventually led to this restorative justice conference.

Tyson committed and was charged with a relatively minor felony: trespassing. When he was a senior in high school, he and three of his friends (also high-school seniors) broke into a vacant apartment that they mistakenly believed was a classmate's home. With the busted front door jammed behind them, locking them in the apartment, the boys shimmied down the balconies of the building to escape.

---

[260] As with individuals who participated in this research, I have also chosen to use pseudonyms for the counties described here. Revealing the names of the counties would enable readers to identify rather easily many of the study participants through simple internet searches.

[261] Because I was unable to take notes during the conferences that I observed, quotations from the actual proceedings are reconstructed from my memory. Immediately after every conference, I noted particularly memorable phrases and moments in the conference. I would then type full notes into a word processing document or make an audio recording in which I recounted the events of the conferences. I only put words in quotation marks that I am fairly certain are accurate representations of the words of study participants. When paraphrasing, I do not use quotation marks. Quotations from interviews are direct quotations from audio recordings.

Neighbors who saw them fleeing the apartment reported their license plate number to the police, and the teenagers were arrested.

Unfortunately for Tyson, while his three friends were legal minors, he was eighteen-years-and-three-months old. His friends entered the juvenile justice system, but Tyson's case was sent to the adult criminal justice system in Foothills County, where he was sentenced to ten weeks in the county jail and ten weeks in a half-way house as well as probation until his twenty-second birthday—three years from now. In contrast, his friends spent a few months on juvenile probation and were never incarcerated, although one of them had an extensive juvenile record. Tyson decided to participate in the restorative justice program as a condition of his probation. In telling the story of his offense and his entrance into the restorative justice program, he admitted responsibility for what he did and said that it was the stupidest thing that he had ever done. His parents agreed.

Once Tyson finished recounting this story, his parents entered the conversation in earnest, describing their family's experience with the criminal justice system after their son's arrest. To say the least, they were frustrated. Anne cried as she talked about feeling "dehumanized" and "stigmatized" by everyone they encountered in the system. The report from the family's attorney that the district attorney wanted a "pound of flesh" from Tyson particularly upset her. Anne said repeatedly, "He's a person, not a piece of meat." She felt that her son had been singled out unfairly for this crime.

Jake, Tyson's father, agreed, citing the divergent sentencing between his son and the other boys. He wondered, if the criminal justice system is sometimes willing to say that thirteen- to seventeen-year-old kids ought to be tried as adults, why then can it not recognize that sometimes an eighteen-year-old young man is so immature that he ought to be treated as a juvenile: "Why can't it work the other way around too?" The law seemed "too inflexible," "too rigid" to Jake. He wanted the police, lawyers, and judges to pay more attention to the "particular circumstances" of Tyson's situation. In a poignant moment, Jake lamented that if the point of the criminal justice system is in part "to make better citizens," then in his son's case it failed miserably: Tyson is a high-school dropout who has a hard time holding down a job in a fast-food restaurant, who lives at home, and whose situational anxiety disorder, exacerbated by his time incarcerated, has reached a state where he is afraid to return phone calls—an especially troublesome vice for someone who must be in constant contact with his probation officer.

In the course of this discussion, the members of the community seemed receptive to the concerns of Tyson and his parents. They nodded, leaned forward, gave Anne tissues to wipe away her tears, offered words of solace and support: "That must have been very difficult for you to see, as a mother." But while the community members showed this understanding, they also did not criticize the criminal justice system in the same ways as Tyson's family, reminding them that even though the system had perhaps responded harshly to Tyson, it remains an ongoing reality with which they must simply cope for now. The facilitator, Patrick—notably the husband of a former district attorney—said that the main task for the group was to focus on moving forward, to identify the harms that have been done, and to look for ways to repair those harms.

After the conference, I asked several of the participants what they thought about this part of the conversation, where Tyson and his family described their frustrations with the criminal justice system. Patrick confirmed my suspicion that he empathized with the family, but that his empathy only extended so far. He said,

> I heard a lot of excuses and a lot of victimhood, is what I heard. Now I could get why they were feeling it, and I also felt the importance that they needed to go there, but if that's where it stops, that's the problem. So as a problem solver in life, I was already thinking, okay, how can I get them out of this victimhood, or at least perceived victimhood, because I don't know, I don't know what the situation was....I had empathy for them, but not enough that I would, like, say, "Oh

my God! Woe is me! You are a complete one hundred percent victim." It was more like, well, "Some crappy stuff happened. How do I get you to get away from that and focus on the harm?"

Patrick distinguished between the "crappy stuff" that happened in the criminal justice system and the "harm" that he thought should be the focus of the restorative justice conference. For him, that harm seemed to be limited to the harm caused to victims and communities, not the harm sometimes experienced by offenders and their families.

In contrast to Patrick, the co-facilitator, Kenneth, described a greater sense of the pain caused to Tyson and his family and validated that pain as harm worthy of discussion in the restorative justice conference. He also located their pain within a broader context of the criminal justice system and its treatment of other cases that he had encountered. Kenneth responded to a question about his assessment of this conference:

My reaction is that we see too much of that in our system, whereby the defendant simply by virtue of the fact that he's two days shy of, or two days past the point of being considered a juvenile, the system just hammers him and makes him do things...and requires him to do things that are just staggering. And to label clients like that so early in the game, rather than trying to work with the each client on an individual basis instead of just slapping that offender, and saying, okay, this is your offense, this what the charges are, this is what's going to happen, these are the consequences. And the system, I don't know if it's simply the sheer numbers that they have to deal with that they can't operate on that basis, but it's very dehumanizing and it puts clients more behind the eight ball than it does rehabilitate them.

Kenneth agreed with Jake's assessment of the criminal justice system: it pigeonholes offenders based on seemingly arbitrary criteria, like one's date of birth rather than one's actual capacities as an adult, without ever attending to individual differences that might make a difference in understanding the circumstances of a crime. As a result, he found that the system tends to treat many offenders too harshly, leading to degradation and an inability to return to society productively. Immediately after the conference, when Tyson, Anne, and Jake had left, Kenneth commented to the other participants, "The human aspect is totally missing from the system."

Linda, another community member (probably the most experienced community member and facilitator that I met in this study), agreed with Kenneth's assessment of the harm done to Tyson and his family by the criminal justice system, but also noted her frustrations with the response of the participants in the conference to this situation:

> Now here's what I need to say to you about that particular group of experiences. I like to make sure that the heart is really brought in and that there's a real sense of inclusion for those who come in. I want them to feel real comfortable with the group, and then we can really look at the whole case.... The conference we were in the other night, I just felt like the heart was missing from that, and I sort of...I think in most of the conferences I sit in there is great heart and there's warmth and there's great stuff going on.

For Linda, "heart" involves attending to all of the harms associated with an offense, "really focusing on community harm, victim harm, family harm, and offender harm." Creating heart requires "getting a full picture," "understanding and working on repair," "seeing different perspectives," and "having compassion and caring." This group failed to bring in the heart in Linda's view because it did not adequately empathize with the harm caused to the offender and his family, and because it could not deal with their issues, the group could not then turn to the harms caused to the victim and community. According to Linda, the discussion of repairing the harm in Tyson's conference was "too broad" to address the specific harms discussed by Tyson, Jake, and Anne.

Despite the frustrations of many of the participants in this conference, at the end of the conversation, Tyson's father, Jake, said that this process was not what he had expected. The family seemed relieved to have someone listen to their stories, and they lamented that they hadn't had any other opportunities to express some of their concerns. No one else had listened to them and sometimes people who worked in the criminal justice system—police, attorneys, probation officers—had specifically told them not to say anything.

Time was running out, and the group had not progressed far in the process. Everyone decided that they should wait until the first follow-up discussion to identify all of the harms associated with the crime and to construct an agreement, the typical pattern of most conferences. Patrick emphasized that the group would be looking at the harms to the community and the victim in the next meeting. Linda, however, expressed a concern that Tyson and his family may need some support in the coming month before the next session, but no one seemed sure about what form this support should take or volunteered to offer it. Despite this challenge, the entire family seemed gratified as they walked out, and they all said that they were glad to have had their stories heard. Even Tyson, who had not said much during the entire conference, said that he looked forward to coming back to meet with this group in a month, to sit with them in a circle of industrial chairs in a stuffy room in the county courthouse on what would in all likelihood be another beautiful, sunny Colorado summer evening—but maybe next time without his parents.

ETHNOGRAPHIC STUDY: FINDING MORAL IMAGINATION IN PRACTICE

I observed and participated in Tyson's conference in the process of ethnographic research with restorative justice programs in five counties in Colorado: Plains, Foothills, Desert, River, and Mountain Counties. The goal of this research is to explore whether and how participants in restorative justice practices draw on the narratives, metaphors, and symbols of restorative moral imagination, in contrast with retributive and rehabilitative moral imaginations described by advocates (cf. table 3 in chapter three). By examining participants' use and negotiation of these different types of moral imagination in their processes of ethical discernment, I hope to understand how elements of each type of moral imagination relate to practices of moral imagining, particularly to efforts to enter into others' stories and appreciate their perspectives, to draw connections across particular cases, and to consider myriad possibilities of how to respond to a situation (cf. figure 1 in chapter two). If the adoption of restorative images of the world and its possibilities among participants is connected to more vivid and expansive moral imagining in concrete cases, then we could suppose that participation in restorative justice practices may contribute to greater attention to the particulars of specific cases and thus to more equitable responses to crime (cf. table 2 in chapter two). As I proceeded through this research, I therefore examined the relationship among three distinctive variables:

1) the use and negotiation by participants in restorative justice of narratives, metaphors, and symbols of restorative, rehabilitative, and retributive moral imaginations;
2) activities of moral imagining in the practices of restorative justice participants; and
3) the responses of participants to stakeholders in restorative justice conferences, especially the extent to which they addressed the particulars of a situation in their processes of

ethical discernment and therefore may have been equitable in conferences.

Examining the interrelationship of these variables reveals the extent to which participants in practice take on the type of imagination described by restorative justice advocates, the strengths and weaknesses in specific circumstances of these images of the world and its possibilities, and the degree to which aspects of restorative moral imagination foster vivid and expansive moral imagining, and thus, better enable participants to realize justice as equity.

The ethnographic research presented here employs three qualitative methods: participant-observation, semi-structured interviews, and examination of primary documents such as training manuals, case records, and program evaluations given to me by program coordinators. The restorative justice programs selected for this study were found in part through community contacts and in part through internet research. The programs employ various restorative justice practices, including victim-offender mediation and dialogue, community conferencing, and citizen- and neighborhood-accountability boards as well as hybrids among these practices in which facilitators draw on what they view as the best elements of each (for the sake of ease, I will refer to all of these practices as "conferences"). Although these five programs go about their work in different ways, they also share much in common because they are well connected to each other, often drawing on similar training resources and consulting with each other regularly in quarterly meetings among their coordinators.

Two of the programs—those in Foothills and Plains Counties— have much higher rates of referral and many more cases than the other three programs because they are more well-established in their communities, their referral processes are better instituted within their local criminal and juvenile justice systems, and they are in counties with larger urban centers, and thus more offenses to address. These two programs address two to six cases per week. The programs in River, Mountain, and Desert Counties did not have any referrals for cases during the times when I was in Colorado for research. As a result, I engaged in participant-observation of restorative justice conferences in only the two larger programs, although I interviewed participants in and examined the primary documents of all five programs.

Because the programs in Foothills and Plains Counties draw on the resources of the same consultant, they use a similar hybrid practice of restorative justice that combines aspects of community conferencing, sentencing circles, and citizen- and neighborhood-accountability boards. In the practices of these programs, stakeholders in the crime—victims, offenders, and their supporters—typically meet with one or two facilitators in a pre-conference interview in the week or so prior to the conference in order to learn more about restorative justice and to prepare for the conversation. The rhythm of the conference described here involves only the offender; I did not see any conferences in which victims were present, although the program directors invite victims to participate whenever possible. During the conference, offenders and their supporters meet with the facilitators and a panel of three to six community members who are regular volunteers with the programs and many of whom have also been trained as facilitators.

Conferences begin with short introductions, followed by one of the facilitators asking the offender to share a little bit about himself—his interests, work, family, etc. The facilitators then ask the offender to tell the group about the offence. When his story is complete, community members have the opportunity to ask him informational questions, which generally focus on what the offender was thinking at the time of the offense, whether he was targeting particular victims or choosing random victims, whether he accepts responsibility for his wrongdoing, or how his life has changed since the offense. Community members try to ask questions in ways that are not accusatorial and that promote the sharing of stories and information. For example, one community member and facilitator, Judy, described these questions as ideally beginning with the phrase "I wonder" rather than with "why." "I wonder" questions, she explained, encourage participants to explain what happened instead of requiring them to defend themselves, a common result when asked, "Why did you...?" Once a clear picture of what occurred surfaces, the conference moves toward an account of the harms associated with the offense, including harms to victims, family and friends of the offender, the offender himself, and the community. After a comprehensive list of harms has been generated, participants begin to brainstorm about ways to "repair the harm," culminating in the creation of an agreement or written contract that lists the responsibilities of all parties (but primarily the offender). When the group reaches consensus about the agreement, they sign it and celebrate with cookies and punch.

These two programs also use follow-up conferences, for which the stakeholders return on a monthly basis, usually for three or four months, to check on progress on the agreement. Follow-up conferences generally last only about twenty to thirty minutes and include all of the participants in the initial conference rather than just the facilitator or program director. The innovation of the follow-up conference is unusual among restorative justice programs, which typically rely on individual facilitators to follow up with all parties.

While Plains County deals primarily with juvenile offenses, Foothills County works mostly with adult crimes, although most offenders are still fairly young, typically in their late teens or early twenties. Offenses are mostly misdemeanors or minor felonies, including breaking and entering, marijuana possession, burglary, forgery, theft, and status offenses for juveniles such as bullying or carrying a weapon (in one case, a butterfly knife) on school property. In total, I engaged in participant-observation in twelve conferences.

Within all five of the programs, I generated a sample of interviewees through two primary strategies. First, in the conferences in which I engaged in participant-observation, I asked all of the participants—facilitators, community members, victims, offenders, and supporters—whether they were willing to be interviewed by me. The second strategy for recruiting participants was snowball sampling with multiple starts; that is, I asked a small group of initial contacts to refer me to two or three people who have participated in restorative justice practices, who then referred me to two or three others, and so on. Together, these techniques balance selection bias that might lead me to only the most "experienced" or "outstanding" participants in the eyes of my initial contacts. But more than correct for selection bias, they led me to some participants whose voices may not have been heard otherwise and whose perspectives and experiences may have differed from more central players in these programs. I conducted several interviews with community members and facilitators, three with offenders, one with a family supporter of an offender, and none with victims (again, no victims attended these twelve conferences; also, the categories of victim, offender, community member, and facilitator often overlapped because individuals had often occupied more than one of these roles at various times in their lives). While a few other offenders agreed to be interviewed, they did not show up for their interviews and efforts to reschedule were unsuccessful. In the future, attending to the voices of offenders—whose voices, along with victims, are the least frequently heard in qualitative studies of restorative justice—may further illuminate their experiences of restorative justice.

In generating this sample, I hoped to speak with people who were well-acquainted with restorative justice in order to see how someone deeply involved in these practices drew on restorative narratives, metaphors, and symbols in approaching particular cases as well as how he or she would guide others through these practices. I also hoped to speak with people who were just getting to know restorative justice in order to get a sense of how they experienced the use and negotiation of restorative images of the world and its possibilities in their first encounters with these practices. To be included, interviewees had only to have participated in at least one restorative justice conference. I interviewed twenty people in all; some had participated in "hundreds" of cases and some had only participated in one or two.

Fourteen of the interviewees were female and six were male; they ranged in age from seventeen to eighty-five. Their employment backgrounds included education, banking and finance, mediation, law, union organization, Christian ministry, life coaching, and secretarial work; lawyers (three) and middle- and high-school teachers (four) were most common in this sample. Seven participants were retirees, although one had retired in his mid-thirties after a short and successful career in finance and two had retired in their fifties because of disabilities. All but three of the interviewees were white, non-Hispanic; the other three were white and Hispanic. The racial and ethnic representation in this sample reflects the breakdown of the counties where these programs are located. As a facilitator of a restorative justice program not included in this study noted to me, "Snow isn't the only thing in Colorado that's white." In 2007 in these counties, between 92.5 and 96.1% of the populations were white; between 6.4 and 16.9% of the residents identified themselves as Hispanic.[262]

My sample of interviewees, conferences, or programs is not representative of all restorative justice participants, practices, or organizations. My conclusions, therefore, may not be generalizable. To a certain extent, my sample of interviewees reflects some self-selection bias as some people did not agree to be interviewed, some did not return phone calls after agreeing to be interviewed, and some did not show up even after an interview had been scheduled. These people included community members, offenders, and supporters, although meetings with offenders and supporters were much more difficult to schedule than community members. In addition, the practices of restorative justice programs vary too much to suppose that these programs could stand in for all other programs in other locations, and the hybrid model adopted by these particular programs is rather idiosyncratic, tailored for the specific needs and capacities of their communities. Moreover, the selection of conferences in which I was a participant-observer may not be representative of the cases with which the programs in Plains and Foothills Counties work. In many ways, the

---

[262] See the U.S. Census Bureau, *State and County Quickfacts*, http://quickfacts.census.gov/qfd/states/08000.html.

conferences that I observed were interesting, but not especially astounding; my description of them does not resemble many of the accounts that one may find in restorative justice literature of dramatic and dazzling transformations among victims, offenders, and community members. Many of the participants could recount conferences where such changes did occur, and at least three of them recalled the same remarkably memorable conference that followed the traffic death of a bicyclist when a teenager fell asleep at the wheel on a mountain road. So although the outcomes of the conferences in this ethnographic account may not amaze readers, it seems that amazing conferences do occur within these programs. Still, most conferences in day-to-day practice—even those described by participants—are in many ways mundane affairs.

To say that the programs, conferences, and participants described in this ethnographic account are not necessarily representative, however, is not to say either that they are necessarily atypical. And to say that my conclusions are not generalizable is not to say that they are uninformative. In interviews, I asked participants to tell me about their most recent conferences, and with one exception, the conferences they described did not involve dramatic and dazzling transformations but real-world, everyday challenges for ethical discernment.[263] This pattern suggests that the conferences in which I was a participant-observer were not unusual in these programs. Also, even though these programs, conferences, and participants may not necessarily reveal externally valid conclusions about all restorative justice practices, programs, and participants, enough of what I saw and heard during this ethnographic study resembles other accounts in the literature to indicate that the findings here are at least analogous to what might be found elsewhere. That is, the conclusions of this chapter may not be generalizable, but they are suggestive of restorative justice practices, programs, and participants outside of this study.

---

[263] See Appendix for more information on interview schedules and methodology.

While I cannot claim that my sample represents all restorative justice practices, programs, and participants, neither can I claim that my data enables an accurate and full comparison between restorative justice and other aspects of our criminal and juvenile justice systems, such as more typical sentencing procedures in a traditional courtroom. This study is not truly comparative; I did not have a similar sample of retributive or rehabilitative practices, programs, and participants in which I traced elements of different types of moral imagination or processes of ethical discernment. As a result, I cannot definitively say that moral imagining in restorative justice conferences is *more* vivid and expansive than in traditional courtrooms. I am certain that many judges, for instance, *do* exhibit vivid and expansive moral imagining in their day-to-day efforts to realize justice and are also often remarkably equitable in light of the demands placed upon them. Nevertheless, many of the participants in this study *did* have experiences with traditional courtroom procedures, and they *could and did* compare those experiences with their experiences of restorative justice. Any comparisons that I make of restorative justice to rehabilitative or retributive practices draw directly on the observations of study participants. Tyson's father, Jake, for example, compared his experience of having been heard by other participants in the restorative justice conference to his experience of being silenced in the courtroom. This datum indicates that moral imagining in the conference was more vivid and expansive than in the courtroom *in this case* and suggests that this pattern may repeat itself in other cases. So again, while the conclusions of this chapter that compare restorative justice to other aspects of our criminal and juvenile justice systems may not be generalizable, they are nevertheless suggestive of the similarities and differences between these sets of programs, practices, and participants.

Another limitation of this study is that it is not longitudinal. I did not observe participants' processes of ethical discernment before or after the restorative justice conferences in which they participated. As a result, I cannot claim that participation in a conference changed participants' images of the world and its possibilities, or that participants used activities of vivid and expansive moral imagining in interactions following the conference. That is, questions about participants' moral character beyond the scope of the conference will not be answered here. Whether participants are equitable in all aspects of their lives, or whether they always attend to the particulars of the realities before them in their processes of ethical discernment, will remain a mystery.

Finally, although evaluation of both processes and outcomes of restorative justice is necessary to understand whether and how its practices repair harm, I concentrate in this study on the processes of ethical discernment used by participants during conferences. I draw conclusions about whether they engaged in activities of vivid and expansive moral imagining that focused their attention on the particulars of a case, thereby enabling them to be equitable in their responses. Whether their decisions actually realized justice as equity remains unanswered; I do not evaluate whether the outcomes arising from these processes avoided mistakes or excessive harshness. It is possible that the outcomes of a conference in which all participants imagined morally in vivid and expansive ways could fail to produce equitable results, as may have been the case with the boy forced to wear an "I am a Thief" t-shirt in Canberra, Australia. Nevertheless, in light of the premise established in chapter two, I believe that engaging in certain activities of moral imagining in our processes of ethical discernment should dispose us to making decisions that are equitable in avoiding mistakes and excessive harshness, that are prone to grace, forgiveness, and mercy. But still the processes in which participants in restorative justice engaged in efforts to realize justice as equity, not the outcomes of those processes, form the center of this text. Evaluation of whether outcomes realize justice as equity must await another study.

Taking into consideration the constraints and possibilities of the ethnographic research presented here, the remainder of this chapter examines the use and negotiation of the narratives, metaphors, and symbols of restorative, rehabilitative, and retributive moral imaginations, first, by participants in Tyson's case and, second, by participants in these five restorative justice programs generally. The use and negotiation of these images of the world and its possibilities serves as the backdrop for exploring how different types of moral imagination relate to various activities of moral imagining. That is, I explore whether and how the narratives, metaphors, and symbols of restorative moral imagination are connected to participants' moral imagining—their efforts to enter into others' stories and appreciate their perspectives, to draw connections across particular cases, and to consider a wide range of images of the world and its possibilities. If the adoption of elements of restorative moral imagination fosters more vivid and expansive moral imagining, then participation in restorative justice practices may contribute to finer understanding of the particulars of cases in efforts to realize justice as equity.

ANALYZING TYSON'S CONFERENCE: RESTORATIVE MORAL IMAGINATION IN PRACTICE

The basic frustration of Tyson, Jake, and Anne was that the criminal justice system in Foothills County had failed to attend to Tyson's particular circumstances, including his all too recent achievement of the age of majority, his struggles with situational anxiety disorder, and his status as a high school student at the time of the offense. As a result, they found that it had treated him unjustly in comparison with his friends. Jake, in particular, protested that the rigidity of the law in distinguishing between juvenile and adult offenders obscured the real similarities between Tyson and the other boys. The legal codes of Colorado were not written with a case in mind where four offenders— three seventeen-year-olds and one eighteen-year-old—worked together to commit a crime; they were formulated too generally to anticipate such a specific situation. The mechanical application of the adult code to Tyson and the juvenile code to his friends resulted in very different treatment of four teenagers. If we can agree that the circumstances of Tyson and his friends were materially alike, *even if not legally alike,* then we can also agree that the criminal and juvenile justice systems of Foothills County did not achieve the highest form of justice. Aristotle's insight that we sometimes need equity to supplement and correct strict legal justice seems apt here. Had the police, attorneys, or judges in the cases of Tyson and his friends taken (or had) the time to attend to the particulars of the situation and to notice the pitfalls of the law, then they might have formulated a more equitable response. As the outcome of this situation stands, however, it illuminates the importance of sometimes looking beyond the law and considering the intentions behind it to discern what justice as equity demands. Kenneth's response, noting that circumstances like Tyson's are all too common, further suggests that the need for equity applies not only here, but in scores of other cases pursued in our criminal and juvenile justice systems.

In light of the challenges presented in Tyson's conference about the relationships among law, justice, and equity, participants' use and negotiation of restorative, rehabilitative, and retributive moral imaginations reveal some of the challenges of ethical discernment in a restorative justice conference. On the one hand, the community members and facilitators commonly drew on narratives, metaphors, and symbols associated with restorative moral imagination described in chapter three, based on the writing of restorative justice advocates. For example, all of the facilitators and community members used the term "harm" to describe the crime and its affects, although some participants focused more on harms to the community and victim while others attended to harms to Tyson and his family. At one point in the conference, Patrick paused to explain that we should think of the initial crime as a pebble dropped into a pond, with the ripples representing the harms extending throughout Tyson's family, the victim, and the wider community. The metaphor of the rippling pond evokes similar metaphors used by restorative justice advocates describing communities as relational webs. Also, especially as Anne and Jake described their experiences, community members offered other restorative metaphors for crime, commenting that the incident "wounded" the family and "broke their relationships." They emphasized that this family could use the conference as a tool for "healing" some of the damages caused to their family by both the initial offense and the response of the criminal justice system. This search for healing is particularly apparent in Linda's suggestion that the group work to find ways to support the family in the coming month. Finally, a holistic understanding of Tyson as a human being and as a person is evident in the practice in the beginning of the conference of asking him about himself before asking him about his offense. Kenneth's comment about the missing human element in the system also reveals this understanding of victims and offenders as human beings and as persons in restorative justice.

Alongside this use of elements of restorative moral imagination in Tyson's conference, however, participants also negotiated both retributive and rehabilitative visions of the world and its possibilities. On the whole, participants in this conference drew a sharp contrast between restoration and retribution. Just as Tyson was viewed as "a piece of meat" or "pound of flesh" by the district attorney, many participants viewed the criminal justice system as a "meat grinder," a term introduced by Anne, but reiterated by others in the conference. In this view, the criminal justice system was perceived as primarily retributive, bent on destroying this young man for the sake of vengeance. Linda also commented that the drive for retribution in the system "pummeled" Tyson and other offenders in similar situations. Despite this contrast with the "healing" offered by the conference, participants recognized that at least partial cooperation with the criminal justice system was a necessary evil for restorative justice. This program depended on attorneys, judges, and probation officers for referrals, and as Linda remarked, pushing the point about the harshness of the system would not endear the program to their referral sources. She continued by recommending that participants approach their legislators about reforming sentencing practices rather than haranguing the people who worked in the criminal justice system. The best that this particular conference could accomplish in terms of dealing with a retributive system, in Linda's assessment, was to mitigate some of the effects of harsh sentencing on Tyson, Jake, and Anne. More systemic responses fell outside of the mission and capacities of the program.

While participants took a largely negative view of retributivism, they also contrasted restorative justice with rehabilitative approaches to crime. Despite this contrast, participants in this conference, as opposed to the opinions of restorative justice advocates, did not seem to think that the differences between restorative and rehabilitative perspectives implied a negative view of the latter. Instead of a necessary evil, rehabilitation was generally seen as necessarily different from restorative justice, but also a good, something that could appropriately address the needs of many of the offenders and victims who came through the program. Kenneth, for example, said several times that the purpose of the criminal justice system is to rehabilitate offenders. On one occasion, he commented, "That's been an issue I've brought up time and time again, that defendants are often victimized to the point by the system to where they become more habitual offenders, than *what the system is intended to do, which is to rehabilitate.*"[264] An interesting aspect of this remark is that even though Kenneth had attended numerous restorative justice trainings and conferences, he did not view the primary goal of criminal and juvenile justice systems to be restoration, or the repair of harm in the aftermath of crime. Rather, in his assessment, rehabilitation ought to be the central focus of these systems, and restorative justice complemented the work of rehabilitation (at least when these systems actually did rehabilitative work instead of fixating on retribution) by addressing the needs of victims and communities in addition to offenders.

Although many participants in this conference recognized rehabilitation as a necessary good that often complements restorative justice, they also held that rehabilitation lay outside of the purview of restorative justice. Patrick expressed this point plainly: "You know, we're not therapists!" He elaborated on this comment, remarking that

---

[264] Emphasis mine.

he was originally attracted to the idea of restorative justice specifically because it was not therapy and therefore not "soft on crime." Patrick said, "Once I figured out that it wasn't therapy and there was a little bit of teeth to it, that's when I got the picture." For him, restorative justice ought to distinguish itself from rehabilitation, first, because its participants do not possess the capacity to offer therapy, and second, because therapy is a "touch-feely" response to crime that fails to address issues of accountability and responsibility to victims and communities. Patrick saw a role for therapy and rehabilitation, but not in restorative justice.

Kenneth would agree with Patrick about the inability of restorative justice practitioners to offer therapy and rehabilitation. Commenting on Tyson's case, he remarked,

> That is something that we as volunteer community members can't tackle because we've been down that path before. There are issues that only, that have to be addressed in that particular case, and I think only trained professionals can deal with. And you know, when I make a statement, it is obvious that it's not really fair because I'm not a professional therapist or psychiatrist, and I really believe that's a track that the parents have to follow with their son because he, he has obviously some anxiety issues that he has to deal with. At one time, we were going down that path, and that is not our role.

From Kenneth's perspective, it seems that restorative justice and rehabilitative services can parallel each other in criminal and juvenile justice systems, each offering different, but complementary, responses to crime. For both Patrick and Kenneth, rehabilitation is important, but because of the lack of training of facilitators and community members, it is impractical for restorative justice to tackle therapeutic issues.

While Kenneth and Patrick rejected primarily for practical reasons the idea that restorative justice conferences should provide therapy, Linda offered more ideological reasons for contrasting rehabilitation and restorative justice. When asked about the distinctive characteristics of restorative justice, Linda replied by distinguishing it from rehabilitation—not retribution—observing that with restorative justice, there should be "a focus on repair of harm, more so than rehabilitation." She continued,

> I think sometimes people get confused. There can be some rehabilitation, but our major role is to provide, is to give people an opportunity for repair, which can include rehabilitation, but that's not the major goal.... Repair of harm is focused as much on other as self. Rehabilitation is like therapy, and our job isn't to do therapy. Our job may be to refer for therapy, or to find resources for everyone, victims, offenders, and sometimes even the community, to help them rehabilitate, but sometimes the repair of harm is broader than rehabilitation. So I see rehab as more [concerned with the] self.

Linda clarifies the difference between restorative and rehabilitative responses to crime in terms of the centrality of the self versus the other. From a rehabilitative perspective, the focus is on the self of the offender, without consideration of the needs of victims or community members. For Linda, much like restorative justice advocates discussed in the previous chapter, this focus is too narrow; it occludes the experiences of the other stakeholders in a crime. While recognizing that therapy for mental illness and drug and/or alcohol dependence may sometimes be necessary (she suggested after Tyson's conference that family and individual therapy might be helpful in this case), she maintains that restorative justice conferences are not the appropriate place for treatment—not because facilitators and community members are not trained professionals, but because restorative justice should encourage all participants to look outside of themselves to the experiences of others.

Participants' use and negotiation of elements of restorative moral imagination in contrast with retributive and rehabilitative alternatives seem to correlate with their activities of moral imagining. At least as far as Tyson and his parents were concerned, they found that these practices enabled the other participants in the conference to enter into their stories more than anyone in the Foothills County criminal justice system had. Tyson, Jake, and Anne seemed to agree that participants in this conference appreciated the perspectives of this family, even if they may have disagreed with the some of their conclusions. One reason that the group did not reach an agreement in this first session was that the facilitators and community members kept asking the family questions, trying to create for themselves an accurate picture of the particulars of Tyson's case. Whereas Jake and Anne objected that the lawyers, probation officers, and judges had not only failed to hear their stories but also explicitly told them not to share their stories, they found in the restorative justice conference a group of people who listened and elicited more information from them in a nonjudgmental manner. Jake and Anne especially found people who empathized with them; several participants, for example, cited similar experiences with parenting. Tyson, however, may have found that fewer of the participants could as easily relate to his story, as only one other person in the room, a community member named John, had ever been through the criminal justice system as an offender. Nevertheless, Tyson's conference involved a concerted effort by participants to imagine what it would be like to have lived through Tyson's, Anne's, or Jake's experiences and to appreciate their perspectives. The co-facilitator, Kenneth, described the work of moral imagining involved in entering others' stories as restoring "the human aspect" that he finds lacking in the "harshness," "anonymity," and "blindness" of the criminal justice system.

At the same time that the facilitators and community members tried to appreciate the perspectives of Tyson and his parents, many of them also tried to imagine the perspectives of those who were not present at the conference: the victim and her direct neighbors in the apartment complex. Patrick, for example, in describing the ripple effect of the crime, wondered aloud about how the renter felt about hearing that someone had broken into her apartment, even if she had been moving out at the time of the offense. He tried to encourage Tyson to enter into her story and to appreciate how she might have reacted to this violation. Furthermore, Patrick tried to introduce the perspectives of her neighbors. About his attempt to highlight their perspectives for Tyson, he later said,

> [The community] is affected, you know. Sure if you bang down a door, I get it. But you also came down from the second or third floor through other people's lofts and balconies. Well, you know what? I sure wouldn't feel good about that, you know, if I had a bunch of kids going down my loft.

Patrick also described the task of introducing these perspectives as helping "that person look beyond their own little spirit world," indicating that one of the roles of facilitators in restorative justice conferences, in his view, is to foster in other participants practices of imagining the world from someone else's point of view.

Another activity of vivid and expansive moral imagining is drawing connections across particular cases. This practice involves highlighting important similarities and differences between experiences and builds upon the appreciation of others' stories and perspectives. In order to see how various cases deviate from and adhere with each other, one must be able to recount the experiences of parties involved in each case, noticing relevant factors in how and why their narratives took shape and recognizing when and why one case is like another case. Jake, Anne, and Tyson indicated that no one in the Foothills County criminal justice system attempted to examine Tyson's case with an eye toward its connections to the cases of his friends. Or, it may be that the points on which participants in the criminal justice system could draw any connections in these cases were limited only to those points deemed legally relevant; the central legally relevant point of comparison between the cases was the ages of the offenders. Aside from this consideration, other points of comparison—such as the motives and actions of the young men, their common social standing as seniors in high school, Tyson's problems with mental illness—fell outside of the stories that participants in the criminal justice system could tell about these cases, and so limited the connections that they could draw between them. For Tyson's parents, however, the ages of the offenders seemed like the least relevant point of the case, the aspect of his experience that would tell onlookers the least about their son, his friends, and their situations.

Participants in this restorative justice conference were not limited by concerns of legal relevance, and so freely considered points of comparison other than age between Tyson and his friends. They worked at expanding their imagining of Tyson's case through questions that helped them compare his circumstances with those of his friends. They asked Tyson, for example, to describe his motives alongside his assessment of the motives of the other boys in committing this offense. He explained that one of his friends sought revenge against a classmate who had stolen a videogame from him and who they believed lived in the apartment. He added that he was not sure what his friend had in mind in terms of revenge and that he just went along "to hang out" with the guys. Community members also asked what Tyson did exactly throughout the course of the crime, and he answered that he and two of the other boys mostly stood back and watched as their friend did everything. He recognized that even being present was wrong, but also said his level of involvement was different from that of the other boy, who was more of a ringleader. Asking these questions of Tyson enabled participants in this conference to add greater detail to their images of his crime and to gauge which points of comparison—mostly, motive and action—they found most relevant in their discernment processes.

Other questions that participants asked Tyson helped them draw connections also between his case and other cases that they had encountered through the restorative justice program. They focused on locating Tyson's offense within the larger context of his life, both before and after the crime. One community member, for example, asked Tyson about his experiences with work, school, and baseball prior to the offense. Many of these questions helped to establish a sense of Tyson's trajectory through life had he not committed this crime, particularly his hopes and goals after graduation from high school. Establishing this trajectory—and comparing it to the patterns of other young men who had gone through the program—enabled this community member to consider what Tyson may have lost in terms of life plans diverted and postponed. In contrast, John, the community member who had also once been an offender, focused his questions on Tyson's life after the offense. He compared his own experiences of lawyers, jail, half-way houses, and probation officers to Tyson's, illuminating common encounters in the Foothills County criminal justice system. Although John did not suffer from any mental illnesses, noting this difference in his experience also highlighted for the group the challenges Tyson would face in complying with probation with the added roadblocks of situational anxiety disorder. Drawing connections such as these between Tyson's case and other cases familiar to participants in this conference underscored the particularities of this young man's experience. It also gave the participants a greater sense of morally salient similarities and differences of this case in addition to the different ages of the boys, allowing them to consider in their discernment processes a more particularized picture than the facts of the case alone presented.

The final activity of vivid and expansive moral imagining for consideration is contemplating a wide range of possibilities for how to respond to a situation. These possibilities may include relatively small-scale concerns, such as hopes for a single offender in the direct future. Participants in this conference exhibited some effort to consider various possibilities of how Tyson's world could be different, although much of their effort seemed frustrated by impediments created by the retributive actions of the Foothills County criminal justice system and by the psychiatric needs of Tyson. Several participants, encouraged by

Linda, began the process of brainstorming with Tyson's family what the group could do to improve their situations in the coming month. During this phase of the conference, toward the end of the session, Linda and the other community members tried to keep their brainstorming focused on the future, rather than dwelling upon what might have been different in the past had Tyson not committed his offense or had the criminal justice system not responded so harshly to him. They also tried to concentrate on concrete actions that could begin to help Tyson cope with his experiences, such as offering assistance with communicating with his probation officer.

Despite this effort to come up with different possibilities for handling Tyson's case, at the end of this conference, the group seemed overwhelmed and paralyzed by the weight of the realities before them. Although they wanted to work with Tyson to affect change in his immediate future, specific strategies for doing so remained unclear to the group. In later interviews, Patrick and Kenneth both acknowledged that one reason for this frustration was that they saw many of Tyson's problems as requiring mental health therapy, which falls outside of the capacities and mission of the restorative justice participants. But they also saw the damages caused by the criminal justice system as another impediment, as they perceived Tyson's family as to be unable to move on to next steps to address their situation until they had the opportunity to air their grievances about their experiences. Imagining together possibilities for Tyson's future needed to wait until the next session.

Contemplating possibilities for the future may also address larger-scale matters, such as the reform of criminal and juvenile justice systems as a whole over the course of time. Participants in Tyson's conference also exhibited moral imagining around more systemic issues in response to their evaluations of his experience. Most of their consideration of these issues occurred outside of the time and space of the conference, mostly immediately afterwards, when Linda, John, and Kenneth discussed the "pummeling" of offenders by the criminal justice system. Their consideration of different possibilities for the future of the criminal justice system indicated that they hoped for a gradual transition toward a restorative system through the creation of new legislation that would combat the "nail-'em-and-jail-'em" approach of our current systems, in the words of Kenneth. Although these off-the-cuff reactions after Tyson's conference may seem somewhat rudimentary and nascent, failing to offer much in the way of specific strategies for bringing about a restorative system other than lobbying one's legislators, the consideration of the possibility of an alternative approach to crime by the participants in this conference is important in their activities of moral imagining. Linda, John, and Kenneth, in particular, see that the ways of the criminal justice system now—the ways of "pummeling," "hammering," "nailing and jailing"— are not the ways that the system has to be.

The discussion of this conference indicates the need for justice as equity where the law sometimes fails to respond to the particulars of certain situations, in this case, to Tyson's shared circumstances with his friends despite his different age. In their responses to this case, participants often drew upon the narratives, metaphors, and symbols of restorative moral imagination used by restorative justice advocates. At the same time, they also negotiated elements of retributive and rehabilitative moral imaginations. Although participants drew a sharp line between retribution and restoration, echoing restorative justice advocates, many of them saw rehabilitation and restoration as more complementary, even if still distinct. Participants' use and negotiation of these types of moral imagination seems to coincide with certain activities of vivid and expansive moral imagining, such as entering the stories of others and appreciating the perspectives of Tyson and his parents, drawing connections among particular cases, and considering various possibilities of how the world could be different, in terms both of Tyson's experience and more broadly-based systemic change. This work of moral imagining took significant conscientious effort on the part of participants, and sometimes the realities of our current justice systems frustrated their efforts. Nevertheless, in their immediate responses to their conference, Tyson and his parents seemed to value the efforts of the facilitators and community members. Their responses indicate that where they found that the system failed to realize justice in Tyson's case, restorative justice offered them hope that some level of equity could be restored to their situation.

EXPANDING ANALYSIS: RESTORATIVE MORAL IMAGINATION IN FIVE PROGRAMS

Analysis of other aspects of the five Colorado restorative justice programs reveals similar patterns as surfaced in Tyson's case, beginning with frustration with our criminal and juvenile justice systems. Many other cases in these programs, for example, illuminate failures of local systems to attend to the particulars of individual circumstances, and therefore, to respond to offenders in seemingly inequitable—even if legal—manners.

John, the community member in Tyson's conference who had also once been an offender, for example, recounted his own arrest with great frustration. According to John, after attending a major league baseball game, where he had drunk a few beers, he took a cab home. The cabdriver asked to use the restroom. When they entered the house, the cabdriver—who was significantly larger than John, a slight man in his mid-thirties—assaulted him. John escaped momentarily to retrieve a gun. The cabdriver fled the house, and both men called the police. Upon their arrival, the police questioned John and arrested him for "prohibited use of a weapon," a misdemeanor charge based on his use of alcohol prior to using a handgun. Although John had broken this law, in light of the circumstances, it seems that arresting him, jailing him overnight, and placing him on probation with a two-year suspended sentence when he had been trying to defend himself (even if arguably in a misguided manner) were responses that ignored the particulars of John's circumstances.

Another case that reflected lack of attention to particulars in the criminal justice system involved Josh, a 23-year-old man who pled guilty to check forgery. When Josh received a deposit refund on an apartment that he felt was too small, he added a "two" to the front of it—changing the check from $84 to $284. The police called six weeks later and asked him to come to the station. The officer explained to Josh that he had been caught, but since he would not be arrested for the offense (although still charged), Josh would have the opportunity to make things right. Josh went home, called his landlord, apologized, and got a money order to repay him. The landlord accepted the apology and asked that the charges against Josh be dropped. But when Josh called the police officer to report his efforts, he learned that the district attorney had decided to press charges anyway. Josh turned himself in, spent a night in jail, and was sentenced to two years on probation. Although this young man had attempted to repair the harm that he had caused and the victim accepted his efforts, the criminal justice system in Foothills County pressed forward with its prosecution without consideration of the particulars of Josh's situation and his work to rectify his wrongdoing.

In John's and Josh's cases, the effects of the refusal of the criminal justice system to look at the particulars had relatively minor consequences. They did not go to prison; probation presented at most a serious inconvenience to them. Both men had resources available to them, especially education, legal advice, money, and family support, to be able to cope with their sentences with comparable ease. Harshness of sentencing due to failure to attend to particulars, however, may have more drastic effects if offenders do not have these resources available to them. Stephen, for example, was fourteen, a freshman in high school, when he was arrested for bringing a weapon, a butterfly knife, onto school property. He was expelled and sentenced to pay a fine, serve two years on probation, and spend 96 hours on a residential work crew. In the years after massacres at Columbine and Virginia Tech, zero tolerance of this offense from both schools and juvenile justice systems may seem reasonable, even necessary. In Stephen's case, however, due diligence in paying attention to the particulars would have revealed that his pockets held not only a butterfly knife, but also all of his belongings that he could fit in his cargo pants—including his toothbrush. The night before, Stephen had moved out of a friend's house, where he had been staying because his father's parental rights had been terminated and his mother was addicted to methamphetamines. When he had a disagreement with his friend, he packed everything he could into his school bag and pants, went to school, and moved into his locker. A classmate saw him put the knife in his locker and reported him to her father, who then called the principal and the police. By responding to Stephen with zero tolerance, the school district and the juvenile justice system ignored the broader context of residential instability and adult unreliability (to be generous) that troubled this young man's life. They overlooked the particulars of his case, and as a result, not only let him fall through the cracks, but perhaps even pushed him down the cracks a little bit farther.

Although these three cases, along with Tyson's, cannot definitively prove that the criminal and juvenile justice systems in Foothills and Plains Counties are inequitable, they at least suggest a pattern of failing to attend to particulars of cases, potentially resulting in dire consequences for people caught up in them. The refusal to try to understand the circumstances in which these crimes took place may be traced in part to the adversarial nature of criminal justice systems (and increasingly, juvenile justice systems), which tends to shut down any attempts to engage in activities of vivid and expansive moral imagining. A more charitable assessment of this situation acknowledges that these systems and the people working in them are overburdened, often by relatively minor crimes that tie up the time of police, attorneys, and courts, rendering them unable to engage in these activities even when they would want to do so.

In these four cases, it seems that no one in these systems attempted to appreciate the stories and perspectives of these offenders (or, notably, their victims), to draw connections between their cases and others, or to consider possibilities other than mandatory or routine sentences. John's comments about his experiences in the system illuminate many ways in which moral imagining was narrowed and deadened in his case. He said,

I don't think anybody really cared about my story. All the stuff you see on TV about sitting down with a detective to find out what really happened—that doesn't happen. I didn't even know what I did, why I was arrested until the next morning. That night of the incident, I remember telling the police what happened...until I realized, like, they thought I had done something. It shut the story *right* down because I was, like, don't talk to the police until you see a lawyer. That is when I shut up.

John's experiences of remaining silent in light of suspicions about him and of not finding anyone to listen to him continued into the courtroom:

There was no one to tell my story. No one cared. I didn't say anything. And then there was the next day when they actually do the bond hearing. The DA said something about "pulled a gun on a cabdriver," and there was no mention that it was in my house or anything like that. And I thought, I should say something, and the judge actually told me to be quiet because I shouldn't discuss the specifics of my case without my lawyer present.

Even with his own lawyer, John's story remained untold. The attorney recommended that John plead guilty because a trial would be more bothersome than accepting a deal. Also, the lawyer explained, by pleading guilty, John would probably receive a suspended sentence that could eventually be expunged from his record. About this outcome, John remarked,

I think one of the things, the justice system, even in [Foothills County] where there's plenty of time and plenty of money, it's just very quick. Like, I got to say nothing. I felt like I didn't have any say in the matter. I never spoke more than a few words in court. "Guilty," my age, my level of education.

John's reflections about justice systems were echoed by Tyson, Josh, and Stephen, although the comments by John were more extensive, perhaps because he is older and, as a result, more reflective. While John's experiences, along with the experiences of these three young men, are troubling in themselves, they evoke serious concern in terms of what they suggest about the experiences of people who do not have the same resources as John in particular. If someone who is white, male, college educated, and financially secure cannot get the particulars of his case noticed in justice systems, then it seems that more marginalized people would have little chance.

These cases, however, may present mere anecdotal evidence of failures among participants in these criminal and juvenile justice systems to imagine morally in vivid and expansive ways or to attend to particulars in processes of ethical discernment, resulting in inequities. Nonetheless, other participants in this study, especially community members and facilitators, who have in total encountered hundreds of cases, express concerns about the limitations of their local justice systems on these points. One area of alarm is the adversarial nature of these systems, which can lead to unwillingness to explore or share the details of an offense in order to arrive at some level of truthfulness on all sides. Two community members, who had also been criminal defense attorneys earlier in their law careers, clarified the problems created by this sense of opposition. Susan, who had been a federal defense attorney, explained bluntly her reasoning as a lawyer for preventing her clients from telling their stories: "I tell my clients, 'Don't admit anything. Don't admit.' Because once admissions come in [that is, into evidence], you're pretty much hosed." Cathy would probably concur. She described her experiences as a criminal defense attorney in terms of "the machine of vengeance":

> I am frustrated by, in general, I'd say the "machine of vengeance" that…makes my client a whole lot more positional than they necessarily would be if someone actually cared about why he or she did what he or she did.

Cathy and Susan reveal the impediments to moral imagining created by the severity of sanctions within criminal justice systems. Because offenders may get "hosed," "pummeled," or "crushed" by "the machine of vengeance" if they told their stories, they must often take a defensive stance behind lawyers that prevents others from entering into their stories or appreciating their perspectives or understanding their cases in light of other situations.

Another worry among participants in this study about the limits of moral imagining in criminal and juvenile justice systems regarded the limitations placed on these systems by factors such as time, money, and legislation. Even if police and probation officers, attorneys, and judges *would* attend to the particulars of cases before them, participants worried that they *could not* do so because the system is overburdened. Cathy explained,

> I acknowledge that judges that I respect a lot, that it's hard for them to really understand everything that's going on in every case. It really just gets to be pleading a class three felony drug possession down to a class five, and this is what you're doing, and they don't have time to care about all of this…. It doesn't take into account the individual. It does nothing whatsoever to heal people.

Judy, a retired middle-school teacher who serves on a judicial commission and regularly observes courtroom proceedings, said of the burdens on the local system, "I'm just overwhelmed by the numbers. I have to remember, I just have to keep telling myself, it's one little drop, but if you can change that drop for one or two kids, it's important." She reflected further on the constraints placed on judges by the number of cases presented to them and the images of young people generated by these constraints. Judy remarked,

> It's mind-boggling to me to be a judge and sit there, and I have several friends who are judges.... It's a rare perspective because...you know, like in the classroom, I would have a whole cross-section [of young people]. They get one end of that cross-section, and that's all they see for the most part. Some of the judges amaze me how much they'll talk and really try to give sound, thoughtful consequences, but they're pretty limited, and that's discouraging to me.

Judy's and Cathy's assessments of judges highlight the limitations that they must confront in order to engage in thorough ethical discernment, even while many of them do their best to attend to the particulars before them and to deliver just and equitable decisions. In addition to adversarial practices hiding the stories of offenders (as well as victims), the demands on courts often prevent judges and attorneys from entering into the stories of people who go through their courtrooms, comparing those stories to anyone's outside of the system, or considering possibilities other than mandatory or routine sentences. Justice becomes "formulaic," in the words of Karen, another community member who also works as a dispute mediator.

These failures—whether of individual moral character or of overburdened systems—may contribute to mistakes in efforts to realize justice. John's case arguably entailed a miscarriage of justice with the accusation of a victim of crime who was trying to defend himself. At least one other case in this study involved mistakes in the system. Matt was a college student who went into the wrong house when he was intoxicated—a surprisingly common offense in Foothills County. The district attorney charged him with felony burglary because of a miscommunication with the couple who owned the house, although Matt should have been charged more appropriately with misdemeanor trespassing. About this situation, one of the facilitators in Matt's conference, Ruth, said,

> The whole thing got blown way out of proportion. He lost a lot. He lost a $50,000 scholarship because of this, because the city prosecutor decided to file it as a felony.... In one of the sessions we had, [Matt] found out that because of a misunderstanding, he was prosecuted as a thief as opposed to a trespass. And when he found out that it was a mistake somewhere along the line, he was extremely hurt because it cost him so much.

Failing to attend to the particulars of cases, to stop and listen carefully to victims and offenders can result in oversights that may have grave long-term negative effects on the stakeholders in a crime.

In addition to mistakes, these failures can also contribute to excessive severity in our criminal and juvenile justice systems. Reflecting on her perception that prosecutors in Foothills County increasingly charge young people with felonies because they do not look at the broader context in which they committed their crimes, Ruth commented on this harshness: "Well, the thing that we see more and more often is that young people are being tagged with these felonies, and felonies follow you through the rest of your life and can really mess up work and all sorts of things." For Ruth, these problems could be addressed better by using restorative justice practices earlier in the process, prior to adjudication, because "we have to *understand* before things go too darned far." One reason for refusal to understand, and therefore, for harsh responses to offenders, is the demonization of offenders. Martha, a facilitator, recalled a case in which a young man had stayed up all night as a designated driver for his friends. He had told his parents about his plan to keep his friends out of trouble, and they had consented. While driving home in the morning, he fell asleep at the wheel and killed a bicyclist. About this case, Martha said,

Of course, when something tragic like that happens, the victims have no idea from court and from police reports what to make of this young man who killed somebody with his car. And so the offender becomes a monster, and his family becomes irresponsible. Everything that you can imagine negative is attributed to the offender.

She explained further that entering into the story of the offender can put a stop to this demonization *and* help victims cope with the situation: "You can see the assumptions falling away that are non-truths, and you just wouldn't see any of that if he had just gone to court and been thrown away in jail." In this case, Martha saw the father of the bicyclist recognize the humanity of the driver and his remorse. As a result, the father came to see the situation not as work of a monster, but as a horrific tragedy, and he began to be able to forgive the young driver.

The reports of these facilitators and community members suggest that both the culture of and the demands placed on our current criminal and juvenile justice systems limit the possibilities of vivid and expansive moral imagining by their participants. Even the best-intentioned and most conscientious police and probation officers, attorneys, and judges are stretched to attend to the particulars of every case before them, and as a result they sometimes make mistakes and seem to assume a "tough on crime" stance in most circumstances. Achieving justice as equity under these conditions is a Sisyphean task.

In response to their frustrations with our justice systems, participants in restorative justice practices in these programs—like participants in Tyson's conference—use narratives, metaphors, and symbols of restorative moral imagination while negotiating elements of retributive and rehabilitative moral imaginations. Thus, like Linda, Kenneth, and Patrick, other participants draw a sharp line between restoration and retribution. The discussion of participants' responses to deficiencies in criminal and juvenile justice systems already reveals some of the perspectives on retributive visions of the world and its possibilities. Some of the most colorful phrases include "meat grinder" and "the machine of vengeance." Other terms used by participants included "anonymous," "impersonal," "adversarial," "oppositional," and "formulaic." Many participants wanted to dissociate themselves and their identities from any desire for retribution. For example, one community member, Sheila, said repeatedly in her interview, "I'm not a punitive person." Another community member, Bea, discussed her rejection of previous retributive impulses, leading to a desire to become less punitive:

> [Before getting involved in restorative justice], I would have thought they [offenders] should be punished before I heard the story, which is terrible to be so judgmental, but now I wait until I hear what happened, what caused it, and how it was repaired. It's just made me more, um, open, but I guess I haven't always been that way.

For Bea, participation in restorative justice practices led to her conversion from being punitive to being open and interested in the stories behind criminal incidents. Through involvement in this program, she finds that her capacities to enter into others' stories and appreciate their perspectives have developed so that her apprehension of particular cases is more detailed. In her own assessment, Bea became less "judgmental" because of this openness.

These descriptions point to a propensity among participants in all five programs to reject the ideal narrative of responding to crime in retributive moral imagination. According to this narrative, justice is realized when offenders receive punishment proportionate to their offense against the law through state sanction. Nearly every community member and facilitator questioned this narrative, expressing dissatisfaction with the way it resolves problems precipitated by crime. In several ways, they challenged this narrative as lacking substance. Participants expressed this challenge, for example, by juxtaposing punishment with "real change." Patrick called the motto "tough on crime" a "bromide," a sentiment many other participants echoed. Sheila commented, "Sometimes the criminal justice system alone can be nothing but punitive, but that doesn't change behavior, and so I think it depends on what you want. Do you want punishment, or do you want change?" Judy, the woman who serves on the judicial commission shared Sheila's perspective:

> I ran around with a judge about this, and I said, "There's more programs that work. I'm just wondering why you don't use them." And she said, "They don't work. If they've driven drunk for a third time, they need to go to jail." And I said, "In particular, I mean, have you found that to be successful in stopping them?" And she couldn't answer that.

If retributive justice depends upon a narrative in which punishment leads to reformed behavior, the participants in these programs simply do not find the ending of the story believable. This image of the world and its possibilities in their opinions is a mere fantasy—a useless, but harmful, fiction.

One of the reasons that many participants reject this narrative of retribution is that they have seen too many cases like Tyson's in which offenders felt victimized by their punishment. Tom, the director of the program in Mountain County, summarized this assessment with respect to zero-tolerance policies in schools and juvenile justice systems:

> Zero tolerance can lead to and has led to a reaction that is negative, and the kids feel punished or picked on or unfairly treated. And they want to retaliate or they want to see the punisher as a bad person or a negative in their lives as opposed to learning anything…. Don't punish them because you're not actually disciplining or teaching them anything. You're teaching them negatively.

A community member in Mountain County, Megan, confirmed Tom's concern about the feeling of victimization among offenders in response to punishment. She said,

> The thing is...when we have the regular justice system, the blame and the anger can be directed at the justice system, the judge, the lawyer, and all that. Well, then, the offender, he has someone to blame and be angry at, and take the fall for him. And the offender can put himself in the victim role.

For Tom and Megan, one of the falsehoods of the retributive narrative is that offenders reform their behavior in response to punishment. Instead, they find that offenders refuse to change or even to see the need for change because they come to see themselves as victims rather than empathizing with the people whom they harmed.

In their discussion of this problem, facilitators and community members find a new narrative based on the concepts of "accountability" and "responsibility." Offenders do not get off easy in restorative justice, they aver; restorative justice "has teeth to it," as both Judy and Patrick would say. Megan continued her comments: "With this process [restorative justice], offenders become accountable.... They get to participate and say, 'Yes, this is what I want to do to repair the harm.'" Many participants suggested that "real change" comes about not through punishment, but through taking responsibility for one's actions and being accountable to others. They replaced the ideal narrative of retributive moral imagination with a narrative compatible with restorative moral imagination. Patrick summarized this alternative narrative in a way that reiterates Megan's account:

> All the parties, you know, the offender, the victim, and the community come together, and you think it's soft on crime, where you actually have to sit a few feet from the person and look them in the face and really hear about how you might have ruined their life? You've got to open your eyes, and hear

all of that pain, and then take steps accordingly. And that's not soft of crime.

Through this process, Patrick finds that offenders "really have to face up" to the impact of the offense. For participants in these programs, the true story, the real narrative that accounts for the realities of crime and reformation centers around responsibility and accountability, not punishment and retribution. Thus, as in Tyson's case, where participants rejected retributive justice as opposing the vision of the world and its possibilities within restorative moral imagination, community members and facilitators in all five programs also held retribution and restoration in stark contrast with each other.

Even though community members and facilitators contrasted retribution and restoration, offenders may not necessarily have agreed with them that these practices are so different. After all, offenders still receive sanctions in restorative justice conferences and are burdened to fulfill the agreement if they are to be responsible and accountable. Just because community members and facilitators do not believe that these burdens are punishment does not mean that offenders do not perceive them as punishment. However, when I asked the three offenders in this study (admittedly a very small sample) whether they found the agreements of their conferences to be fair and whether they would recommend restorative justice to a friend, they did not seem to find the demands of their agreements to be punishing. Josh, the young man who forged the deposit check, contrasted the feelings he had in response to his conference with his feelings in response to his probation officer:

> [With restorative justice], you're in an environment where you are not being constantly reminded of what you did or, you know, that you're a criminal. You know, going to a P.O., the P.O.'s, they just see people all day. They don't care. They're just cold, and just...they make you feel hated.

Josh described his conference as providing him with a sense that he was not merely a criminal deserving punishment, but someone who had simply made a bad decision that he needed to make right. John similarly found that participation in restorative justice was more of a relief from the criminal justice system than a punishing burden. He commented that he particularly appreciated writing the letter of apology to the cabdriver because it helped him think about his own responsibility: "The letter of apology was just a good way to think about what happened, the results of my actions, so I think that it was fair and a good thing to do." Stephen, the boy with the butterfly knife, drew the starkest contrast between restorative justice and retributive punishment:

> I think the court system is more about consequences for what you did, you know...it's punishment.   But the restorative justice is talking about what you did and seeing how it affected a group of people, like the school board, for example. They could've freaked out about, you know, Columbine, or other stuff that could happen in Colorado with knives, guns, what have you.   I think restorative justice is almost the opposite.   It's not punishment, it's, um, it helps you in a way.

For Stephen, the difference between restorative justice and his experiences with the juvenile justice system could be found in that restorative justice helped him rather than punished him. As far as these three offenders were concerned (and more offenders should be asked these questions), the contrast held by community members and facilitators between restoration and retribution accurately reflected their own experiences.

In contrast to retribution, just as participants in Tyson's case saw more redeeming value in rehabilitation, so other community members and facilitators found that rehabilitative approaches differ from, but could possibly complement restorative justice.   On the one hand, many participants reiterated Patrick's attitude that they were not involved in restorative justice to provide therapy. This conclusion is especially apparent in the comments of two facilitators who had served therapeutic roles in previous careers. Karen had been a counselor and social worker. She commented that one of the most challenging aspects of training to become a facilitator was her recognition of the distinction between restorative justice and therapy and how this distinction would affect her practice:

> You know, as a social worker, I've done therapy groups where my job was to repeat back what someone said. And about three days into the training, it struck me that I wasn't, I mean, they didn't want *me* to be repeating back to clarify when the victim said something. They called on the offender to say, "What did you hear?" Then repeat it back. I was like—it took three days of training to get that!

Megan, the facilitator in Mountain County, had a similar experience with shifting her practices in light of differences between restorative justice and life coaching. Regarding her difficulties with training, she said, "My first thing was I had to be careful about learning not to coach during a conference, and there was a time that I had to turn off part of my training and just shut up." Because of their professional backgrounds, Karen's and Megan's experiences may reveal a heightened sensitivity to the distinction between rehabilitation and restoration, between therapy and repairing the harm, than most of the other facilitators and community members conveyed. Nevertheless, their reflections illuminate the care with which participants avoided providing therapy within restorative justice conferences, even when qualified to do so.

While participants avoided confounding restoration and rehabilitation, on the other hand, the distinction became fuzzy at times. Outside of the context of conferences and out of earshot of stakeholders in an offense, many facilitators and community members would offer diagnoses of the problems of offenders, often using the terminology of pop psychology or twelve-step treatment. Judy analyzed the dynamics within one family in which a fifteen-year-old boy broke into a neighbor's home. About the boy's mother, she said, "His mom to me is an enabler, and that's okay, and that worked really well when the kids were three years old, but it doesn't work so well when they're fifteen." Ruth spoke of Matt, the young man who lost his scholarship when he mistakenly went into a neighbor's house when drunk: "I have the feeling that he was self-medicating for ADHD [Attention-Deficit/Hyperactivity Disorder] with his alcohol, and that is something that happens so often." Although community members and facilitators recognized that they are not therapists, and that the purpose of restorative justice is not therapy, they still drew on elements of a rehabilitative moral imagination to understand and assess particular cases.

The distinction between restoration and rehabilitation was blurred to the greatest extent in the program in Mountain County. A large proportion of the cases referred to this program involve minors-in-possession tickets for people under the legal drinking age caught with alcohol. To address these cases, in which no apparent victim can be identified, facilitators have constructed a sort of hybrid conference that includes both a sentencing circle and an educational presentation on the effects of alcohol consumption on young brains. The coordinators of this program, Tom and Megan, have found that pairing these components allows the program to divert young offenders from not only retributive aspects of the juvenile justice system, but also rehabilitative aspects, such as extensive drug and alcohol counseling in response to what they often view as a youthful dalliance, at least for first-time offenders. In this program, participants have continued to maintain that restorative justice and rehabilitation are distinct, but they have also been most explicit and conscientious among all of the programs about how these two approaches to offending can complement each other.

Despite the willingness in Mountain County to unite restorative and rehabilitative frameworks, two participants in this study, together possessing decades of experience in facilitation, worried that confusing restorative justice with rehabilitation would result in partial (in both senses) responses to crime. By failing to attend to the experiences of victims, Susan and Linda maintained, rehabilitation fails to repair all of the harms associated with a crime and tends to answer the needs only of offenders. Quoted above, Linda criticized rehabilitation as too focused on the self of the offender, without concern for victims and community members. Susan would concur: "Under a retributive or mental health [that is, rehabilitative] framework, you would never, I mean, who cares what the victim's background is?" For these two women, engaging the experiences of victims is necessary to achieve restoration; without attending to their stories, the narrative of a crime will always be incomplete. Although they did not comment on "victimless" crimes, such as minors in possession of alcohol, their concerns suggest that they would find that the mishmash of restorative justice with rehabilitation could undermine the holistic vision of the world and its possibilities sought by restorative justice.

Participants in these restorative justice programs thus sharply contrasted restorative and retributive justice, but found the distinction between restoration and rehabilitation more difficult to maintain, with the exceptions of Linda and Susan. In negotiating these alternative ways of imagining crime and the people involved in it, community members and facilitators rejected the punitive narrative idealized by retributive moral imagination and suggested that "real change" comes about through the "accountability" and "responsibility" involved in literally facing the people harmed by an offense. At the same time, however, a rehabilitative narrative about facing one's challenges with family dysfunction, mental illness, and drug and alcohol abuse may also be important for "real change," and so rehabilitation—in the perspectives of many participants—may appropriately complement restorative justice.

While negotiating elements of retributive and rehabilitative moral imaginations, participants also used images of the world and its possibilities presented in restorative moral imagination. In many instances, they also expanded upon those images, introducing their own narratives, metaphors, and symbols while engaged in restorative justice practices. For example, restorative justice advocates most frequently refer to crime as harm caused by one person against another, presenting an opportunity to address conflicts that disrupt our relationships. Although all of the facilitators and community members used "harm" to refer to crime, they most frequently used the terms "bad choices," "bad decisions," or "mistakes." This usage could conjure retributive accounts of crime as a willful violation of the law by free agents responsible for their wrongdoing, and may connect to participants' emphasis on responsibility and accountability. However, in using these terms, many facilitators and community members distinguished between choices and persons, thereby setting their perspectives apart from retributive moral imagination. In Judy's words, "The focus is repairing the harm, not whether the person is good or bad." Or in Cathy's words, "Clearly, there's some sense of who's right and who's wrong, but you don't have the side where one person's good and the side where one person's bad." Participants also admitted the possibility that environmental factors could contribute to these mistakes and perhaps mitigate the severity of the offense. As Sheila noted, "In my opinion, I think they're going to continue to make poor choices until you get at the crux of the real problem." The image of "bad choices" subtly allows participants in restorative justice practices to maintain a view of offenders as inherently good, with their crime representing aberrations of judgment rather than ongoing faults in moral character. Especially with younger offenders, this terminology permits community members and facilitators to see particular crimes as the result of kids' underdeveloped decision-making capacities; that is, they see youthful offenders as "kids being kids," not unlike themselves when they were younger.

The image of crime as bad choice, therefore, enables these participants in restorative justice to maintain a view of offenders as human beings and as persons who have long histories that cannot be reduced to their offense. Many community members expressed the need to understand the context in which offenders made bad decisions, and thus, often wanted to hear the entire stories of offenders' lives and their offenses. Kenneth commented,

> I think of [offenders] differently because each case is so different, and the circumstances surrounding the person who is the offender, in terms of their background, their culture, their own personal experiences, all contribute to what has brought them to where they are today.

Cathy, one of the attorneys, similarly talked about a desire to explore the background of "bad choices" and what led offenders to make them:

> I want to spend a lot of time on what people were thinking when they did something. So if there's not enough time spent on that, and when people are just trying to get to, "Well, what are we going to do?," I get frustrated by that. I like to get inside of these people and what they're thinking about. I think it's relevant. I don't think it's just because I'm curious. It's because I know that it's important.

For Cathy and Kenneth, the stories of offenders are not merely voyeuristic windows into lives of crime. These stories reveal that offenders cannot be reduced to their crimes, that they are *persons* who are also offenders, to borrow Kenneth's phrase. Viewing offenders as persons, as human beings leads Kenneth, Cathy, and other participants in these programs to engage in the activity of moral imagining of entering into others' narratives in order to understand the particulars of their cases. They believe that their processes of ethical discernment and their efforts to realize justice in restorative justice conferences are stunted unless they do so.

Beyond their own responses to offenders, many facilitators and community members conveyed hope that restorative justice could humanize offenders for other participants as well. Several participants told stories of cases where victims and other community members overcame stereotypes of offenders that either pathologized or demonized them. Judy recalled a case where three boys caused a wildfire when playing with fireworks on a grassy hillside, leading to thousands of dollars of property damage for several victims, including ranchers, a power company, and a local open-space organization. A rancher caught them and then came to their conference as a victim. Judy said that when the rancher caught the boys,

> He said to the kids, "I've got my gun here, and if you move off the truck, I'll shoot you like a dog." And they knew he would do it. That's why they waited for the police to come. And [in the conference], he turns around and says, "You can always come over to my house at any time. You are welcome at my door. I will always say 'hi' to you now."

Judy seemed proud of this turn of events in the conference; she remembered it as her most outstanding experience with restorative justice. For her, the transformation of the rancher so that he saw the boys as human beings marked a significant success. Other community members, especially Tom, Linda, Susan, and Martha, shared similar pride about other cases in which offenders were humanized for victims and community members. They tended to agree that adopting this perspective not only allowed offenders to reintegrate into the community, but also helped victims and community members to move past their anger and grief, if not to forgive. About the conference of the young man who killed the bicyclist, Martha said,

> [Based on court and police reports], the offender becomes a monster.... Restorative justice was such a powerful tool for helping forgiveness begin with this case because hearing his story...allowed the father of the victim a lot of grief to flow out and a lot of healing to begin.

These participants believe that seeing the humanity and personhood of offenders benefits all stakeholders in an offense—offenders, community members, *and* victims.

Another benefit to victims, according to many facilitators and community members, is that offenders will begin to see them as human beings and as persons in turn. Participants already seemed to assume this status for victims; the "real change" involved, in part, getting offenders to recognize this status as well and to empathize with victims. Kenneth, for example, described a case similar to Matt's, in which a drunken young man went into a neighbor's house at night. Unfortunately, the neighbor was a young woman who had been raped, and her previous victimization exacerbated her sense of fear and vulnerability in reaction to the new violation. For Kenneth, the most remarkable aspect of that conference occurred when the offender was to able to appreciate the victim's perspective:

> You know, I mean, the emotions in that room were unbelievable, and he literally broke down and cried. And he said, "I had no idea of, you know, the trauma that I made you relive as a result of my actions." And so that was a pretty, pretty profound experience.

Through the restorative justice conference, according to Kenneth, this young man was able to imagine the experience of this woman, and therefore, to empathize with the pain he caused her within the context of her entire narrative.

Other community members and facilitators recounted similar experiences as especially meaningful, including Judy. She recalled a conference where a school bully finally saw one of his victims as a person:

> One moving conference was with this girl that was real overweight and pretty ugly, and she was just devastated about this kid. He was saying things to her, and he really had no

idea. And it was so important for him to hear, and he looked right at her, and said, "I'm really sorry. I haven't even known you, but you're actually a really nice person.".... And it was wonderful for her to hear that.

Judy's comments indicate that getting offenders to recognize that their victims are human beings and persons not only helps offenders empathize more. It also can give victims a sense of vindication, reduce their feelings of isolation, and allow them to share their stories in a setting where they have the potential to be heard.

Despite the importance that community members and facilitators found in offenders seeing the humanity and personhood of victims, this concern often seemed less prevalent than the desire among participants to see offenders as human beings and as persons. In conversation, the latter issue received much more attention from community members and facilitators. Perhaps they assumed the significance of recognizing the humanity and personhood of victims; maybe they found this issue so obvious that they felt it did not warrant as much discussion. Empathizing with offenders may be more challenging, and so worthy of more contemplation. Regardless of the reasons, it bears noting that participants generally paid greater attention to challenges of entering offenders' stories and appreciating their perspectives than those of contemplating the stories and perspectives of victims.

The images of community and its possibilities among restorative justice participants also reveal some of the difficulties involved in drawing upon restorative moral imagination in practice. Many community members and facilitators could speak with great facility about images of an ideal community, but also found that cultural, social, and institutional barriers often constrained the realization of this ideal. One aspect of an ideal community identified by participants was "immediacy" to the stakeholders in a crime. According to participants, the tighter knit that the web of relationships could be drawn to stakeholders, the greater likelihood that stakeholders would find their experiences with restorative justice "meaningful." Linda reflected on the problems with bringing together an ideal community in Tyson's conference:

> There's not a lot of compassion and concern about how to provide support to [Tyson]. So let's say, if he had offended and a community group had been able to surround him in some way, to help him understand what was going on for him and figure out, how do we hold him accountable, you know, and work with him. We need to say, who else is in your neighborhood that can provide this support? Or is there a church community or whatever? So if we had more time, we would really search out for that group that's really going to be meaningful for him.

Linda's comments summarize the desire among participants to find more ideal community members based on their relationships to stakeholders. Finding a tightly knit community, however, foundered on obstacles such as lack of time for coordinators to find meaningful community, poor connections of victims and offenders to particular communities, and absence of strong communities within a particular jurisdiction.

Many community members and facilitators also worried that if the web of community were too loose, then participants in a conference would not be able to enter adequately into the stories of victims and offenders and appreciate their perspectives. In order to save time within an already packed administrative schedule, the programs in Foothills and Plains Counties drew on a regular group of volunteers to represent the community. These volunteers usually did not have any direct connection to an offense other than that they lived in the same county. They also typically had vastly different social statuses from most offenders; they were mostly middle to upper-middle class, mostly women, and mostly in their late-forties and beyond. Community members and facilitators were thus often separated from victims and offenders by both geographic and demographic distance. Judy commented on this challenge: "We often get, we really struggle with really getting community people that at all identify [with offenders]." She further described one volunteer, a white male in his twenties, whom she would ask to "dress young and scruffy, pull down your pants a little bit, look a little less white suburban" so that it would seem that someone in the room could relate to the experiences of young offenders.   The need for community members to connect to the experiences of offenders is also revealed in comments by John and Stephen. In his role as a community member, John talked about his own experiences as an offender in order to enter into the stories of other offenders better, to draw connections for other community members, and to show offenders that someone in the room shared some of their experiences.   Stephen noted that in his conference, "They were all pretty old. They were, like, sixty-five.... But they were all women. I was surprised that there were no other men there from the community, but I guess we just don't care, most of the time." These reflections by Judy, John, and Stephen suggest that being more tightly bound to stakeholders at least in terms of demographic similarity might enable participants to relate to each others' stories more easily, perhaps enhancing the vividness and expansiveness of moral imagining in a conference.

Realizing an ideal community composition in a conference affects not only the moral imagining of participants, however. Facilitators and community members generally agreed that the wrong kind of community also can lessen the effectiveness of restorative justice in addressing the harms associated with a crime.   First, as Linda's comments above indicate, not having meaningful community participation can take the "heart" out of a conference, resulting in lack of support for both offenders and victims. Judy echoed Linda in her reflections on the Foothills County program:

> We've really taken an easier way for a lot of reasons, and we've had to....   But when you have true community members, that are someone who lives in the neighborhood, or,

you know, something, often when it comes up that we need to mentor this guy, we need someone to take this guy, they all step up to the plate in order to do that, and that, to me, is a huge function of community—that they're willing to step in and be another person in this village to raise this kid.

Community members who are not bound more tightly to an offender, Judy and Linda intimate, are not invested enough in him to get involved in his life, build a relationship, and address the harms associated with his offense. To draw themselves into action on his behalf, community members need to be able both to imagine the experiences of an offender vividly and expansively and to perceive their connections as meaningful enough to warrant ongoing relationship.

A second effect of failing to include an ideal community in a restorative justice conference, according to some participants, is that communities do not build upon restorative justice programs to develop the capacities necessary to address crime in their midst and perhaps to prevent future crime. Patty, the coordinator of the Desert County program, conveyed this concern:

Getting the community involved is so important. I think it creates understanding on behalf of the community people about what's really happening in our communities—the struggles that some of the really young adult members of the community are facing—and maybe some better dialogue about how we might address some of these problems.

Linda would probably agree with Patty. She observed that the involvement of community is necessary to address the problems that contribute to crime, but also that if restorative justice conferences that do not include community members closely liked to an offense, this goal will remain out of reach. Linda said,

We can do conference after conference, but if we never address the root causes—which is what we want the community to do. And the building of the capacity of the community is to have them take responsibility for their own community members and begin also to do problem solving, to put more reliance back on citizens.... So I think that's one of our greatest challenges, how we do community involvement. If I had my way, we'd have a program in each of the neighborhoods, and we'd pull together community from those neighborhoods, as well as community that's most intimately involved with [the offender]. And that then would be the perfect model. Someday.

With this ideal community, Linda and Patty project, participants have the opportunity, first, to assess the current status of their communities, and then, to imagine possibilities for new ways of relating in those communities that would build their capacities and create responses to problems that generate crime. For Linda and Patty, it is not enough that restorative justice practices expand and vivify the moral imagining of participants; they must do so with the *right* participants, members of an ideal community closely tied to both victims and offenders, in order to create broadly-based systemic change beyond victims and offenders.

While participants in these programs used and negotiated elements of restorative moral imagination in contrast with retributive and rehabilitative alternatives, they also endeavored to imagine morally in a vivid and expansive manner. The activities of appreciating others' stories and perspectives and of considering myriad possibilities for the future were most apparent in conferences and interviews, although participants also frequently drew connections among various cases in their experiences. Several instances of these activities have already been noted above. Cathy and Kenneth, for example, described their desires to appreciate the stories and perspectives of offenders in order to understand why they made a bad decision. Other facilitators and community members also emphasized the importance of this aspect of moral imagining. Linda indicated the danger that people will be "harshly judgmental" if they do not know the "whole story" of an incident: "It lets people step out of having any heart and just say whatever nasty thing might be on their mind and don't have to be responsible for any of it." For Susan, one of the attorneys, entering into each other's stories allows restorative justice participants to find meaning in an offense, to understand differing perspectives, and to recognize commonalities again. Regarding a case in which a young man was reconciled with his family through a restorative justice conference after serving four years in juvenile detention for killing his uncle in self-defense, she remarked,

> You realize that each person is a book, and oftentimes they both have losses in that crime, and that loss will trigger their past losses. And so it was a wonderful experience to be able to participate in that and to witness a family starting to mend.

Patty found similar value in stories and their power to reveal the humanity of participants in restorative justice practices:

> To me, restorative justice brings us to this common humanity of sharing our stories, or what happens when we share our stories, and we sit down and really talk about things....it's got to be, kind of, a fresh look at things.

Martha spoke of the capacity of restorative justice to reveal the complexity of different stories, and therefore, the need to attend carefully to each new story:

> Every conference you do, you learn more about people. Everybody's reality is a little bit different. Everybody's truth is a little bit different. You never really have the full story, and they don't know that story either.

Several other participants in these restorative justice programs also discussed the significance of appreciating others' stories and perspectives for their processes of ethical discernment in conferences. The value that they placed in these activities, however, is most evident in the tendency for conferences to run overtime because of their efforts to hear and understand victims and offenders. Where criminal and juvenile justice systems often "shut down" the story, to use John's terms, the practices of these programs fostered the sharing of stories, and therefore, the expansion and vivification of moral imagining— sometimes for hours on end.

Participants in these programs, however, did not univocally agree that appreciation of others' stories and perspectives always occurred in these restorative justice programs. They flagged two main barriers to their efforts. Patrick summarized one danger:

> I hear a lot of bullshit actually, I would say…. That has come up a little bit in some of the stories that I've heard. So it's kind of like, you know, why are you wasting my time, if you're kind of BS-ing me a little bit? I'm actually kind of curious if in three years I get a little jaded and stop believing people who might be genuine.

In short, people lie, especially when they are in trouble. And reasonable skepticism about the stories they hear in restorative justice conferences may lead facilitators and community members to question the veracity of any story they hear, especially from offenders, rather than enter into them more openly. Nevertheless, Patrick's reflections may prove the rule that participants in these programs strive to hear and appreciate others' stories and perspectives. They just want these stories and perspectives to be "genuine."

Another barrier to participants' abilities to enter into others' stories and appreciate their perspectives is their recognition that their own stories and perspectives often differ significantly from those of offenders. This issue was highlighted above in terms of the dangers of looseness in the web of community, both geographically and demographically. Facilitators and community members worried that their social distance from offenders could hinder them from entering into their stories as fully as others who are closer in age, socio-economic class, gender, and racial or ethnic background. As with the first barrier, this issue reveals that participants strive to enter into others' stories, but that they also try to recognize when their own efforts are inadequate and to formulate ways to compensate for their inadequacies. Judy encouraged young men to volunteer, John brought up his experiences as an offender, and Linda dreamed of a program that could be more neighborhood oriented. Despite their occasional difficulties with entering into others' stories and appreciating their perspectives, participants envisaged ways in which they could do better, and doing so shows how much they valued this activity of moral imagining.

Community members and facilitators also endeavored to consider myriad possibilities for change in their world. Their consideration generally addressed two levels of change: interpersonal and social. On the one hand, participants tried to break free from the constraints of mandatory or routine sentencing in order to formulate agreements that responded to particulars revealed in conferences. Many community members and facilitators drew on aspects of the stories they heard as foundations for envisioning other possibilities. Sheila, for example, participated in the conference of Eric, a young man arrested for marijuana possession. As a former school counselor, she asked Eric to research vocational and educational programs as part of his agreement so that he could gain a sense of direction and purpose in his life. In the case of Joaquin, a fourteen-year-old boy who had stolen fifteen cars because he was "bored," one community member heard in his initial story that he had used to like to read. She suggested that reading a book be part of his agreement so that he could find other ways to deal with boredom. In Stephen's case, Linda recognized a young man who had made a mistake by bringing a knife to school, but who had also successfully struggled through many issues with which other young offenders also dealt. She asked him in his agreement to return to another conference as a community member. Although conferences usually generated a few standard items in agreements, such as letters of apology and community service, participants tried to match their responses to both the offenses and the needs and strengths of the offenders. They often had to be creative, avoiding "one-size-fits-all and cookie-cutter responses," to use one community member's words. In formulating individualized responses to particular cases, community members and facilitators considered the stories and perspectives of offenders, generated images of their potential, and made plans to help them achieve certain possibilities.

On the other hand, participants also considered possibilities for change in broader terms, particularly with respect to criminal and juvenile justice systems and to communal relationships. The comments of Linda and Patty above disclose their visions of communities as tighter knit and as empowered with capacities necessary to address local problems. Other participants echoed their vision, including Tom, who spoke of restorative justice helping participants "to imagine a different way of behaving in a community in a moral and ethical approach." Beyond communal relationships, participants also considered other possibilities for how we as a society could respond to crime. Participation in a restorative justice program itself suggested an imaginative leap among community members and facilitators, intimating that the adversarial and punitive practices of our justice systems are not the only possibilities for realizing justice in our society. Although many community members and facilitators conveyed this sentiment, Susan best summarized it. Formerly a federal defense attorney, she said that her involvement in restorative justice "opened a huge window in my brain":

> I just thought it was refreshing that you could sit down and realize that you could actually have personal accountability and use creativity outside of the constricted rules of evidence to solve problems. It was great realizing that there are other

ways to resolve pretty serious conflicts outside of the legal system, outside of the constriction of the dominant legal system. That was totally refreshing. Even though I knew that, I'd forgotten it. So I got to learn that over again.

For Susan, restorative justice represents and presents other possibilities for what the world could become. Participation in these practices allows her to look at the world as it is critically, especially the limitations of our justice systems, and to propose a different sort of world where stories are heard, stakeholders in a crime are empowered, community problems are solved, and justice is realized.

CONCLUSION

The ethnographic data collected in these five programs reveal a complex account of participants in restorative justice practices using aspects of restorative moral imagination and negotiating retributive and rehabilitative alternatives while confronting the difficulties of criminal and juvenile justice systems. Most participants conveyed frustration with these systems' failures to consider particulars of cases, often resulting in either errors in judgment or in excessive harshness. Whether because of an adversarial culture or because these systems are overburdened, numerous cases in this study as well as the reflections of participants suggest that our criminal and juvenile justice systems can often narrow and deaden moral imagining. In the experiences of participants in this study, few people in these systems listen to the stories of victims and offenders; few draw connections across cases to understand the effects of varying circumstances on offending; few consider possibilities outside of mandatory and routine sentencing. The resulting mistakes and harshness, according to participants, could hardly be described as equitable.

In responding to the inequities that they see in criminal and juvenile justice systems, participants in these restorative justice programs tend to reject elements of retributive moral imagination, especially the narrative that punishment (as opposed to responsibility and accountability) can lead to substantive transformation of the lives of victims, offenders, and community members. They distinguish less sharply between rehabilitation and restoration, finding some useful resources in the former for addressing needs of offenders struggling with drug and/or alcohol abuse, family dysfunction, or mental illness. But they still insist that restorative justice requires that the needs of victims and communities be addressed in addition to those of offenders. In practice, participants often used narratives, metaphors and symbols of restorative moral imagination as described by advocates (such as "crime as harm"), but they also contributed their own concepts (such as "crime as bad choice"). They employed images of victims and offenders as human beings and as persons, although they frequently emphasized the need to see these qualities in offenders more than in victims. Participants, furthermore, struggled with questions of how to create realities that could correspond to the images of the world and its possibilities in restorative moral imagination, particularly with respect to ideal community involvement in conferences. Finally, participants recognized that their success in translating these images into reality in their processes of ethical discernment could affect the outcomes of restorative justice conferences. Failing to include the right community members or to recognize the personhood of an offender would hinder participants' abilities to attend to the particulars of each case, and therefore, to respond equitably.

While participants in these programs used and negotiated aspects of restorative, retributive, and rehabilitative moral imaginations, they strove to attend to particulars of cases with vivid and expansive moral imagining. They expressed commitment to entering the stories and appreciating the perspectives of stakeholders in an offense, sometimes spending hours in conversation with them—as opposed to the few minutes often spent on cases in typical courtroom procedures. Community members and facilitators worried that two main barriers in restorative justice practices could stifle or limit this aspect of moral imagining: skepticism about the truthfulness of stakeholders and geographic and demographic distance from the experiences of stakeholders, especially offenders. Participants tried to overcome these barriers through several means, including involvement of more ideal community members that are more tightly bound to victims and offenders in a relational web.

Another component of vivid and expansive moral imagining apparent in the practices of these restorative justice programs is the consideration of myriad possibilities for what the world could become. On an interpersonal level, by seeing the humanity and personhood of offenders, participants recognized that these young people possessed not only a past that led to their bad choices, but also a future that could lead them away from a life of crime. They imagined them as potentially productive and contributing members of the community who could find a vocation, learn to appreciate literature, and act as a mentor to other young people with similar struggles. Community members and facilitators refused to be limited by the possibilities of mandatory and routine sentencing and worked at responding to the particular strengths and needs of participants. They sometimes resorted to standard responses such as letters of apology and community service, but even here participants tried to be creative to avoid "cookie-cutter" answers. On a social level, participants hoped to foster more empowered and active communities as well as justice systems in which people would be responsible and accountable for their wrongdoing. Refusing to be limited to more traditional rehabilitative and retributive ways of thinking about crime, they worked to establish new ways of realizing justice by repairing the harms associated with crime, attending to particulars of individual cases, and striving to be equitable.

Examination of restorative justice practices in this ethnographic chapter thus supports the overall argument: restorative justice entails processes of ethical discernment that encourage vivid and expansive moral imagining among its participants, enabling them to attend to particulars of cases before them in their efforts to realize justice as equity. As participants in these practices use and negotiate the narratives, metaphors, and symbols of restorative, rehabilitative, and retributive moral imaginations, they engage in activities of entering into others' stories, appreciating their perspectives, drawing connections across various experiences, and envisioning myriad possibilities for change. In light of these observations, many questions remain about how restorative justice ought to contribute to reform of our criminal and juvenile justice systems; how restoration, retribution, and rehabilitation can and should relate to each other as we change these systems; and what cultural, social, and institutional shifts will be necessary to support restorative justice in criminal and juvenile justice responses to crime. Based on the argument about the moral imagination of restorative justice thus far, the concluding chapter explores these issues.

CHAPTER 5

The Moral Imagination of Restorative Justice

The current crises in our criminal and juvenile justice systems in the United States present massive problems for the realization of justice in our society. These problems raise serious questions about the meaning of justice and what the nature of these systems should be. Restorative justice has represented one possible response to these questions. In restorative justice, many advocates have found the basis for critique of rehabilitative and retributive models of criminal and juvenile justice, which they view as underlying the crises in these systems today. By adopting a new "lens" or "paradigm" with restorative justice, they hope that these systems may become more humane and personal, better able to address the needs of all stakeholders in an offense, and thus more likely to "repair the harm" in the aftermath of crime.

Writing as a Christian social ethicist, but drawing on interdisciplinary resources, I have offered tempered support for restorative justice as an answer to how criminal and juvenile justice systems ought to be reformed. On the one hand, the qualification of my hope arises from my doubt that any one movement to change these systems can address all of their problems. Charles Dickens's admonition of nineteenth-century penitentiaries lingers with me: we might be kind, humane, and aspiring for reformation, but we still might not know what we are doing, and our ignorance can cause much suffering for people caught up in our criminal and juvenile justice systems. This admonition reminds us that we must be cognizant not only of the possibilities of any reform efforts, but also of their potential dangers. We live in a complex, fallen world, and we ought not to assume that our reforms will be a panacea to the problems of these systems. Patterns in the history of criminal and juvenile justice in our nation reveal that in all likelihood, our children and grandchildren will have to correct the mistakes of our attempts at reform. Serious reflection about the possibilities and dangers of any reform efforts requires conversation with participants in these systems (both those who work within and those who are constrained by them) as well as with scholars in various disciplines studying these problems, especially sociologists and criminologists. Without these interdisciplinary conversations, we risk not knowing what we are doing when we make our recommendations, and therefore perhaps contributing to the suffering of already marginalized people.

Dickens's admonition also reminds me that in recommending any reforms, theories and practices must be placed in dialogue. Sometimes even high-minded theories do not translate well into practice, and often our best-designed practices need theoretical guidance when our shared activities become confused, ambiguous, or troubled in their implementation. As a Christian social ethicist, I have endeavored to allow the bodies of theoretical literature explored here and the practices of restorative justice to challenge, illuminate, and correct each other. Through the facilitation of this dialogue, the possibilities as well as the dangers of these theories and practices may surface. The theories and practices underlying suggestions that restorative justice can reform our current justice systems can then mutually improve each other. These methodological commitments value and demand the inclusion of diverse perspectives on the strengths and weaknesses of restorative justice practices and the use of theoretical frameworks that elevate experience as a primary source of knowledge. The dialogue between theory and practice in this text reveals the complexity of restorative justice as a movement for the reform of criminal and juvenile justice systems, and thus the difficulties faced by any single movement seeking change in these systems.

While my support of restorative justice is therefore tempered by consideration of the challenges of criminal and juvenile justice reform, on the other hand, I share much of the hope of restorative justice advocates that restorative justice can transform our justice systems if carefully and appropriately implemented. Through restorative justice, I believe that the impacts of criminal and juvenile justice systems upon the members of our communities who have increasingly been seized in their grasp can be lessened. Restorative justice can be used as a diversion of people away from much more invasive and detrimental responses to crime such as incarceration in jails and prisons. As it does so, this movement could also help to loosen the ever-tightening grip of these systems on marginalized groups of people in our society— especially black and socio-economically disadvantaged people, and increasingly, women and youth. I hope that restorative justice can affect the lives not only of individuals such as Tyson and John, Stephen and Josh. I also envision the possibility that restorative justice can fundamentally change our criminal and juvenile justice systems as a whole so that they may better realize justice.

One way in which restorative justice can bring about this change on both individual and systemic levels is through the cultivation of vivid and expansive moral imagining among its participants. The narratives, metaphors, and symbols of a restorative moral imagination allow and encourage people who draw upon them to engage in activities of moral imagining in their processes of ethical discernment. Since the realization of justice as equity requires vivid and expansive moral imagining, restorative justice practices that foster these activities better enable their participants to be equitable in their responses to stakeholders in particular cases. As participants in restorative justice enter into each other's stories and appreciate one another's perspectives, as they draw connections among their experiences, and as they envision myriad possibilities for a different future, they are empowered to attend to the particulars before them. As a result they are more likely to realize justice as equity than if they were restricted to mandatory or routine sentencing options that occlude the particulars of each case. In responding to individual cases equitably, participants may come to recognize the mistakes and harshness of our current criminal and juvenile justice systems, and so envision possibilities for transforming these systems as well.

Based on this conclusion, this chapter suggests strategies for carefully and appropriately implementing restorative justice for the reform of our criminal and juvenile justice systems. Drawing on insights both from other disciplines as well as from the dialogue between theory and practice, this discussion indicates the strengths of restorative justice in transforming criminal and juvenile justice on both individual and systemic levels. Together the evaluative data discussed in chapter three and the ethnographic data discussed in chapter four indicate that while our criminal and juvenile justice systems should move away from the predominance of retributivism, restorative justice could properly work with appropriate rehabilitative interventions to address the needs of victims, offenders, and communities. We ought also to discuss strategies for increasing inclusion and diversity in the community contexts of restorative justice in order to decrease the demographic and geographic differences that sometimes challenge the moral imagining of participants in these practices, as well as to consider contexts in which restorative justice could be inappropriate, and perhaps even dangerous, and certain steps to mitigate these dangers. This chapter concludes by highlighting unanswered questions about restorative justice that will require the attention of sociologists and criminologists, participants in and advocates of restorative justice, and participants in other academic disciplines such Christian social ethics in the future. Despite these caveats and lingering questions, I leave this topic with a qualified hope in restorative justice for furthering reform of our criminal and juvenile justice systems.

REALIZING A QUALIFIED HOPE IN RESTORATIVE JUSTICE

The argument of this text grew out of an initial insight that the different practices of restorative justice versus more common sentencing procedures in our criminal and juvenile justice systems entail different processes of ethical discernment. Restorative justice involves empowering people with a direct interest in a conflict to participate in an inclusive procedure that enables them to come to an agreement about how to "repair the harm" associated with crime. In contrast, our justice systems over the last three decades have increasingly restricted the processes of ethical discernment in sentencing procedures within a typical courtroom, limiting the discretion of judges with the charts and logarithms of legislated guidelines. Understanding restorative justice as a reform of criminal and juvenile justice systems thus requires understanding these differences in ethical discernment, especially when compared with the rehabilitative and retributive models of criminal and juvenile justice systems that have predominated. We cannot know whether and how restorative justice better realizes justice, and therefore, whether it is a worthwhile reform, without consideration of its processes of ethical discernment and their capacity to draw participants' attention to the particulars of the cases before them.

The normative foundation upon which I have built this examination of ethical discernment in restorative justice is based in the two bodies of theoretical literature discussed in chapter two: Aristotelian virtue ethics and works on moral imagination. Exploration of this literature established that a legalistic interpretation of justice (exemplified in practices in our current criminal and juvenile justice systems such as the use of sentencing guidelines) is faulty in two central ways. First, it depends on an inadequate account of ethical discernment in which reason reigns to the exclusion of other important moral faculties such as emotion, perception, and imagination. Second, strict legal justice fails to recognize the limitations of law, which because of its necessary generality will inevitably make mistakes or prove excessively harsh in certain cases. Due to these limitations, justice as equity is needed to supplement and correct law. With this alternative interpretation of justice, being equitable requires that we attend to the particulars of specific cases, that we look at the intentions of legislators in the context in which they wrote the laws, that we understand someone's actions within the context of his entire story and consider his intentions, that we give weight to the positive aspects of our relationships, and that we consider possibilities for our responses that do not necessarily fall within the strict demands of the law. An equitable interpretation of justice, therefore, acknowledges the significance of emotion, perception, and imagination in addition to reason in processes of ethical discernment, and compensates for the limitations of law.

Moral imagination is an especially important faculty in efforts to realize justice as equity specifically and in processes of ethical discernment generally. Moral imagination empowers human beings to create images of their world and its possibilities. We use these images to organize and give meaning to our experiences arising from embodied relationships within the world. The narratives, metaphors, and symbols that form the schematic maps or frameworks of our moral imaginations are generated as we engage in practices embedded in our cultural interactions, social arrangements, and institutional structures. Certain types of moral imagination encourage the people who carry and draw upon them to participate in activities of vivid and expansive moral imagining: entering into others' stories and appreciating their perspectives, drawing connections across diverse experiences, and envisioning myriad possibilities for what the world could become. A person's capacity to imagine morally in a vivid and expansive way depends, in part, on the types of moral imagination that she uses to interpret her experiences. In turn, the types of moral imagination available to her depend, in part, upon her cultural, social, and institutional location as well as the practices in which she participates there. Making one's moral imagining more vivid and expansive, then, may involve exposure to different types of moral imagination; shifts in cultural, social, or institutional location; or participation in other practices. With respect to questions of justice, the various activities of vivid and expansive moral imagining enable us to empathize with others, to locate specific incidents within broader contexts, and to consider possibilities outside of the strict demands of legal codes—all requirements of being equitable. The realization of justice as equity therefore requires vivid and expansive moral imagining in our processes of ethical discernment. This premise provides the normative foundation for my examination of ethical discernment in restorative justice.

Our current criminal and juvenile justice systems seem to conform largely with a legalistic interpretation of justice in their common sentencing and adjudication procedures. Evidence for this claim can be found in the prevalence of sentencing guidelines, discussed more extensively in chapters one and two. These procedures tend to limit the possibility that their participants can attend to the particulars of the cases before them. They reduce ethical discernment to reading charts and calculating logarithms, thereby discouraging activities of vivid and expansive moral imagining among the participants in these systems. Given the central premise of this text, we could then expect that these systems tend to limit the capacities of their participants to realize justice as equity. Reports in chapter four of mistakes made in criminal and juvenile justice systems and their excessive harshness indicate that such is the case at least in two Colorado counties. Participants in these restorative justice programs conveyed their frustrations that even if police and probation officers, lawyers, and judges in their counties would want otherwise to attend to the particulars in the cases with which they dealt, the severity of these systems and the demands placed upon them often discouraged them from doing so. The predominance of a legalistic interpretation of justice in these systems seems to correspond with a lack of equity as well as deadened and narrowed moral imagining within them.

A higher form of justice than strict legal justice demands that equity supplement and correct the law in sentencing procedures. Justice as equity requires that we attend to the particulars of cases through activities of vivid and expansive moral imagining. An equitable interpretation of justice thus has the potential of mitigating some of the mistakes and harshness of a legalistic interpretation of justice in our current criminal and juvenile justice systems. Reform must involve reassessment of the relationships among restorative, rehabilitative, and retributive moral imaginations; changes in the practices of sentencing; and cultural, social, and institutional shifts in these systems. These are the prerequisites for fostering more vivid and expansive moral imagining in our responses to the moral situations precipitated by crime, and thus, for better realizing justice as equity in both individual and systemic terms.

Restorative moral imagination as presented by advocates was the focus of chapter three, where I found that the narratives, metaphors, and symbols of restorative images of the world and its possibilities have the potential to vivify and expand the moral imagining of the people who draw upon them in their efforts to realize justice. This type of moral imagination, in contrast with rehabilitative and retributive moral imaginations, should allow for more nuanced accounts of the ambiguity, diversity, and complexity of experiences of crime. It should generate greater awareness of the limitations of the law in particular cases, and thus, encourage people who use restorative moral imagination to find ways to supplement and correct the law. This type of moral imagination should then better enable participants in restorative justice to realize justice as equity as they partake in activities of vivid and expansive moral imagining in their processes of ethical discernment.

The practices of restorative justice in which participants use and negotiate restorative, retributive, and rehabilitative moral imaginations in their responses to the particulars of a case were the concern of chapter four. In these practices, participants tended to reject retributivism, especially the narrative that punishment rather than responsibility and accountability can change the lives of stakeholders in crime in any meaningful ways. While still distinguishing between restoration and rehabilitation, in contrast, they found the latter useful, but limited in terms of addressing the needs of victims and communities as well as offenders. They also concluded that the goals of rehabilitation fell beyond their capacities as facilitators and community members, although they recognized some cases in which appropriate rehabilitative services would be useful to offenders. Participants in these practices often used images of the world and its possibilities described by restorative justice advocates, but they also developed their own narratives, metaphors, and symbols in response to their experiences. In their use and negotiation of these different types of moral imagination, participants also endeavored to share in activities of vivid and expansive moral imagining, especially entering others' stories, appreciating their perspectives, and considering myriad possibilities for the future—on both individual and systemic levels. As a result, they attended to the particulars of the cases before them, and therefore, seemed more equitable in their efforts to realize justice in response to victims, offenders, and community members during conferences. Examining restorative justice practices with an eye toward the relationship between moral imagination and justice as equity thus suggests that these practices involve processes of ethical discernment that encourage vivid and expansive moral imagining among their participants, a necessary condition for being equitable.

Aside from whether restorative moral imagination and practices of restorative justice contribute to vivid and expansive moral imagining in efforts to realize justice as equity, many other questions abound about the potential of this reform of criminal and juvenile justice systems, especially with respect to the cultural, social, and institutional shifts necessary to support it. Addressing these shifts in the nature of these systems requires consideration of what the relationships among retribution, rehabilitation, and restoration ought to be. It also involves examination of ways to encourage diversity and inclusion in the community contexts of restorative justice. Another issue in implementing restorative justice is whether some contexts ever militate against its use because of particular dangers to its participants. These broader concerns fall outside of the scope of my argument thus far. Nonetheless, elements of the previous chapters indicate some features of the shifts needed to support restorative justice as well as some challenges to bringing them about.

Restoration versus Retribution

First, our criminal and juvenile justice systems ought to move away from the retributive framework that has come to dominate them over the last four decades. This claim is supported in part by evaluative evidence presented in chapter three that excessively punitive responses to crime such as incarceration in jail or prison may actually increase recidivism. Restorative justice advocates also convincingly argue not only that retributive justice often harms offenders and augments the likelihood that they will re-offend, but also that it often fails to attend to the needs of victims and communities, ignoring the call to repair the harms done to them. Moreover, participants in the restorative justice programs in this study cited problems with "the machine of vengeance" in their counties that led both to mistakes and to excessive harshness in the failure of these systems to realize justice. On the whole, it seems that criminal and juvenile justice systems dominated by retributivism have few redeeming qualities.

Rejection of retributivism in the cultural interactions, social arrangements, and institutional structures of these systems, however, is not a simple matter. Retributive justice has become predominant in recent years as politicians have run on platforms of being "tough on crime" and as money has flowed into ever larger criminal and juvenile justice systems. Meanwhile, restorative justice programs have struggled and compromised to find any foothold in these systems from which they could offer an alternative. Along the way, indispensable allies—including people who work as police and probation officers, attorneys, and judges, who also find hope in restorative justice—have made room for these programs to do their work. Even so, too frequently stakeholders in crime are mistreated before they can get to the door of a restorative justice program. As a result, victims often feel re-victimized by these systems, and offenders often come to see themselves as victims of these systems. Because of the massive influence of retributivism on our criminal and juvenile justice systems, and because of the dependence of restorative justice programs on these systems and the people who work within them, participants in these programs, especially facilitators and community members, have limited power to bring about change from within them. Often they must simple cope—like Tyson's family—with the situation at hand until change comes from the outside.

Despite these difficulties, some of Linda's comments in response to Tyson's case indicate one strategy for transforming our criminal and juvenile justice systems: legislation. Linda indicated that because restorative justice programs must often work with allies in criminal and juvenile justice systems, and because these allies often have limited control over the systems in which they work, the best way to affect change in these systems is through changes in the law. At times in this text, it may have seemed that I gave law short-shrift. While I still find with Aristotle that law is limited because of its inherent generality, it still offers important summaries of our assessments of right and wrong, good and evil in our societies. Furthermore, law dictates the practices of our criminal and juvenile justice systems, and thus, the processes of ethical discernment and efforts to realize justice within them. Changes in legislation concerning sentencing practices could provide a larger opening for restorative justice to change these systems. They could also signal a social and cultural shift toward restorative images of the world and its possibilities. In Colorado, some of these shifts have been captured in the revision of the Children's Code, which governs juvenile justice systems. Democratic Governor Bill Ritter signed the code into law in the spring of 2008, and it now gives judges the authority to offer accused juvenile offenders the legal option to participate in restorative justice processes voluntarily in lieu of more common juvenile justice procedures. Legislative reforms in other jurisdictions and pertaining to adult offenders as well may be the most effective means of transforming our criminal and juvenile justice systems away from retributive justice.

At least two major barriers, however, may thwart legislative changes: costs and votes. When comparing the costs of sentencing procedures alone, restorative justice may not seem cost effective. Whereas a single judge supported by courtroom staff can make a decision in a matter of minutes in more common sentencing procedures, restorative justice requires hours of making phone calls and sending emails to coordinate stakeholders, of pre-conference meetings, of conferencing itself, and of following-up to make sure that all parties fulfilled the agreement. When our criminal and juvenile justice systems are already overburdened, it may seem unreasonable to spend more time and money on individual cases. Then again, the comparison of time spent in more common sentencing procedures versus restorative justice practices hides many of the costs of the former. If processing in justice systems results in harsher, more expensive sanctions, and if restorative justice is used as a diversion for certain offenders— especially the low-risk, younger offenders who commit serious violent and property crimes with whom it has been shown to be most effective—then sentencing through restorative justice and the resulting sanctions can be less expensive on the whole. Furthermore, even if restorative justice is no more effective than more punitive responses are at reducing recidivism (and evidence discussed in chapter three indicates that it *is* more effective), then it is still more cost effective in producing the same or better results.[265] To avoid increasing costs, net-widening must be avoided with restorative justice. That is, it ought not to be used with minor cases that otherwise would not be pursued through retributive justice. Provided that this condition is satisfied, legislators could be assured that restorative justice is not only more

---

[265] Sherman and Strang (2007), 87.

effective than more common sentencing procedures at reducing recidivism; it is also a more efficient allocation of our public resources.

Of course, the re-allocation of public resources always stirs up controversy. Spending money on restorative justice may mean not paying some of the people who currently operate our criminal and juvenile justice systems as their jobs become obsolete in a restorative system. To mitigate resistance from these people, who may oppose restorative justice more because it affects their livelihood than anything else, reform of these systems could provide re-training of police and probation officers, attorneys, and judges so that they too can participate in restorative justice and become more allies to the movement. Restorative justice programs have operated primarily on a volunteer basis. The long-range sustainability of these programs depends on hiring more paid staff to organize and facilitate conferences. People who already work in criminal and juvenile justice systems may be useful resources in these efforts to realize justice, and so shifts in these systems need not mean that they are put out of work—provided they can adopt the images of the world and its possibilities of restorative justice in their approaches to particular cases.

The other main barrier to shifting from retributive to restorative justice is the support of the electorate. Legislators may worry that a vote for restorative justice may make them seem too soft on crime and hurt their chances for re-election. Contrary to these expectations, many studies suggest that the retributive streak within the public is less virulent than often assumed.[266] In addition, individuals and communities who have had positive experiences with restorative justice could lobby their representatives to consider this alternative to our current systems. They could effectively report on their perceptions of the problems with these systems and the promise of restorative justice. Participation in these practices could thus not only lead to change in individuals' lives, but also could be tapped to mobilize stakeholders in

---

[266] John Doble Research Associates, Inc. (1994); Peachy (1992); Wright (1989).

political efforts to achieve systemic reform. Moreover, at a time of economic crises in many states, being tough on crime may be a lower priority among legislators than using tax dollars wisely. During the recent recession, some states have looked to intermediate sanctions, such as those offered by restorative justice, to replace and reduce incarceration, which has become one of the most significant drains on public coffers in many states.[267]   Although the recent economic downturn has caused a great deal of suffering in many people's lives, we may also look at this hardship in state budgets as an opportunity to re-evaluate the ways we spend our money and to re-direct our resources to different kinds of criminal and juvenile justice.

While I agree with most restorative justice participants and advocates that we ought to shift our justice systems away from retributivism, I would like to raise one caveat to this argument. Many of the procedures of retributive systems arose from commitments to guarding the rights of all citizens, including offenders, and to maintaining both the rule of law and equal protection under it. Sentencing guidelines, for example, grew out of a desire to guarantee that different judges because of their own individual idiosyncrasies did not treat similar offenders unequally and that individual judges did not treat different offenders unequally because of some sort of prejudice. I venture to guess that very few people would want to live in a society in which these commitments were not valued.

Restorative justice practices in themselves, however, do not offer many protections against outcomes such as unequal treatment in different jurisdictions or prejudiced responses to offenders. I worry that the attention to particulars enabled in restorative justice practices may permit participants to consider particulars that should be irrelevant to entering into others' stories or appreciating their perspectives, such as their attributes of race or ethnicity, gender, class, or sexual

---

[267] Jennifer Steinhauer, "To Cut Costs, States Relax Prison Policies," *New York Times*, March 25, 2009.

orientation.[268] To preserve commitments to human rights, the rule of law, and equal protection, we will still need some of the safeguards offered by our criminal and juvenile justice systems from arrest through conviction. Moreover, systematic review of outcomes from restorative justice programs, perhaps by a judicial panel, may help to monitor the outcomes of their practices and to ensure against treatment that places undue burdens on certain groups of people because of prejudices among participants in restorative justice practices. This relationship between restorative justice and aspects of our criminal and juvenile justice systems may reflect the Aristotelian ideal that law in its generality is indispensable for a well-ordered society, although justice as equity is necessary to supplement and correct a legalistic interpretation of justice. It may also find support in Bazemore and Walgrave's goal-focused definition of restorative justice, which emphasizes that "doing justice" requires the legal protection of the procedural rights of all participants in these practices as citizens of a

---

[268] Asking restorative justice participants not to allow the particulars of another person's race and ethnicity, gender, class, or sexual orientation to influence their processes of ethical discernment regarding that person may seem hypocritical here. After all, have I not been arguing for the importance of attending to the particulars all along? I make a fine distinction, however, between one's attributes and how responses to those attributes affect one's experiences, and I find only the latter relevant in processes of ethical discernment. While I do not believe another's *attributes* of race or ethnicity, gender, class, or sexual orientation in themselves should be morally salient features in her story or perspective, I do maintain that *experiences* of racism, ethnic difference, sexism, class bias, and homophobia may be morally salient features of her story or perspective, and may be mitigating or aggravating factors for consideration of her case in restorative justice conferences. That is, I am not trying to erase these attributes among the participants in restorative justice, but to encourage understanding of how social, cultural, and institutional responses to these attributes shape the individuals who bear them. Prejudices regarding another's attributes alone, whether positive or negative, should not determine her treatment or others' approaches to the particulars of her experiences.

particular jurisdiction, thereby permitting legal review of restorative justice processes and outcomes.[269]   Some of the commitments that underlie sentencing guidelines and other aspects of retributive justice then must be upheld, but we should try to find ways to uphold them within a restorative system.

Restoration and Rehabilitation

We must also reconsider the relationship between restorative justice and rehabilitation in the shifting nature of our criminal and juvenile justice systems.   Advocates of restorative justice are correct in distinguishing between these two conceptions of crime and our responses to it.   Restorative and rehabilitative moral imaginations are distinct.   The practices from which they arise and that they support are also very different.   Nevertheless, I find it compelling that, in practice, many of the participants in the restorative justice programs in this study who recognize these distinctions still find value in offering offenders rehabilitative services outside of restorative justice.   On the one hand, they are right to note that some problems lie beyond their skills as well as exceed the practices of restorative justice: they are not therapists and a conference should not offer therapy.   Offenders who assume accountability and take responsibility for their wrongdoing, however, may still need assistance in dealing with aspects of their experiences that contributed to their wrongdoing, such as family dysfunction, mental illness, or drug and/or alcohol abuse.   Some advocates of restorative justice would perhaps agree with this conclusion, although they tend to draw starker lines between rehabilitation and restoration. But Howard Zehr, for example, cites the responsibility of restorative justice to explore the harms that offenders may have experienced that could have contributed to their crime.[270]   Some of these harms may call for communities to provide appropriate rehabilitative services.

---

[269] Bazemore and Walgrave (1999b), 49.
[270] Zehr (2002), 30.

On the other hand, participants in restorative justice practices are also right to acknowledge that restorative justice is still worthwhile even in cases where rehabilitation may be necessary as well. Using restorative justice in cases where offenders receive rehabilitative services as well could help these offenders to be accountable and responsible for their wrongdoing, avoiding some of the dangers of pathologizing them. Furthermore, complementing rehabilitation with restorative justice may also help address the needs of victims and community members as well as those of offenders, avoiding some of the dangers of ignoring victims and communities in a rehabilitative framework. Evaluative evidence discussed in chapter three indicates that restorative justice and rehabilitation might readily complement each other, addressing offenders according to their varying needs. Restorative justice effectively reduces re-offending among low-risk offenders who commit both violent and property offenses. But the greatest reductions of recidivism come about through appropriate rehabilitative interventions in community contexts with high-risk offenders. Although reducing recidivism ought not to be the only concern of our criminal and juvenile justice systems, all members of our communities and societies, including offenders, benefit from crime reductions. Rehabilitation and restorative justice do not necessarily mutually exclude each other. Acceptance of one need not mean rejection of the other, and so the two may be drawn together to address the various needs of offenders, victims, and communities.[271]

Drawing on the practical insights of participants in restorative justice practices as well as those of criminologists, I suggest an ideal for criminal and juvenile justice systems that would rely on the strengths of both rehabilitationism and restorative justice in reducing recidivism as well as in achieving other goals distinctive to each model.

---

[271] Tony Ward and Robyn Langlands make a similar recommendation for restorative justice and rehabilitation working alongside each other in their article, "Repairing the Rupture: Restorative Justice and the Rehabilitation of Offenders," *Aggression and Violent Behavior* 14 (2009): 205-214.

Each set of practices should focus primarily on those populations with which they are most effective at reducing recidivism. One way to accomplish this goal is to screen offenders for rehabilitative services through restorative justice programs. John Braithwaite offers a model for such a process in his pairing of restorative justice with "responsive regulation" to determine when *not* to use restorative justice, although I would adapt his model so that regulations beyond restorative justice aim at rehabilitation and incapacitation, rather than at deterrence and retribution (see figure 2).[272]

Figure 2. Pyramid of Restorative Justice, Rehabilitation, and Incapacitation.

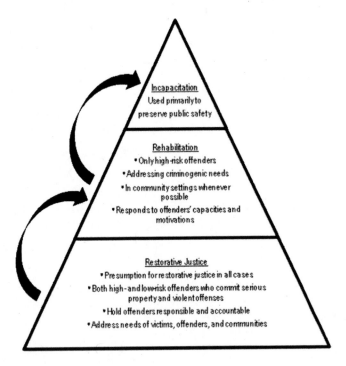

---

[272] Braithwaite (2002).

This model supposes that we should always offer restorative justice as the first response to offenders, regardless of the seriousness of their offenses. Only when offenders fail to respond to restorative justice (for example, if they deny responsibility, if they refuse participation, or if they display predatory behaviors) should other interventions be employed. In this way, low-risk offenders would only be required to complete the terms of the agreement reached in their conferences. But high-risk offenders could be referred through restorative justice programs to appropriate rehabilitative services that would address their criminogenic needs (such as substance abuse and mental illness) in ways that respond to their capacities and motivations. These services would preferably be offered in community settings in all cases where concerns for public safety did not require the use of commitment or incarceration to incapacitate offenders. By responding to all offenders with restorative justice practices first and progressively requiring rehabilitation and incapacitation only as needed, the sanctions placed on all offenders could respond more appropriately to their levels of risk, needs, and responsiveness to treatment. Moreover, the numbers of people that we incapacitate in our prisons and jails could be greatly reduced as more people are diverted to restorative justice programs to create agreements to repair the harm caused by their crime or are enrolled in rehabilitative programs suited to them.

Despite the emphasis here on reducing recidivism, a criminal or juvenile justice system based on a pyramid of restoration, rehabilitation, and incapacitation would address other concerns as well. Justice as equity requires that we begin with practices of restorative justice that entail processes of ethical discernment that respond to the particulars of every case. We must begin then with the assumption of offenders' humanity and personhood, and only by attending to their particular circumstances can we draw conclusions about any disorders or illnesses that must be confronted through either rehabilitation or incapacitation. When we presume that all cases in which offenders admit guilt and participate willingly would be addressed first by restorative justice, the particulars of each case would receive attention in a conference that includes community members and preferably victims whenever possible, and so these case would be more likely to receive equitable responses. By beginning with restorative justice, the goals of these practices beyond reducing recidivism can be met. By allowing for rehabilitation, and when necessary, incapacitation, recidivism can also be reduced even more, therapeutic needs of offenders can be addressed, and public safety can be protected.

One benefit of this model of relating restorative justice and rehabilitation is that it gives high- and low-risk offenders the opportunity to take responsibility and assume accountability for their wrongdoing and to address the needs of their victims and communities through restorative justice while also attending to the underlying illnesses or disorders that may have contributed to the wrongdoing of high-risk offenders. Pairing restorative justice and rehabilitation in this way may also make the responses of restorative justice participants more effective at preventing re-offending. Instead of focusing on non-criminogenic aspects of offenders' experiences, such as having low self-esteem, participants in restorative justice practices in formulating their agreements could attend to aspects of offenders' experiences that actually contributed to the crime. Although self-esteem is important, restorative justice may prove better at reducing recidivism if it borrowed from appropriate rehabilitative interventions an understanding of the causes and control of crime. Restorative justice participants, especially facilitators, would also need to be able to refer all stakeholders to therapeutic resources and social services that lay outside of their capacities and responsibilities.

More strident advocates of restorative justice might protest against this model, claiming that because restorative justice and rehabilitation involve completely different images of the world and its possibilities, they are irreconcilable in practice. Although I would clearly agree that moral imagination affects practice (and vice versa) and that we ought not to ignore differences in types of moral imagination and their implications, I maintain a much more nuanced understanding of moral imagination than these advocates would suppose. We draw on different types of moral imagination all of the time depending upon our social, cultural, and institutional settings. As we cross between different settings and engage in the various practices associated with them, we often employ different narratives, metaphors, and symbols that describe the world and its possibilities—sometimes even in contradictory ways. Using different types of moral imagination is not necessarily a problem; we simply need other faculties such as perception, emotion, and even reason to sort out the most adequate images of the world and its possibilities for responding to the particulars of varying circumstances. Drawing on a restorative moral imagination thus does not exclude the possibility that rehabilitative narratives, metaphors, and symbols might sometimes prove better at resolving ambiguity, conflicts, and disturbances within our experiences. Many of the participants in restorative justice practices discussed in chapter four regularly drew upon aspects of both restoration and rehabilitation and still were able to respond to the particulars of the cases before them with vivid and expansive moral imagining in their efforts to realize justice as equity.

In using both rehabilitative and restorative practices, however, we still ought to keep the distinctions between them and their moral imaginations in order to maintain the separate strengths and to remember the weaknesses of each. For example, as I mentioned in chapter three, both rehabilitative and restorative moral imaginations use metaphors for crime that connote the need for "healing" in our responses to crime. But with rehabilitation, "healing" pertains to the underlying illnesses or disorders of offenders. With restorative justice, it concerns the wounds or injuries sustained by the stakeholders in a crime. As long as the different ways of applying these metaphors in interpreting our experiences remain apparent, their differences need not imply that rehabilitation and restorative justice cannot work together. Certain images within these different types of moral imagination may require more consideration, especially if they are more conflicted. Within rehabilitative moral imagination, the metaphors of offenders as disordered or ill, for instance, suppose their lack of moral agency and emphasize their determination within cultural, social, and institutional settings. Restorative justice, with its emphasis on accountability and responsibility, recognizes the possibility of formation within these settings, but emphasizes that offenses are "bad choices." In bringing rehabilitation and restorative justice together, we may need to ponder new images of the world and its possibilities that can account for both individual agency and the impact of our various settings on our actions. Other narratives, metaphors, and symbols within each type of moral imagination may also require reassessment as we face the complexities of working with both rehabilitative and restorative frameworks.

Diversity and Inclusion in the Community Contexts of Restorative Justice

In addition to evaluation of the relationships among retribution, rehabilitation, and restoration, the cultural, social, and institutional shifts necessary to support restorative justice will have to account for its community contexts. Disputes among restorative justice advocates about the definition of community and who comprises it indicate that achieving the ideal community composition in any restorative justice conference is not an obvious or easy matter. Furthermore, the reflections of participants in the five Colorado programs indicate that translating theories about "meaningful" and "immediate" community into practice often founder on logistical problems. Participants frequently found that these difficulties contributed to greater cultural, social, and institutional differences among stakeholders in a conference. These differences led to geographic and demographic distance in communal webs of relationship. The extent of these challenges varied from county to county depending on the cities and towns within their jurisdictions. Despite these differences, all of the programs struggled, first, with identifying appropriate community members, and then, with getting them to come to conferences.

The efforts of coordinators in Foothills and Plains Counties reveal some of the tensions in dealing with community issues. On the one hand, they concluded that providing conferences at all in their large programs required better management of their time, particularly with regard to making the phone calls and writing the emails necessary to coordinate every conference. They solved this issue by organizing groups of regular volunteers to offer conferences on certain nights each month. This solution guaranteed that the programs could offer prompt conferences to every referred offender, although with community members who might not know either the victims or the offenders. On the other hand, participants often observed that this solution failed to bring ideal community members into the restorative justice programs— community members who could more readily identify with both victims and offenders because of less geographic or demographic distance from them. They sought ways for community representation to be more diverse and inclusive.

One way to deal with this tension is to provide more staffing resources to these programs. With more time, staff would be able to make the local contacts necessary to address the particulars of each case. It seems that with even two or three more staff members in the largest programs to coordinate conferences, many more community members with more direct stakes in an offense could participate. Providing more staffing, however, would also require the commitment of allies in local criminal and juvenile justice systems to direct the necessary funding to restorative justice programs.

Another solution is to tie community involvement to smaller geographic areas than large Western counties that include multiple cities and towns. One county in Colorado not included in this study divides its largest city into six neighborhood districts. Restorative justice conferences in this county are held in whichever neighborhood the offense occurred, thereby cutting down the geographic distance among all of the participants. By bringing in more tightly knit communities geographically, this strategy may also cut the demographic distance among participants as each neighborhood is relatively homogeneous when compared with the aggregate jurisdiction. Members of the same neighborhood are more likely to share similar experiences, as well as similar racial, ethnic, and class backgrounds, and so may be better prepared to enter into each other's stories and appreciate one another's perspectives.

The inclusion of community members who are closer geographically and demographically to offenders and victims may also require financial resources in addition to more staffing of programs. Poverty can create roadblocks to participation in programs such as restorative justice. Socio-economically disadvantaged people may need help with transportation, for instance, so that they can go to and from conferences. They may also have less flexibility in their work schedules and may work long shifts and extra jobs to make ends meet. If they need to take time off work in order to participate in a conference as a community member, then perhaps they should be compensated for their time. One way to orchestrate this plan may be to offer a small flat rate for all community volunteers, allowing those who wish to donate privately their compensation back to the program if they feel that they do not need it. As minorities are socio-economically disadvantaged at higher rates than whites, this strategy may also encourage more racial and ethnic diversity within restorative justice conferences as well. While a common policy with probation and parole is to require offenders to pay for various services, I would discourage this plan for generating money to pay community members in restorative justice. Doing so may lead poorer offenders to opt out of restorative justice only because of their poverty. Instead, funding for community members should be incorporated in program budgets as part of a commitment to fostering inclusion and diversity within restorative justice programs.

Another way to realize more ideal community participation may be to tap into already existing local institutions and organizations, including businesses, schools, unions, non-profits, and religious congregations. Many of the programs in Colorado already draw on these resources by seeking volunteers among other organizations or by using community buildings, such as church fellowship halls or school cafeterias, to host conferences. In Foothills County, for instance, one group of volunteers was recruited from a United Methodist church after Sunday school sessions on restorative justice in their congregation. In Plains County, a Lutheran church hosted restorative justice conferences. But restorative justice programs could employ the resources of local organizations and institutions more strategically. For example, rather than using the same church fellowship hall for all conferences in a county, coordinators could map out religious congregations in neighborhoods throughout the jurisdiction and host conferences in the congregational building nearest the location of the offense. Assuming that members of congregations may live close to their places of worship (which may not always be the case), some of them could also be appropriate community members. Among congregations tied to denominations, especially denominations that have expressed support for restorative justice as a criminal and juvenile justice reform, restorative justice coordinators could find networks for communication and recruitment across neighborhoods within their towns and cities. When working with religious congregations, programs should be clear that restorative justice is not religiously associated and that proselytization is inappropriate in a conference. Other local organizations and institutions might also prove helpful in ways similar to religious congregations, including YMCAs and YWCAs, Boys' and Girls' Clubs, schools, businesses, and unions. One downside with this strategy, however, is that neighborhoods with the highest crime rates also often lack the social organization to support these local organizations and institutions.[273] Nevertheless, efforts

---

[273] On the challenges of social disorganization and its ties to community crime rates, see Clifford R. Shaw and Henry D. McKay, *Juvenile Delinquency and Urban Areas* (Chicago: University of Chicago Press, 1942); Ernest Burgess, "The Growth of the City: An Introduction to a Research Project," in *The City*, edited by Robert E. Park, Ernest Burgess, and Roderick D. McKenzie (Chicago: University of Chicago Press, 1969 [1925]); Robert J. Bursik and Harold G. Grasmick, *Neighborhoods and Crime: The Dimensions of Effective Community Control* (Lanham, MD: Lexington Books, 1993); John Kasarda and Morris Janowitz, "Community Attachment in Mass Society," *American*

should be made to consider how restorative justice programs could find local allies in order to encourage more meaningful and immediate community participation. Local organizations and institutions could in turn benefit as their members become aware of crime in their areas and are empowered with ways to respond to it.

Commitment to inclusion and diversity in restorative justice programs ought not to arise only from a desire to realize ideal community participation in some sort of politically correct vision. Rather this commitment should stem from recognition, first, that sometimes our moral imagining is inhibited by social, cultural, and institutional differences, and second, that inclusion and diversity probably increase the effectiveness of restorative justice in addressing harms, building community capacity, and realizing justice. These justifications for this commitment were highlighted by various participants in the Colorado restorative justice programs who noted that sometimes the geographic and demographic distance among stakeholders in conferences made entering into others' stories and appreciating their perspectives more difficult. They also worried that the wrong kind of community members can take the "heart" out of a conference, and that if community members were too far removed from an offense, then their empowerment in the wake of crime would be less relevant and effective.

But another, closely related, reason to foster inclusion and diversity in restorative justice is that all people are influenced by the racist, ethno-centric, class-biased, sexist, and homophobic types of moral imagination that unfortunately fill our cultural consciousness, regardless of whether we prefer or disdain these images. Moreover, these narratives, metaphors, and symbols can complicate our use and negotiation of restorative moral imagination. Negative images of black young men and their possibilities in our society and culture, for

---

Sociological Review 39 (1974): 328-339; and Ruth Rosner Kornhauser, *Social Sources of Delinquency: An Appraisal of Analytic Models* (Chicago: University of Chicago Press, 1978).

example, may sometimes occlude our vision of a particular boy in a conference. The inclusion of community members who could more easily relate to his experiences of race and ethnicity, class, gender, and sexuality may help to mitigate the danger that his attributes rather than his story or perspective will determine the responses of other participants to him. Diversity among restorative justice participants may also better enable them to draw connections among different experiences, to see both the underlying commonalities among all people and the important differences that prejudice makes in our experiences of the world. Commitment to inclusion and diversity in community representation may thus not only make the activities of moral imagining among participants in restorative justice more vivid and expansive, and thereby make their processes of ethical discernment more equitable. It may also help to combat the influence of racist, ethno-centric, class-biased, sexist, and homophobic types of moral imagination on the efforts to realize justice within restorative justice practices. Restorative justice programs would be well-advised to address issues of prejudice openly and honestly, trying to repair the harms that these dangerous images of the world and its possibilities pose to restorative moral imagination.

Dangerous Uses of Restorative Justice

Even while recommending restorative justice practices that embody commitment to inclusion and diversity, I also recognize that in some contexts where racist, ethnocentric, class-biased, sexist, or homophobic images of the world and its possibilities dominate, these practices may be inappropriate, or even dangerous, for addressing crime. In such settings, prejudices based on individuals' attributes may so distort participants' attention to the particulars that these practices cannot realize justice as equity, and may even create grave injustices.

An example of such a setting could be found on Pitcairn Island in the South Pacific. After the mutiny on the Bounty in 1789, Fletcher Christian led the mutineers to this isolated island and established what became a British colony with young girls they had kidnapped from Tahiti. Over the next two centuries, a small society (currently only forty-eight individuals from nine different families) developed in which the rape of young girls became acceptable, partially because of images of the girls in the culture that implied that they are temptresses of older men. In the early part of this century, British authorities became aware of the situation and prosecuted seven Pitcairners, including the mayor, for child rape.[274] This context may have proven impossible for restorative justice because its images of the humanity and personhood of the young girls could not combat the sexist images that dominated Pitcairn society—narratives, images, and symbols so ingrained in residents that they accepted the rape of their own daughters by their neighbors. The stories and perspectives of the victims may have been perceived as lies by the offenders and other community members who had long tolerated, and even encouraged, this behavior.

While the example of Pitcairn Island may be extreme, it still suggests that for restorative justice to combat dangerous types of moral imagination, the cultural, social, and institutional context must already demonstrate some commitment to human rights, the rule of law, and equal protection. Where these conditions are not met with respect to either victims or offenders, more traditional sentencing procedures that offer more support and protection of these commitments may be necessary. Furthermore, where such dangerous types of moral imagination are less dominant but still present—as in our own setting in the United States—the use of judicial review of restorative justice practices and outcomes again may help to guarantee that these commitments are still upheld.

---

[274] For a fascinating account of the history of Pitcairn Island and the sexual abuse trials, see Kathy Marks, *Lost Paradise: From Mutiny on the Bounty to a Modern-Day Legacy of Sexual Mayhem, the Dark Secrets of Pitcairn Island* (New York: Free Press, 2009).

ONGOING QUESTIONS AND CONCLUSIONS

Several questions remain about restorative justice as a reform of our criminal and juvenile justice systems. Answering them will require more interdisciplinary work as well as ongoing efforts to place theory and practice into dialogue. Some of these questions demand the attention of criminologists and sociologists trained with using both quantitative and qualitative methods. In addition to issues of recidivism and stakeholder satisfaction, other goals of restorative justice should be evaluated, including its capacities to protect participants' legal rights; to repair the material, physical, psychological, relational, and social harms caused by crime; to include stakeholders in responding to crime; to provide a forum for victims to express anger and fear; to re-establish the social efficacy and cohesion of communities; and to re-integrate both victims and offenders in a safe and secure environment. Beyond these goal-oriented questions, other questions have also arisen about which aspects of restorative justice practices contribute to certain effects as well as about how restorative justice relates to retribution and rehabilitation in practice on interpersonal, organizational, and institutional levels. It remains to be seen, for example, if a plan that combined restorative and rehabilitative elements could reduce recidivism at even higher rates than either could alone or how such a plan would work with different types of offenders and offenses. The contributions of criminologists and sociologists will be indispensable in seeking answers to these questions.

The input of participants in restorative justice practices is also imperative for understanding this reform of our criminal and juvenile justice systems. Out of necessity, this study has drawn primarily upon the experiences and reflections of facilitators and community members. The voices of offenders and victims are remarkably and regrettably absent in the vast majority of literature on restorative justice. Understanding all of the complexities of moral imagining in the ethical discernment processes among participants in restorative justice (among other questions) demands consideration of these marginalized stories and perspectives. Of central interest in attending to the stories and perspectives of offenders and victims is whether they imagine the moral situations precipitated by crime and the responses generated in restorative justice conferences in the same ways as community members and facilitators. Of particular concern should be whether offenders perceive the sanctions in a restorative justice agreement as punitive, therefore suggesting that the distinctions between restorative justice and retribution may not be as sharp as community members, facilitators, and advocates might hope.

We should also examine the experiences and reflections of all participants in restorative justice over time. Many restorative justice advocates make claims of dramatic and enduring transformation of participants in these practices. Interpreting the impact of restorative justice in the weeks, months, and years after a conference will probably require more than consideration of recidivism rates. Qualitative data collected longitudinally may provide us with a greater sense of the long-term effects of the intangible and mysterious aspects of restorative justice described by Braithwaite and others. It may also prove helpful to compare such data with qualitative studies of the experiences and reflections of participants in more common sentencing and adjudication procedures in our criminal and juvenile justice systems, which are ignored even more than the voices of offenders and victims in restorative justice. Attention to all of these perspectives is necessary not only in epistemological terms to further our understanding of restorative justice. In light of my ethical methodology, it is a moral imperative to listen to the people who would be most affected by any reforms of these systems.

Several cultural, social, and institutional shifts are necessary to support restorative justice practices and the images of the world and its possibilities from which these practices arise and that they generate. First, our criminal and juvenile justice systems ought to move away from the retributive model that has come to dominate them. These changes will most likely be realized through legislative reforms driven, in part, by citizens calling for more equitable systems and, in part, by budget revisions in response to the escalating costs of these systems in the midst of economic crises.

Instead of retributivism, our criminal and juvenile justice systems ought to become more restorative, and in response to the needs of some offenders, more rehabilitative. While maintaining the distinctions between these two models, these systems ought to begin sentencing procedures through restorative justice practices, allowing offenders to take responsibility and assume accountability for their wrongdoing in efforts to repair the harm associated with crime. But where their criminogenic needs require therapeutic attention, offenders must also have access to appropriate rehabilitative services. Incapacitation through incarceration ought only to be used as a matter of public safety. This strategy would also permit victims and community members to participate in sentencing procedures, allowing their needs to be addressed as well.

In implementing restorative justice in this way, programs should encourage community participation that is diverse and inclusive, minimizing the geographic and demographic distance among stakeholders. Doing so may reduce the danger that different cultural, social, and institutional locations among stakeholders will inhibit their moral imagining or decrease community capacities to respond to crime. Inclusion and diversity may also help to combat the influence of racist, ethno-centric, class-biased, sexist, and homophobic types of moral imagination on processes of ethical discernment among participants in restorative justice practices. To ensure that these prejudices do not undermine efforts to realize justice as equity in restorative justice, judicial review of these practices and their outcomes may help to secure commitments to human rights, the rule of law, and equal protection.

Many more caveats and questions about restorative justice and its implementation remain. Any efforts to bring about reform of our criminal and juvenile justice systems must venture daring proposals for how we might better realize justice. But we must also do this work humbly, remembering that we live in a fallen world and that the next generation of criminal and juvenile justice reformers will probably need to correct our mistakes. For now, along with other reform efforts, restorative justice has the potential to create criminal and juvenile justice systems that better realize justice as equity as well as that expand and vivify the moral imagining of the people who participate in these practices. That is, in restorative justice, we can place a qualified hope.

Methodology, Interview Schedules, and Analysis

B eyond my argument specific to the moral imagination of restorative justice, I have endeavored in this study to demonstrate the importance of moral imagination for the work of ethicists more generally. This demonstration has been largely implicit, based on the example I have provided by examining this faculty in theories and practices relevant to restorative justice specifically. I trust that ethicists interested in consideration of moral imagination in their own work would benefit primarily from reading the text, finding in these pages a model for the incorporation of moral imagination in "doing ethics." But given the implicitness of the implications of the methodology in this study for ethicists, I include here some reflections on the significance of moral imagination in both the processes of ethical discernment and the methodology of ethics in which we bring theory and practice into dialogue.

Contrary to the bulk of Western moral philosophy and theology, I have shown that failing to consider moral imagination in our processes of ethical discernment would be gravely misguided. When people face moral situations and ask themselves, "What ought I to do?," they have already imagined the particulars of those situations in ways that will affect their reasoning, emotions, and perceptions. Analyzing the principles and goals that inform their answers to this question is thus insufficient; we must also look at their use and negotiation of moral imagination. Aristotle and his modern interpreters have supported this claim especially in terms of efforts to realize justice as equity, although their reflections pertain to other processes of ethical discernment as well. Similarly, moral imagination authors have demonstrated that principles and procedures of various disciplines sometimes do not adequately guide practices within their fields. Practitioners well-grounded in these principles and procedures often must also imagine morally in vivid and expansive ways in order to discern how principles apply to the particulars of any given circumstances and how to achieve the goals outlined by their procedures. Furthermore, examination of the experiences and reflections of participants in restorative justice practices has illuminated how their use and negotiation of restorative moral imagination related to their activities of moral imagining, and thereby, affected their efforts to realize justice as equity. Together this theoretical and practical evidence supports the conclusion that when ethicists ignore moral imagination, we occlude an essential feature of our processes of ethical discernment.

In approaching issues other than our current criminal and juvenile justice systems, I therefore propose that ethicists use "moral imagination" as one category of analysis in their interpretations of processes of ethical discernment. As we examine the practices of people engaged in processes of ethical discernment, we ought to look at the types of moral imagination upon which they draw to interpret and organize their experiences. Another important question is whether and how different practices arising from and generating these images of the world and its possibilities encourage their participants to imagine morally in vivid and expansive ways. Ethicists must also consider the various virtues associated with different sets of practices and the relationships of these virtues to vivid and expansive moral imagining. That is, in this study, I established the premise that the realization of justice as equity requires this faculty. But it remains for ethicists to show that moral imagination is as important for other virtues such as courage or compassion or prudence.

Finally, ethicists ought to explore the cultural, social, and institutional locations of practices and how these settings affect the types of moral imagination used by participants, their capacities for moral imagining, and their abilities to embody various virtues. Understanding moral situations and our processes of ethical discernment in responding to them requires more than appreciation of how people use reason to apply principles or calculate consequences. We must also attend to the complexity of moral imagination as they participate in multifaceted processes of ethical discernment in their common practices.

As we look at other issues through the analysis of moral imagination, I believe that ethicists will come to recognize that finding answers often depends less upon logical reasoning within any particular framework than upon using a different set of images of the world and its possibilities. Restorative justice advocates have argued that addressing our criminal and juvenile justice crises requires something other than more thorough or consistent application of retributive or rehabilitative models of justice. We must instead come to use different narratives, metaphors, and symbols in our assessment of the moral situations precipitated by crime. But examples of other issues also demonstrate the difference moral imagination can make in finding answers. In his account of physician and anthropologist Paul Farmer's work to address global drug-resistant tuberculosis epidemics, for instance, Tracy Kidder illustrates that answers do not necessarily lie in more rigorous application of public health policies and procedures. Rather solutions will depend on new images of disease, poverty, care, health resources, doctors, and patients as well as of possibilities for how the relationships among these realities can change.[275]

---

[275] Tracy Kidder, *Mountains Beyond Mountains: The Quest of Dr. Paul Farmer, A Man who Would Cure the World* (New York: Random House, 2003).

Environmentalists, perhaps best exemplified by Lynn White Jr., have long argued that addressing our environmental crises will depend significantly on revising the narratives, metaphors, and symbols that we use with reference to human beings, our ecologies, and the relationships between people and the earth.[276] In addition to issues of criminal justice, public health, and environmental degradation, consideration of moral imagination as an analytical concept may prove helpful for understanding processes of ethical discernment with respect to countless other topics, including economic disparities, war and peace, political agency, racial and ethnic divides, inter-religious dialogue, gender discrimination, and homophobia.

But more than treating moral imagination as an analytical concept, I hope that this book demonstrates that ethicists themselves must be capable of vivid and expansive moral imagining. If we are to bring theories and practices into dialogue, we must first learn to attend to the particulars of practices in which people confront moral situations. Doing so requires a set of skills outside of the more common academic skills of reading texts charitably yet critically (although here too activities of moral imagining play their part). Many of these skills can be developed through introduction to qualitative methods from anthropology and sociology such as participant-observation and interviewing. The practices of these disciplines can enable ethicists appropriately trained in them to attend to the particulars of people facing certain moral situations in their own lives. They can help us to challenge, illuminate, and correct our ethical theorizing as we enter into the stories and appreciate the perspectives of these people. As we consider their stories and perspectives in comparison with each other and in light of our ethical theories, ethicists will need to be able to draw connections across a wide range of experiences. Furthermore, as we try to understand the principles, goals, and virtues that shape responses to

---

[276] Lynn White Jr., "The Historical Roots of Our Ecological Crisis," in *Western Man and Environmental Ethics: Attitudes toward Nature and Ecology*, edited by Ian G. Barbour (Reading, MA: Addison-Wesley, 1973).

more immediate questions of "What ought I to do?," ethicists must be able to envision myriad possibilities of what the world could become—in terms both of individual responses and of broader systemic transformation. Without expansive and vivid moral imagining, we will not be capable of seeing the value of putting theory and practice into dialogue or of attending to the particulars in making more general moral claims.

To foster vivid and expansive moral imagining in the methodology of ethics, we will need to examine types of moral imagination used and negotiated by ethicists as we go about our work; the practices that generate and arise from these images of the world and its possibilities; and the social, cultural, and institutional settings in which we engage in these practices. Many of these factors shaping our activities of moral imagining depend upon our professional locations within academia. Ethicists must then not only analyze moral imagination with respect to various moral issues. We must also consider how our own moral imaginations shaped through academic training may affect our abilities to attend to the particulars of those issues. In particular, we must assess how this training shapes our images of knowledge and where it is created and can be found. What we discover has moral as well as epistemological implications as these images indicate whether we will search for moral knowledge in practices as well as in theory, and therefore, whether we will speak to people outside of academia and in other disciplines about the nature of the good and the right.

These reflections on moral imagination in the discipline of ethics and the necessity of vivid and expansive moral imagining in a methodology that places theory and practice in dialogue will remain merely indicative here. They are the seeds for an entirely different project than this study. Nevertheless, I hope that my project demonstrates the value both of using "moral imagination" as an analytical category for understanding processes of ethical discernment and of activities of moral imagining in ethical methodology.

Beyond theoretical justification of using an ethical methodology that attends to moral imagination, this project presented numerous practical problems in terms of how one studies moral imagination. In designing interview schedules for this study, I faced several challenges in trying to understand the moral imaginations of participants in restorative justice practices. I could not simply ask participants, "What does your moral imagination look like?" or "What role does moral imagination play in your processes of ethical discernment in a conference?" First, "moral imagination" does not have a single, clear meaning in common parlance, and its most frequent usage, it seems to me, refers to a capacity to see beyond the mire of a particular situation to find an inventive solution or response. This usage, for example, marks the most famous use of "moral imagination" in the Final Report of the 9/11 Commission, which cited a breakdown of moral leadership based on a lack of imagination in the intelligence community as a major contributing factor in the failure to prevent the tragedies of that day. Although this usage of "moral imagination" is related to my definition of the term as the cognitive faculty that empowers us to create images of the world and its possibilities, I use this term in a more specialized, technical way than common parlance allows.

As a result of this usage in common parlance, when I would ask participants questions involving the term "moral imagination," they did not disclose the narratives, metaphors, and symbols that they used to organize and interpret their experiences of the world and its possibilities. Those few people whom I asked these questions, usually at the end of interviews, instead talked about the inventiveness of restorative justice in the face of the mire of our criminal and juvenile justice systems. While this response is important, it does not necessarily reveal what I wanted to know about how they use and negotiate different types of moral imagination in their processes of ethical discernment in response to moral situations precipitated by crime. Thus, even if I asked participants about moral imagination, they would not necessarily use this term in the same way that I do and so their answers would not necessarily be particularly revelatory of their images of the world and its possibilities.

A second challenge in designing the interview schedules for this study was discerning how to operationalize "moral imagination." That is, I had to figure out how I would know moral imagination when I saw it being drawn upon by participants, and I found an answer in the schematic organization and interpretation of experience through moral imagination based upon the use of the tools of narrative, metaphor, and symbolism. I maintain that different types of moral imagination involve different sets of narratives, metaphors, and symbols that people draw upon in forming their images of the world and its possibilities. Because of the schematic character of moral imaginations, these different types have some level of coherence. But I also recognize that we all use and negotiate different types of moral imagination as we engage with others in various cultural interactions, social arrangements, and institutional structures. Even though different types of moral imagination may have some level of coherence, we thus often find multiple sets of images useful for explaining and interpreting different aspects of our experiences in varying situations. Examining how individuals use and negotiate these images in moral situations should illuminate how they understand themselves, others in a situation, and their relationships, thus revealing how they organize and interpret that experience in their processes of ethical discernment. In designing the interview schedules, I therefore needed questions that would help uncover the narratives, metaphors, and symbols that participants used to organize and interpret their experiences specifically of responding to crime through restorative justice practices.

I did not assume literary definitions of "narrative," "metaphor," or "symbol" in this study. While people may sometimes draw upon literary narratives, metaphors, or symbols in their moral imaginations, I understand these figures more broadly to be our tools for organizing and interpreting our experiences in different ways. As I argue in chapter two, narratives, for instance, imply causality: "First, A happened, then B." They also suggest anticipation: "Given that A happened, previous experience tells me that B should happen next." Metaphors, alternatively, draw connections by indicating resemblance, but not identity, among experiences: "A is like B, but A is not B." Both similarities and differences between two experiences bear meaning.   In contrast, symbols are concrete representations of something else, usually something invisible and intangible: "A is B, but B is not contained in A." These tools therefore specify different kinds of relationships among our experiences.   In order to uncover the narratives, metaphors, and symbols that participants use and negotiate to organize and interpret their experiences in restorative justice practices, I wanted to find out how they saw a particular experience causing, resembling, or representing other experiences, which may not involve their explicit use of narratives, metaphors, or symbols in a literary sense.

Another challenge in designing interview schedules for this study was that participants could give me the answers that they thought I would want to hear, rather than presenting their own views on their experiences.   Interviews in many ways are "performances," opportunities to display one's accomplishments or skills in a particular arena. In encountering a researcher who has expressed an interest in restorative justice, some of the participants could have wanted to prove to me that they are thoroughly engrained in restorative justice. Offenders, for example, may have picked up terms and phrases in their conferences or meetings with facilitators and community members and used them in their interviews with me to demonstrate that they "got it" in their conference and now they are doing the right things and seeing the world in the right way. I worried that offenders would use phrases such as "repair the harm" because they thought that I wanted to hear that they understood restorative justice and not because they would actually use that phrase in describing their experiences in other contexts.   Facilitators or community members could similarly use narratives, metaphors, and symbols that they picked up in training sessions or among other facilitators and community members because they wanted to demonstrate their facility with restorative justice, not because they commonly use these images of the world and its possibilities in organizing and interpreting their experiences.   This concern arose especially around the description of conferences, in which facilitators or community members could pick only their most outstanding conferences as demonstrations of the transformative power of restorative justice and their participation in it.

One way that I dealt with this challenge was to check responses of participants in interviews against my experiences of them in restorative justice conferences. By using participant-observation in comparison with the interviews, I was then able to examine whether and how participants used the same narratives, metaphors, and symbols in their practices as they did in conversation with me. While conferences are also in many ways performances as participants assume different roles in interaction with each other, seeing the interviews in light of my participant-observation allows me to see the consistency with which participants in these practices use and negotiate different types of moral imagination.

Another way of dealing with this challenge involved modeling my interview schedules on James P. Spradley's "Taxonomy of Ethnographic Questions,"[277] particularly his recommendation to use descriptive questions that allow participants to speak at length about both typical and exceptional experiences. By encouraging participants to ramble on about their experiences, these questions can "lead directly to a large sample of utterances that are expressed in the language used by informants in the cultural scene under investigation."[278] Increasing the number of utterances of participants may lessen the performance quality across the entire sample of their utterances, thereby increasing the likelihood that interviews reveal their own views on their experiences rather than leading to answers that participants thought that I would want to hear.

My interview schedules thus include questions in which I ask participants to give me a verbal "grand tour" of both typical and

---

[277] See Appendix A in James P. Spradley, *The Ethnographic Interview* (Belmont, CA: Wadsworth, 1979).
[278] Ibid., 90.

exceptional experiences of restorative justice, walking me through their most recent and their most memorable conferences in great detail. I asked them to explain where they were, who was there, how they were sitting, and the entire process of the conferences from beginning to end including who said what and why. Where participants used terms abstractly, I would ask for specific examples of what they meant. For instance, when Linda talked about "heart" in restorative justice conferences, I followed up by asking about a particular conference that displayed heart and one in which it was absent. Frequently I would also ask participants to provide more information about those terms: "Say more about what you mean by 'heart' and how you would use it to describe a conference." While using grand tour questions, however, I also asked participants to provide definitions of certain terms. For example, I asked them how they would describe restorative justice to someone who had never heard of it or to a person that held certain assumptions about it. These definitional questions provided a baseline for me of their understanding of restorative justice from which I could assess their own views on their experiences with these practices.

A final challenge with designing interview schedules was that just as I could not say to participants, "Tell me about your moral imagination," I also could not ask them, "What do you think about the metaphor of community as 'a web of relationships'?" I could foresee answers in which participants would say, "Well, yes, that's a nice metaphor. I had never thought of it that way before." By explicitly using the narratives, metaphors, and symbols of restorative, rehabilitative, and retributive moral imaginations in my questions, I could taint my interviews by introducing terms that participants do not actually draw upon while organizing and interpreting their experiences. Instead I had to figure out ways to ask questions that revealed whether and how participants use and negotiate different types of moral imagination without actually explaining and describing those types to the participants.

In response to this challenge, rather than asking participants about the narratives, metaphors, and symbols of restorative, rehabilitative, and retributive moral imaginations, I drew upon my categories for analyzing these types of moral imagination in chapter three in formulating many of my questions. These questions required participants to reflect upon their understanding of crime, offenders, victims, community, criminal and juvenile justice systems, the state, and types and purposes of sanctions (cf. Table 3). While I did not ask them to define these terms, especially when I asked grand tour questions, I could ask follow-up questions about participants' images of particular crimes, offenders, victims, etc. Their responses to these questions frequently brought up the narratives, metaphors, and symbols that they used in organizing and interpreting their experiences of responding to crime through restorative justice. For example, the metaphor of "crime as bad choice" arose from many participants' descriptions of various conferences in which they observed that the offender was "just a kid who made a mistake" or "a guy who made a bad decision."

My analysis of the interviews also drew upon the framework established with the categories described in table 3. That is, when reading transcripts of the interviews, I would code any reference to "crime," "offenders," "victims," etc. I then collected all references to these categories across all of the interviews and examined them for any common themes as well as for any significant differences among the participants. I put all references to "crime" together, for example, and found the frequent use of "bad choice" among all participants. I also put all references to "types and purposes of sanctions" together and found that participants had less negative assessments of therapy than of punishment as a viable means of bringing about "real change," but also saw "responsibility" and "accountability" as the primary source of transformation. Using this strategy, I was able to generate lists of the narratives, metaphors, and symbols that participants drew upon in describing their experiences with restorative justice with respect to each of the categories that I had used in analyzing restorative, rehabilitative, and retributive moral imaginations. These lists included consideration of ways that participants saw some experiences causing, resembling, or representing other experiences (for example, "responsibility" and "accountability" causing change; or "the machine of vengeance" representing criminal and juvenile justice systems). I could then compare these lists to my schematization of these types of moral imagination in order to understand how participants used and negotiated them in practices of restorative justice.

Finally, in conducting these interviews, I often did not feel constrained by my interview schedules. I viewed these sets of questions as good places to start conversations with participants, but was also open to the possibility that other questions would arise as I spoke with each person. These lists therefore do not fully capture these semi-structured interviews, but they do suggest the general shape of the conversations. Also, I wrote multiple interview schedules because I recognized that the different experiences of community members, offenders, and facilitators required that I find different places to start our conversations. For example, it would not make sense to ask an offender about his training, and it would not make sense to ask most community members about the offense that led them to a restorative justice conference. I did not include an interview schedule for victims because I did not have the opportunity to interview any of them; many of the questions of offenders would resemble the questions that I would ask victims. These interview schedules thus represent my best efforts for uncovering the use and negotiation of different types of moral imagination among participants in restorative justice.

COMMUNITY MEMBERS

(1) Tell me a little bit about yourself. Where are you from? How long have you lived here? What are you doing when you're not participating in restorative justice?

(2) Tell me about how you first heard about restorative justice and decided to become involved with this program. I'd like to know more about your particular story. Who told you about restorative justice and what did he or she say? What were some of your first impressions? Why do you think those were your first impressions? What were some of the first restorative justice practices in which you participated?

(3) What sort of training did you receive after you got involved in restorative justice? Who conducted the training? Who went through training with you? How long was your training? Describe some of the exercises you went through. What is most memorable about your training? What was most important that you learn? If you provided training for other facilitators, what are some of the most important things you would hope that they would learn?

(4) About how many restorative justice conferences have your participated in? Have you always participated as a community member? Have you ever participated as a victim, offender, or facilitator?

(5) Walk me through the last restorative justice conference in which you participated. Who was there and what were they like? What led to the conference? What happened during the conference? How did it all end up? Did you think the outcomes were good?

(6) What is your most memorable or meaningful experience with restorative justice? Walk me through what happened. Who was there

and what were they like? What led to this experience? How did it all end up? Did you think the outcomes were good?

(7) How would you describe the experiences of people who come to restorative justice through criminal or juvenile justice systems? What do you think these systems are like? If you think there are problems, what do you think they are? What do these systems do well in light of the experiences of people you encounter in this program? What does restorative justice do differently?

(8) How do you define restorative justice? If you were telling friends or teaching a class about restorative justice, what are the most important things that they should know? How would you compare restorative justice to "justice"? How does restorative justice differ from other justice practices, for example, criminal court practices?

(9) What is your understanding of the role of community members in restorative justice? Do you think it is important to have community members participate?   How do you think the community goes about offering resources and support? What are the strengths and limitations of including community? Do you think the community gets repair from restorative justice? How so?

(10) What are some of the things that you want to communicate as a community member in restorative justice?   What do you hope offenders will get out of the experience? What are your hopes for victims? What are your hopes for the community?

(11) What do you personally get out of your involvement in restorative justice? Has it taught you anything about yourself? Has it taught you anything about people who might go through these practices? Has it taught you anything about your community?

(12) Do you have any disappointments or frustrations with restorative justice practices? Are there things you would like to change with restorative justice practices to improve them? How so?

(13) Are there any questions that I should have asked you, but didn't?

FACILITATORS

(1) Tell me a little bit about yourself. Where are you from? How long have you lived here? What are you doing when you're not participating in restorative justice?

(2) Tell me about how you first heard about restorative justice and decided to become involved with this program. I'd like to know more about your particular story. Who told you about restorative justice? What attracted you the idea of restorative justice? What were some of the first restorative justice practices in which you participated?

(3) What sort of training did you receive after you got involved in restorative justice? Who conducted the training? Who went through training with you? How long was your training? Describe some of the exercises you went through. What is most memorable about your training? If you provide training for other facilitators, what are some of the most important things you hope that they learn?

(4) Describe this program for me. Who is involved in it? What roles do they have? What does the program do? When do people who are involved with this program get together and what do they do together?

(5) Walk me through the last restorative justice conference in which you participated. Who was there and what were they like? What led to the conference? What happened during the conference? How did it all end up? Were you satisfied with the outcomes?

(6) What is your most memorable or meaningful experience with restorative justice? Walk me through what happened. Who was there and what were they like? What led to this experience? How did it all end up? Were you satisfied with the outcomes?

(7) How do you define restorative justice? If you were telling friends or teaching a class about restorative justice, what are the most important things that they should know? How would you compare restorative justice to "justice"? How does restorative justice differ from other justice practices, e.g. criminal court practices?

(8) How would you describe the experiences of people who come to restorative justice through criminal or juvenile justice systems? What do you think these systems are like? If you think there are problems, what do you think they are? What do these systems do well in light of the experiences of people you encounter in this program? What does restorative justice do differently?

(9) Tell me about some of the common features of participants in this program. What are some of the offenders like? Victims? Describe some of these people and their backgrounds, without identifying information. What do you hope that they get out of this program?

(10) What do you get out of your involvement in restorative justice? Has it taught you anything about yourself? Has it taught you anything about people who might go through one of these practices?

(11) Do you have any disappointments or frustrations with restorative justice practices? Are there things you would like to change with restorative justice practices to improve them? How so?

(12) Are there any questions that I should have asked you, but didn't?

OFFENDERS

(1) Tell me a little bit about yourself. Where are you from? Do you have brothers or sisters? Tell me about your parents. Who are your best friends? What do you do on a typical day or a typical week? What is your biggest hope for your future?

(2) Tell me about how you were referred to a restorative justice program. Who first contacted you? What did s/he say restorative justice was? What were some of your first impressions? Did you think that it was crazy, or that it was something that you just had to get over with, or that it seemed like a good idea? Why do you think those were your first impressions?

(3) Did you have the opportunity to agree to go through the restorative justice program? If so, why did you choose this path instead of something more traditional, like going through the criminal or juvenile justice system? What did you hope would be the result of the restorative justice conference? Have you ever had to go through a more traditional judicial process? How would you say this experience compares?

(4) Did you have any meetings with the facilitator of this program before your restorative justice conference? What happened in those meetings? What did the facilitator tell you about restorative justice? Did he or she ask you to do anything to prepare for the conference? Was the meeting, assignments, etc. helpful?

(5) Now let's talk about your actual conference. I want you to walk me through what happened. What was the room like? When you walked into the room, who was there? Did you know any of them before the meeting? What were some of your first impressions—fear, anger, disinterest, nervousness, skepticism, curiosity? What were the people doing?

(6) How did the conference get started? Who said the first thing? Did a facilitator explain any ground rules? If so, what were they? Did these seem like good rules to you? Would you have added any, taken any away?

(7) What happened next? Did you have an opportunity to tell your story? What did you think about telling your story? What are some of the things that you wanted to communicate to the group by telling your story? How did it make you feel? Did you feel like the people in the room listened to you? If so, what did it feel like to be listened to? What kinds of questions did they ask you? What was the facilitator doing? What kinds of harms were identified?

(8) Was the victim present at your conference? Did you know this person beforehand? If not, what did you think he or she would be like? Did he or surprise you? Did he or she say anything during the conference? What did you learn about him or her? If the victim wasn't there, do you think your experience would have been like if he or she had come? What difference do you think it would have made to have him or her there?

(9) Were there community members there? Can you describe them for me? What was it like for you to have these other people there? What kinds of questions did they ask you? Did any of them say anything that helped you through the process or that helped you learn something new? Had you thought before about connections between the things you do and the effects they have on the community?

(10) What was the outcome of your conference? What did you agree to do to repair the harm caused by the crime? Why did your conference choose this plan? Do you think it was fair? If not, what would be a more fair agreement? What harms do you think this agreement will help to solve?

(11) We talked about some of your hopes for the process. Do you think that this agreement will help fulfill those hopes? Did your hopes change through the process? If so, how would you describe your hopes for the rest of the process as you try to fulfill the requirements of your agreement?

(12) How did the conference end? Who said the last thing? What were feeling when it was all over—relief, remorse, forgiveness, support, love, anxiety, anger? You said that your first impressions of the other people in the room were.... Would you say that you thought the same things about them at the end of the conference?

(13) For offenders who have had a follow-up meeting: How much time was there between your initial conference and the follow-up meeting? What was it like for you to come back and see the same group of people? Now that you know them from your previous conference, what was it like to walk in the room? Do you feel like you kept your part of the agreement? Are there things that you still need to work on?

(14) If you had a friend who got into trouble, would you recommend restorative justice to him or her? How would you describe restorative justice to him or her? What about the process worked best for you? Is there anything that you would want to change, anything that disappointed or frustrated you?

(15) What did you get out of your involvement in restorative justice? Has it taught you anything about yourself? Has it taught you anything about the other people who participated in your conference, for example, your parents and friends, the victim, community members?

(16) Are there any questions that I should have asked you, but didn't?

Bibliography

Acorn, Annalise. *Compulsory Compassion: A Critique of Restorative Justice.* Vancouver: UBC Press, 2004.

Addelson, Kathryn Pyne. *Moral Passages: Toward a Collectivist Moral Theory.* New York: Routledge, 1994.

Allison, Dale. *The Sermon on the Mount: Inspiring Moral Imagination.* New York: Herder and Herder, 1999.

Alschuler, Albert W. "The Failure of Sentencing Guidelines: A Plea for Less Aggregation." *The University of Chicago Law Review* 58.3 (1991): 901-951.

American Law Institute. *The Model Penal Code.* Philadelpia: American Law Institute, 1962.

Andrews, D.A., and James Bonta. *The Psychology of Criminal Conduct*, 4th edition. Cincinnati: Anderson/LexisNexis, 2006.

Andrews, D.A., James Bonta, and R.D. Hoge. "Classification for Effective Rehabilitation: Rediscovering Psychology." *Criminal Justice and Behavior* 17 (1990): 19-52.

Andrews, D.A., Ivan Zinger, Robert D. Hoge, James Bonta, Paul Gendreau, and Francis T. Cullen. "Does Correctional Treatment Work? A Clinically-Relevant and Psychologically Informed Meta-analysis." *Criminology* 28.3 (1990): 369-404.

Annie E. Casey Foundation, The. "2008 KIDS COUNT Message FACT SHEET: A Road Map for Juvenile Justice." The Annie E. Casey Foundation. http://www.aecf.org/KnowledgeCenter/ Publications.aspx?pubguid={29CFCA70-348B-416B-8546-63C297710C5D} (accessed on May 14, 2009).

Anscombe, Elizabeth. "Modern Moral Philosophy." In *Virtue Ethics*, edited by Roger Crisp and Michael A. Slote, 26-44. New York: Oxford University Press, 1997.

Aristotle. *The Basic Works of Aristotle.* Translated and edited by Richard McKeon. New York: Modern Library Classics, 2001.

Arrigo, Bruce A. "Social Justice and Critical Criminology: On Integrating Knowledge." *Contemporary Justice Review* 3.1 (2000): 7-37.

- - -. "Rethinking Restorative and Community Justice: A Postmodern Inquiry."

Contemporary Justice Review 7.1 (March 2004): 91-100.

Babbit, Susan E. *Impossible Dreams: Rationality, Integrity, and Moral Imagination.* Boulder: Westview, 1996.

- - -. *Artless Integrity: Moral Imagination, Agency, and Stories.* Lanham, MD: Rowman & Littlefield Publishers, 2001.

Balanced and Restorative Justice Project. *Guide for Implementing the Balanced and Restorative Justice Model.* Washington, D.C.: Office of Juvenile Justice and Delinquency Prevention, U.S. Department of Justice, 1998.

Basic Principles on the Use of Restorative Justice Programmes in Criminal Matters. United Nations, 2000.

Bazemore, Gordon. "Three Paradigms for Juvenile Justice." In *Restorative Justice: International Perspectives,* edited by Burt Galaway and Joe Hudson, 37-67. Monsey, NY: Criminal Justice Press, 1996.

- - -. "What's New About the Balanced Approach?" *Juvenile and Family Court Journal* 48.1 (1997): 1-23.

- - -. "After Shaming, Whither Reintegration: Restorative Justice and Relational Rehabilitation." In *Restorative Juvenile Justice: Repairing the Harm of Youth Crime,* edited by Gordon Bazemore and Lode Walgrave, 155-194. Monsey, NY: Criminal Justice Press, 1999.

Bazemore, Gordon, and Dee Bell. "What is the Appropriate Relationship between Restorative Justice and Treatment?" In *Critical Issues in Restorative Justice,* edited by Howard Zehr and Barbara Toews, 119-131. Cullompton, UK: Willan, 2004.

Bazemore, Gordon and Dennis Maloney. "Rehabilitating Community Service: Toward Restorative Service in a Balanced Justice System." *Federal Probation* 58.1 (1994): 24-35.

Bazemore, Gordon, and Sandra O'Brien. "The Quest for a Restorative Model of Rehabilitation: Theory-for-practice and Practice-for Theory." In *Restorative Justice and the Law,* edited by Lode Walgrave, 31-67. Cullompton, UK: Willan, 2002.

Bazemore, Gordon, and Mara Schiff, eds. *Restorative Community Justice: Repairing Harm and Transforming Communities.* Cincinnati, OH: Anderson, 2001.

Bazemore, Gordon, and Mara Schiff. "What and Why Now: Understanding

Restorative Justice." In *Restorative Community Justice: Repairing Harm and Transforming Communities*, edited by Gordon Bazemore and Mara Schiff, 21-46. Cincinnati, OH: Anderson, 2001.

- - -. "Paradigm Muddle or Paradigm Paralysis? The Wide and Narrow Roads to Restorative Justice Reform (or, a Little Confusion May Be a Good Thing." *Contemporary Justice Review* 7.1 (March 2004): 37-57.

- - -. *Juvenile Justice Reform and Restorative Justice: Building Theory and Policy from Practice*. Portland, OR: Willan Publishing, 2005.

Bazemore, Gordon and Jeanne B. Stinchcomb. "Restorative Conferencing and Theory-Based Evaluation." In *Family Group Conferencing: New Directions in Community-Centered Child and Family Practice*, edited by Gale Buford and Joe Hudson, 284-297. New York: Aldine de Gruyter, 2000.

Bazemore, Gordon and Mark Umbreit. "Rethinking the Sanctioning Function in Juvenile Court: Retributive or Restorative Responses to Youth Crime." *Crime and Delinquency* 41.3 (1995): 296-316.

Bazemore, Gordon and Lode Walgrave, eds. *Restorative Juvenile Justice: Repairing the Harm of Youth Crime*. Monsey, NY: Criminal Justice Press, 1999.

Bazemore, Gordon, and Lode Walgrave. "Introduction: Restorative Justice and the International Juvenile Justice Crisis." In *Restorative Juvenile Justice: Repairing the Harm of Youth Crime*, edited by Gordon Bazemore and Lode Walgrave, 1-14. Monsey, NY: Criminal Justice Press, 1999a.

- - -. "Restorative Juvenile Justice: In Search of Fundamentals and an Outline for Systemic Reform." In *Restorative Juvenile Justice: Repairing the Harm of Youth Crime*, edited by Gordon Bazemore and Lode Walgrave, 45-74. Monsey, NY: Criminal Justice Press, 1999b.

Beidelman, T.O. *Moral Imagination in Kaguru Modes of Thought*. Washington, DC: Smithsonian Institution Press, 1993.

Benhabib, Seyla. *Situating the Self: Gender, Community, and Postmodernism in Contemporary Ethics*. New York: Routledge, 1992.

Bergseth, Kathleen J., and Jeffrey A. Bouffard. "The Long-Term Impact of Restorative Justice Programming for Juvenile Offenders." *Journal of Criminal Justice* 35 (2007): 433-451.

Blum, Lawrence A. *Moral Perception and Particularity*. New York: Cambridge University Press, 1994.

Bonafé-Schmitt, Jean-Pierre. "Alternatives to the Judicial Model." In

Mediation and Criminal Justice: Victims, Offenders, and Community,
edited by Martin Wright and Burt Galaway, 178-193. London: Sage
Publications, 1989.

Bonta, James, Rebecca Jesseman, Tanya Rugge, and Robert Cormier.
"Restorative Justice and Recidivism: Promises Made, Promises Kept?" In
Handbook of Restorative Justice: A Global Perspective, edited by Dennis
Sullivan and Larry Tifft, 108-120. New York: Routledge, 2006.

Braithwaite, John. *Crime, Shame, and Reintegration.* New York: Cambridge
University Press, 1989.

- - -. "Conditions of Successful Reintegration Ceremonies." *The British
Journal of Criminology* 34 (1994): 139-171.

- - -. "Restorative Justice and a Better Future." *Dalhousie Review* 76.1 (1996):
9-32.

- - -. *Restorative Justice and Responsive Regulation.* New York: Oxford
University Press, 2002.

Braithwaite, John, and Christine Parker. "Restorative Justice is Republican
Justice." In *Restorative Juvenile Justice: Repairing the Harm of Youth
Crime,* edited by Gordon Bazemore and Lode Walgrave, 103-126.
Monsey, NY: Criminal Justice Press, 1999.

Braithwaite, John, and Peter Pettit. *Not Just Deserts: A Republican Theory of
Criminal Justice.* Oxford: Oxford University Press, 1990.

Braithwaite, John, and Declan Roche. "Responsibility and Restorative
Justice." In *Restorative Community Justice: Repairing Harm and
Transforming Communities,* edited by Gordon Bazemore and Mara Schiff,
63-84. Cincinnati, OH: Anderson, 2001.

Brann, Eva. *The World of Imagination: Sum and Substance.* Chicago:
University of Chicago Press, 1986.

Breton, Denise, and Stephen Lehman. *The Mystic Heart of Justice: Restoring
Wholeness in a Broken World.* West Chester, PA: Chrysalis Books, 2001.

Britton, Dana M. *At Work in the Iron Cage: The Prison as Gendered
Organization.* New York: New York University Press, 2003.

Brockway, Zebulon. *Fifty Years of Prison Service: An Autobiography.* New
York: Charities Publication Committee, 1912.

Brown, William P. *The Ethos of the Cosmos: The Genesis of Moral
Imagination in the Bible.* Grand Rapids, MI: Eerdmans, 1999.

Brueggemann, Walter. *Hopeful Imagination: Prophetic Voices in Exile.*
Philadelphia: Fortress Press, 1986.

- - -. *Texts under Negotiation: The Bible and Postmodern Imagination.* Minneapolis: Fortress Press, 1993.

- - -. *The Prophetic Imagination.* 2nd edition. Minneapolis: Fortress Press, 2001.

- - -. *An Introduction to the Old Testament: The Canon and Christian Imagination.* Louisville, KY: Westminster John Knox Press, 2003.

Buford, Gale and Joe Hudson, eds. *Family Group Conferencing: New Directions in Community-Centered Child and Family Practice.* New York: Aldine de Gruyter, 2000.

Bureau of Justice Statistics. "Incarceration Rate: 1980-2005." U.S. Department of Justice. http://www.ojp.usdoj.gov/bjs/glance/tables /corr2tab.htm (accessed on November 14, 2007).

Bureau of Justice Statistics. "Indigent Defense Statistics." U.S. Department of Justice. http://www.ojp.usdoj.gov/bjs/id.htm#defendants (accessed on November 14, 2007).

Bureau of Justice Statistics. "The Number of Adults in the Correctional Population Has Been Increasing." U.S. Department of Justice. http://www.ojp.usdoj.gov/bjs/glance/corr2.htm (accessed on November 14, 2007).

Burgess, Ernest. "The Growth of the City: An Introduction to a Research Project." In *The City,* edited by Robert E. Park, Ernest Burgess, and Roderick D. McKenzie. Chicago: University of Chicago Press, 1969 [1925].

Burrell, Nancy, Rebecca Gill, Lindsay Timmerman, and Mike Allen. "Victim-Offender Mediation: A Meta-Analysis." Paper presented at the NCA 95th Annual Convention, Chicago, IL, November 11, 2009.

Bursik, Robert J., and Harold G. Grasmick. *Neighborhoods and Crime: The Dimensions of Effective Community Control.* Lanham, MD: Lexington Books, 1993.

Bussman, Kai-D. "Morality, Symbolism, and Criminal Law: Chances and Limits of Mediation Programs." In *Restorative Justice on Trial: Pitfalls and Potentials of Victim-Offender Mediation—International Perspectives,* edited by Heinz Messmer and Hans-Uwe Otto, 317-326. Dordrecht, the Netherlands: Kluwer, 1992.

Carrell, Michael R., and John E. Dittrich. "Equity Theory: The Recent Literature, Methodological Considerations, and New Directions." *The Academy of Management Review* 3.2 (1978): 202-210.

Carroll, Gordon. *Cool Hand Luke.* Warner Brothers Pictures, 1967.

Casey, Edward S. "Imagination: Imagining and the Image." *Philosophy and Phenomenological Research* 31.4 (1971): 475-490.

- - -. *Imagination: A Phenomenological Study*. Bloomington: Indiana University Press, 1976.

Caston, Victor. "Why Aristotle Needs Imagination." *Phronesis* 41.1 (1996): 20-55.

Clemetson, Lynette. "Judges Look to New Congress for Changes in Mandatory Sentencing Laws." *New York Times*, January 9, 2007.

Chopp, Rebecca. *Saving Work: Feminist Practices of Theological Education*. Louisville, KY: Westminster John Knox Press, 1995.

Christie, Nils. "Conflict as Property." *The British Journal of Criminology* 17 (1977): 1-14.

Clausen, Christopher. *The Moral Imagination: Essays on Literature and Ethics*. Iowa City: University of Iowa Press, 1986.

Clear, Todd R. "Thoughts About Action and Ideology in Criminal Justice Reform." *Contemporary Justice Review* 7.1 (March 2004): 69-73.

Clear, Todd R. and David R. Karp. *The Community Justice Ideal*. New York: Westview, 1999.

Coates, Robert B. and John Gehm. *Victim Meets Offender: An Evaluation of Victim-Offender Reconciliation Programs*. Valparaiso, IN: PACT Institute of Justice, 1985.

- - -. "An Empirical Assessment." In *Mediation and Criminal Justice: Victims, Offenders, and Community*, edited by Martin Wright and Burt Galaway, 251-263. London: Sage Publications, 1989.

Coles, Robert. *The Call of Stories: Teaching and the Moral Imagination*. Boston: Houghton Mifflin Company, 1989.

Consedine, Jim. *Restorative Justice: Healing the Effects of Crime*. Lyttelton, New Zealand: Ploughshares Publications, 1995.

Cook, Karen S., and Karen A. Hegtvedt. "Distributive Justice, Equity, and Equality." *Annual Review of Sociology* 9 (1983): 217-241.

Cullen, Francis T., and Karen E. Gilbert. *Reaffirming Rehabilitation*. Cincinnati: Anderson Publishing Co., 1982.

Cragg, Wesley. *The Practice of Punishment: Towards a Theory of Restorative Justice*. New York: Routledge, 1992.

Crisp, Roger, and Michael Slote, eds. *Virtue Ethics*. Oxford: Oxford University Press, 1997.

Currie, Gregory, and Ian Ravenscroft. *Recreative Minds: Imagination in*

Philosophy and Psychology. Oxford: Clarendon Press, 2002.

Daly, Kathleen. "Restorative Justice: Moving Past the Caricatures." Paper presented at the Seminar on Restorative Justice, Institute of Criminology, University of Sydney Law School, Sydney, Australia, April 1998a. http://www.gj.edu.au/school/ccj/kdaly.html.

- - -. *South Australia Juvenile Justice (SAJJ) Research on Conferencing: Technical Report No. 1: Project Overview and Research Instruments.* Brisbane, Australia: School of Criminology and Criminal Justice, 1998b. http://www.griffith.edu.au/school/ccj/kdaly.html.

- - -. "Restorative Justice in Diverse and Unequal Societies." *Law in Context* 17.1 (1999): 167-190.

- - -. "Revisiting the Relationship between Retributive and Restorative Justice." In *Restorative Justice: Philosophy to Practice,* edited by Heather Strang and John Braithwaite, 33-54. Aldershot: Ashgate/Dartmouth, 2000.

- - -. *South Australia Juvenile Justice (SAJJ) Research on Conferencing: Technical Report No. 2: Research Instruments in Year 2 (1999) and Background Notes.* Brisbane, Australia: School of Criminology and Criminal Justice, 2001. http://www.griffith.edu.au/school/ccj/kdaly.html.

- - -. "Restorative Justice: The Real Story." *Punishment and Society* 4.1 (2002): 55-79.

Daly, Kathleen and Russ Immarigeon. "The Past, Present, and Future of Restorative Justice: Some Critical Reflections." *Contemporary Justice Review* 1.1 (1998): 21-45.

Davis, Robert C., Martha Tichane, and Deborah Grayson. *Mediation and Arbitration as Alternatives to Prosecution in Felony Arrest Cases: An Evaluation of the Brooklyn Dispute Resolution Center.* New York: Vera Institute of Justice, 1980.

Dickens, Charles. *American Notes.* Introduction by Christopher Lasch. Gloucester, MA: Peter Smith, 1842/1968.

Dongier, Sylvie and Denis van Doosselaere. "Approaching Mediation in Juvenile Court: Rationale and Methodological Aspects." In *Restorative Justice on Trial: Pitfalls and Potentials of Victim-Offender Mediation— International Perspectives,* edited by Messmer, Heinz and Hans-Uwe Otto, 501-512. Dordrecht, the Netherlands: Kluwer, 1992.

Duff, R.A. "Desert and Penance." In *Principled Sentencing: Readings on Theory and Policy,* 2ⁿᵈ edition, 161-167. Oxford: Hart Publishing, 1998.

Dyck, David. "Reaching Toward a Structurally Responsive Training and

Practice of Restorative Justice." *Contemporary Justice Review* 3.3 (2000): 239-265.

Engell, James. *The Creative Imagination: Enlightenment to Romanticism.* Cambridge, MA: Harvard University Press, 1981.

Engmann, Joyce. "Imagination and Truth in Aristotle." *The Journal of the History of Philosophy* 14 (1976): 259-265.

Feld, Barry C. "Rehabilitation, Retribution, and Restorative Justice: Alternative Conceptions of Juvenile Justice." In *Restorative Juvenile Justice: Repairing the Harm of Youth Crime*, edited by Gordon Bazemore and Lode Walgrave, 17-44. Monsey, NY: Criminal Justice Press, 1999.

Fernandez, James W., and Mary Taylor Huber, eds. *Irony in Action: Anthropology, Practice, and the Moral Imagination.* Chicago: University of Chicago Press, 2001.

Fesmire, Steven. *John Dewey and Moral Imagination: Pragmatism in Ethics.* Bloomington: Indiana University Press, 2003.

Forst, Brian. "Prosecution and Sentencing." In *Crime*, edited by James Q. Wilson and Joan Petersilia, 363-386. San Francisco: ICS Press, 1995.

Frede, Dorothea. "The Cognitive Role of *Phantasia* in Aristotle." In *Essays on Aristotle's* De Anima, edited by Martha Nussbaum and Amélie Rorty, 279-295. Oxford: Clarendon Press, 1992.

Freydberg, Bernard. *Imagination in Kant's Critique of Practical Reason.* Bloomington: Indiana University Press, 2005.

Friedman, Lawrence W. *Crime and Punishment in American History.* New York: Basic Books, 1993.

Galaway, Burt. "The New Zealand Experience Implementing the Reparation Sentence." In *Restorative Justice on Trial: Pitfalls and Potentials of Victim-Offender Mediation—International Perspectives*, edited by Heinz Messmer and Hans-Uwe Otto, 55-80. Dordrecht, the Netherlands: Kluwer, 1992.

Galaway, Burt and Joe Hudson, eds. *Criminal Justice, Restitution, and Reconciliation.* Monsey, NY: Willow Press, 1990.

- - -. *Restorative Justice: International Perspectives.* Monsey, NY: Criminal Justice Press, 1996.

Garland, David. *Punishment and Modern Society: A Study in Social Theory.* Chicago: University of Chicago Press, 1990.

Gehm, John R. "The Function of Forgiveness in the Criminal Justice System."

In *Restorative Justice on Trial: Pitfalls and Potentials of Victim-Offender Mediation—International Perspectives*, edited by Heinz Messmer and Hans-Uwe Otto, 541-550. Dordrecht, the Netherlands: Kluwer, 1992.

Gendreau, Paul, Claire Goggin, and Francis T. Cullen. *The Effects of Prison Sentences on Recidivism.* Ottawa: Solicitor General Canada, 1999.

Gendreau, Paul, Paula Smith, and Sheila A. French. "The Theory of Effective Correctional Intervention: Empirical Status and Future Directions." In *Taking Stock: The Status of Criminological Theory*, Advances in Criminological Theory, vol. 15, edited by Francis T. Cullen, John Paul Wright, and Kristie R. Blevins, 419-445. New Brunswick, NJ: Transaction, 2006.

Georgiadis, Constantine. "Equitable and Equity in Aristotle." In *Justice, Law, and Method in Plato and Aristotle*, edited by Spiro Panagiotou, 159-172. Edmonton, Alberta: Academic Printing and Publishing, 1987.

Gil, David G. "Toward a 'Radical' Paradigm of Restorative Justice." In *Handbook of Restorative Justice: A Global Perspective*, edited by Dennis Sullivan and Larry Tifft, 499-511. New York: Routledge, 2006.

Glaze, Lauren E., and Laura M. Maruschak. "Parents in Prison and Their Minor Children." *Bureau of Justice Statistics, Special Report 222984.* Washington, DC: U.S. Department of Justice, 2008.

Gorringe, Timothy. *God's Just Vengeance: Crime, Violence, and the Rhetoric of Salvation.* Cambridge: Cambridge University Press, 1996.

Griffith, Lee. *The Fall of the Prison: Biblical Perspectives on Prison Abolition.* Grand Rapids, MI: William B. Eerdmans, 1993.

Grönfors, Martti. "Ideals and Reality in Community Mediation." In *Mediation and Criminal Justice: Victims, Offenders, and Community*, edited by Martin Wright and Burt Galaway, 140-151. London: Sage Publications, 1989.

- - -. "Mediation—A Romatic Ideal or a Workable Alternative." In *Restorative Justice on Trial: Pitfalls and Potentials of Victim-Offender Mediation—International Perspectives*, edited by Heinz Messmer and Hans-Uwe Otto, 419-430. Dordrecht, the Netherlands: Kluwer, 1992.

Guroian, Vigen. *Tending the Heart of Virtue: How Classic Stories Awaken a Child's Moral Imagination.* New York: Oxford University Press, 1998.

Gustafson, James. "Context Versus Principles: A Misplaced Debate in Christian Ethics." *Harvard Theological Review* 58.2 (1965): 171-202.

Hadley, Michael L. "Spiritual Foundations of Restorative Justice." In

  Handbook of Restorative Justice: A Global Perspective, edited by Dennis
    Sullivan and Larry Tifft, 175-187. New York: Routledge, 2006.

- - -, ed. *The Spiritual Roots of Restorative Justice*. New York: SUNY Press,
    2001.

Haley, John. "Confession, Repentance, and Absolution." In *Mediation and*
    Criminal Justice: Victims, Offenders, and Community, edited by Martin
    Wright and Burt Galaway, 195-211. London: Sage, 1989.

- - -. "Victim-Offender Mediations: Japanese and American Comparison." In
    Restorative Justice on Trial: Pitfalls and Potentials of Victim-Offender
    Mediation—International Perspectives, edited by Heinz Messmer and
    Hans-Uwe Otto, 105-130. Dordrecht, the Netherlands: Kluwer, 1992.

Hall, Pamela M. "Limits of the Story: Tragedy in Recent Virtue Ethics."
    Studies in Christian Ethics 17.3 (2004): 1-10.

Harris, M. Kay. "Reflections of a Skeptical Dreamer: Some Dilemmas in
    Restorative Justice Theory and Practice." *Contemporary Justice Review* 1
    (1998): 57-69.

- - -. "An Expansive, Transformative View of Restorative Justice."
    Contemporary Justice Review 7.1 (March 2004): 117-141.

- - -. "Transformative Justice: The Transformation of Restorative Justice." In
    Handbook of Restorative Justice: A Global Perspective, edited by Dennis
    Sullivan and Larry Tifft, 555-566. New York: Routledge Press, 2006.

Hart, H.L.A. *Punishment and Responsibility: Essays in the Philosophy of Law*,
    2nd edition. New York: Oxford University Press, 2008.

Hayes, Hennessey and Kathleen Daly. "Youth Justice Conferencing and
    Reoffending." *Justice Quarterly* 20.4 (2003): 725-764.

Himmelfarb, Gertrude. *Poverty and Compassion: The Moral Imagination of*
    the Late Victorians. New York: Alfred A. Knopf, 1991.

- - -. *The Moral Imagination: From Edmund Burke to Lionel Trilling*.
    Chicago: Ivan R. Doe, 2006.

Hudson, Barbara. "Beyond Proportionate Punishment: Difficult Cases and the
    1991 Criminal Justice Act." *Crime, Law, and Social Change* 22 (1995):
    59-78.

Hudson, Joe, and Burt Galaway, eds. *Restorative Justice: International*
    Perspectives. Monsey, NY: Criminal Justice Press, 1996.

- - -. "Introduction." In *Restorative Justice: International Perspectives*, edited
    by Joe Hudson and Burt Galaway, 1-14. Monsey, NY: Criminal Justice
    Press, 1996.

Hudson, Joe, Allison Morris, Gabrielle Maxwell, and Burt Galaway. *Family Group Conferences*. Monsey, NY: Criminal Justice Press, 1996.

Immarigeon, Russ. "Restorative Justice, Juvenile Offenders, and Crime Victims: A Review of the Literature." In *Restorative Juvenile Justice: Repairing the Harm of Youth Crime*, edited by Gordon Bazemore and Lode Walgrave, 305-326. Monsey, NY: Criminal Justice Press, 1999.

Ishiguro, Hide. "Imagination." In *British Analytical Philosophy*, edited by Bernard Williams and Alan Montefiore, 153-178. London: Routledge, 1966.

John Doble Research Associates, Inc. *Crime and Corrections: The Views of the People of Vermont*. Waterbury, VT: Report to the Vermont Department of Corrections, 1994.

Johnson, Mark. *Moral Imagination: Implications of Cognitive Science for Ethics*. Chicago: University of Chicago Press, 1993.

Kant, Immanuel. *Groundwork of the Metaphysics of Morals*. Edited and translated by Mary Gregor. Cambridge: Cambridge University Press, 1998.

Karp, David R. "The Offender/Community Encounter: Stakeholder Involvement in the Vermont Reparative Boards." In *What is Community Justice: Case Studies of Restorative Justice and Community Supervision*, edited by David R. Karp and Todd R. Clear, 61-86. Thousand Oaks, CA: Sage Publications, 2002.

- - -. "Birds of a Feather: A Response to the McCold Critique of Community Justice." *Contemporary Justice Review* 7.1 (March 2004): 59-67.

Karp, David R. and Todd R. Clear. "Community Justice: A Conceptual Framework." In *Criminal Justice 2000*, vol. 2 in *Boundaries Changes in Criminal Justice Organizations*, 323-368. Washington, D.C.: National Institute of Justice, 2000. http://www.ncjrs.gov/criminal_justice 2000/vol_2/02i2.pdf.

Karp, David R. and Todd R. Clear, eds. *What is Community Justice: Case Studies of Restorative Justice and Community Supervision*. Thousand Oaks, CA: Sage Publications, 2002.

- - -. "The Community Justice Frontier: An Introduction." In *What is Community Justice: Case Studies of Restorative Justice and Community Supervision*, edited by David R. Karp and Todd R. Clear, ix-xvi. Thousand Oaks, CA: Sage Publications, 2002.

Karp, David R. and Lynne Walther. "Community Reparative Boards in

Vermont." In *Restorative Community Justice: Repairing Harm and Transforming Communities*, edited by Gordon Bazemore and Mara Schiff, 199-218. Cincinnati, OH: Anderson, 2001.

Kasarda, John, and Morris Janowitz. "Community Attachment in Mass Society." *American Sociological Review* 39 (1974): 328-339.

Keane, Philip S. *Christian Ethics and Imagination*. New York: Paulist Press, 1984.

Kekes, John. *Moral Tradition and Individuality*. Princeton: Princeton University Press, 1989.

- - -. *The Enlargement of Life: Moral Imagination at Work*. Ithaca, NY: Cornell University Press, 2006.

Kidder, Tracy. *Mountains Beyond Mountains: The Quest of Dr. Paul Farmer, A Man who Would Cure the World*. New York: Random House, 2003.

Kirk, Russell. *Eliot and His Age: T.S. Eliot's Moral Imagination in the Twentieth Century*. Peru, IL: Sugden, 1988.

Klause, John. *The Unfortunate Fall: Theodicy and the Moral Imagination of Andrew Marvell*. Hamden, CT: Archon Books, 1983.

Kornhauser, Ruth Rosner. *Social Sources of Delinquency: An Appraisal of Analytic Models*. Chicago: University of Chicago Press, 1978.

Kurki, Leena. "Evaluating Restorative Justice Practices." In *Restorative Justice and Criminal Justice: Competing or Reconcilable Paradigms?*, edited by Andrew Von Hirsch, Julian V. Roberts, Anthony Bottoms, Kent Roach, and Mara Schiff, 293-314. Portland, OR: Hart Publishing, 2003.

Larmore, Charles. *Patterns of Moral Complexity*. Cambridge: Cambridge University Press, 1987.

Latimer, Jeff, Craig Dowden, and Danielle Muise. *The Effectiveness of Restorative Justice Practices: A Meta-Analysis*. Ottawa: Department of Justice, 2001. http://www.justice.gc.ca/en/ps/rs/rep/2001/meta.pdf.

- - -. "The Effectiveness of Restorative Justice Practices: A Meta-Analysis." *The Prison Journal* 85 (2005): 127–144.

Lederach, John Paul. *The Moral Imagination: The Art and Soul of Building Peace*. New York: Oxford University Press, 2005.

- - -. *Building Peace: Sustainable Reconciliation in Divided Societies*. Washington, D.C.: U.S. Institute of Peace Press, 1998.

- - -. *The Journey Toward Reconciliation*. Scottdale, PA: Herald Press, 1999.

- - -. *The Little Book of Conflict Transformation*. Intercourse, PA: Good Books, 2003.

Leventhal, Gerald S. "What Should Be Done with Equity Theory?: New
Approaches to the Study of Fairness in Social Relationships." In *Social
Exchange: Advances in Theory and Research*, edited by Kenneth J.
Gergen, Martin S. Greenberg, and Richard H. Willis, 27-55. New York:
Plenum Press, 1980.

Lipsey, Mark W., and Francis T. Cullen. "The Effectiveness of Correctional
Rehabilitation: A Review of Systematic Reviews." *Annual Review of Law
and Social Science* 3 (2007): 297-320.

Logan, James Earl. *Good Punishment?: Christian Moral Practice and U.S.
Imprisonment.* Grand Rapids, MI: Wm. B. Eerdman's Publishing
Company, 2008.

MacIntyre, Alasdair C. *After Virtue: A Study in Moral Theory.* 2nd edition.
London: Duckworth, 1985.

- - -. *Dependent Rational Animals: Why Human Beings Need the Virtues.*
Chicago: Open Court, 1999.

Mackay, Robert E. "Restitution and Ethics: An Aristotelian Approach." In
*Restorative Justice on Trial: Pitfalls and Potentials of Victim-Offender
Mediation—International Perspectives*, edited by Heinz Messmer and
Hans-Uwe Otto, 569-583. Dordrecht, the Netherlands: Kluwer, 1992.

Mackey, Virginia. *Restorative Justice: Toward Nonviolence.* Louisville, KY:
Presbyterian Criminal Justice Program, 1997.

MacKenzie, Doris Layton. *What Works in Corrections: Reducing the Criminal
Activities of Offenders and Delinquents.* New York: Cambridge
University Press, 2006.

Maguire, Daniel C. *The Moral Choice.* Garden City, NY: Doubleday, 1978.

Marks, Kathy. *Lost Paradise: From Mutiny on the Bounty to a Modern-Day
Legacy of Sexual Mayhem, the Dark Secrets of Pitcairn Island.* New
York: Free Press, 2009.

Marshall, Christopher D. *Beyond Retribution: A New Testament Vision for
Justice, Crime, and Punishment.* Grand Rapids, MI: Wm. B. Eerdmans
Publishing Company, 2001.

Marshall, Tony. "Restorative Justice on Trial in Britain." In *Restorative
Justice on Trial: Pitfalls and Potentials of Victim-Offender Mediation—
International Perspectives*, edited by Heinz Messmer and Hans-Uwe Otto,
15-28. Dordrecht, the Netherlands: Kluwer, 1992.

- - -. "The Evolution of Restorative Justice in Britain." *European Journal of
Criminal Policy and Research* 4.4 (1996): 21-43.

Marvell, Thomas B. "Sentencing Guidelines and Prison Population Growth."

The Journal of Criminal Law and Criminology 85.3 (1995): 696-709.

Marvin, Niki. *The Shawshank Redemption.* Castle Rock Entertainment, 1994.

Masur, Louis P. *Rites of Execution.* New York: Oxford University Press, 1989.

Maxwell, Gabrielle M., and Allison Morris. *Family, Victims, and Culture: Youth Justice in New Zealand.* Wellington, New Zealand: Social Policy Agency and Institute of Criminology, Victoria University, 1993.

- - -. "Research on Family Group Conferences with Young Offenders in New Zealand." In *Family Group Conferences: Perspectives on Policy and Practice,* edited by Joe Hudson, Allison Morris, Gabrielle Maxwell, and Burt Galaway, 88-110. Monsey, NY: Criminal Justice Press, 1996.

McCold, Paul. *Restorative Justice: An Annotated Bibliography.* Monsey, NY: Criminal Justice Press, 1997a.

- - -. "Restorative Justice: Variations on the Theme." Paper presented at the Restorative Justice for Juveniles International Conference, Leuven, May 1997b.

- - -. "Toward a Holistic Vision of Restorative Juvenile Justice: A Reply to the Maximalist Model." *Contemporary Justice Review* 3.4 (2000): 357-414.

- - -. "Paradigm Muddle: The Threat to Restorative Justice Posed by Its Merger with Community Justice." *Contemporary Justice Review* 7.1 (March 2004a): 13-35.

- - -. "Paradigm Muddle: A Response to the Responses." *Contemporary Justice Review* 7.1 (March 2004b): 143-146.

McCold, Paul, and Benjamin Wachtel. *Restorative Policing Experiment: The Bethlehem Pennsylvania Police Family Group Conferencing Project.* Pipersville, PA: Community Service Foundation, 1998.

McCold, Paul, and Ted Wachtel. *Restorative Justice Theory Validation.* Paper presented at the Fourth International Conference on Restorative Justice for Juveniles, Tübingen, Germany, 2000.

- - -. *In Pursuit of Paradigm: A Theory of Restorative Justice.* Paper presented at the XIII World Congress of Criminology, Rio de Janeiro, Brazil, August 10-15, 2003. http://fp.enter.net/restorativepractices/ paradigm.pdf.

McCollough, Thomas E. *The Moral Imagination and Public Life: Raising the Ethical Question.* Chatham, NJ: Chatham House Publishers, 1991.

McDowell, John. "Virtue and Reason." *The Monist* 62 (1979): 331-350.

McFarland, Thomas. *Originality and Imagination.* Baltimore: The John Hopkins University Press, 1985.

McFaul, Thomas R. *Transformation Ethics: Developing the Christian Moral*

Imagination. Lanham, MD: University Press of America, 2003.

McGarrell, Edmund. *Restorative Justice Conferences as an Early Response to Young Offenders*. Washington, D.C.: Office of Juvenile Justice and Delinquency Prevention, U.S. Department of Justice, 2001. http://purl.access.gpo.gov/GPO/LPS18711.

McGarrell, Edmund, and Natalie Kroovand Hipple. "Family Group Conferencing and Re-Offending Among First-Time Juvenile Offenders: The Indianapolis Experiment." *Justice Quarterly* 24.2 (2007): 221-242.

McGarrell, Edmund, Kathleen Olivares, Kay Crawford, and Natalie Kroorand. *Returning Justice to the Community: The Indianapolis Juvenile Restorative Justice Experiment*. Indianapolis: Hudson Institute, 2000.

McGowen, Randall. "The Body and Punishment in Eighteenth Century England." *The Journal of Modern History* 59 (1987): 651-679.

Meirs, David, Mike Maguire, Shelagh Goldie, Karen Sharpe, Chris Hale, Ann Netten, Steve Uglow, Katherine Doolin, Angela Hallam, Jill Enterkin, and Tim Newburn. *An Exploratory Evaluation of Restorative Justice Schemes*. London: Home Office, 2001. http://www.homeoffice.gov.uk/rds/prgpdfs/crrs09.pdf.

Merry, Sally Engle. "Myth and Practice in the Mediation Process." In *Mediation and Criminal Justice: Victims, Offenders, and Community*, edited by Martin Wright and Burt Galaway, 239-250. London: Sage Publications, 1989.

Messmer, Heinz. "Communication in Decision-Making About Diversion and Victim-Offender Mediation." In *Restorative Justice on Trial: Pitfalls and Potentials of Victim-Offender Mediation—International Perspectives*, edited by Heinz Messmer and Hans-Uwe Otto, 461-474. Dordrecht, the Netherlands: Kluwer, 1992.

Messmer, Heinz and Hans-Uwe Otto, eds. *Restorative Justice on Trial: Pitfalls and Potentials of Victim-Offender Mediation—International Perspectives*. Dordrecht, the Netherlands: Kluwer, 1992.

- - -. "Restorative Justice: Steps on the Way Toward a Good Idea." In *Restorative Justice on Trial: Pitfalls and Potentials of Victim-Offender Mediation—International Perspectives*, edited by Heinz Messmer and Hans-Uwe Otto, 1-12. Dordrecht, the Netherlands: Kluwer, 1992.

Miller, Richard B. *Children, Ethics, and Modern Medicine*. Bloomington, IN: University of Indiana Press, 2003.

- - -. "On Making a Cultural Turn in Religious Ethics." *Journal of Religious Ethics* 33.3 (2005): 409-443.

Modrak, Deborah. *Aristotle: The Power of Perception.* Chicago: University of Chicago Press, 1987.

Moore, David B., with L. Forsythe. *A New Approach to Juvenile Justice: An Evaluation of Family Conferencing in Wagga Wagga.* Wagga Wagga: Charles Sturt University, 1995.

Moore, Michael. "The Moral Worth of Retribution." In *Responsibility, Character, and the Emotions: New Essays in Moral Psychology,* edited by Ferdinand Schoeman, 179-219. Cambridge: Cambridge University Press, 1987.

Morris, Norval. *Punishment, Desert, and Rehabilitation.* Washington, DC: U.S. Government Printing Office, 1976.

Morris, Norval, and Michael Tonry. *Between Prison and Probation: Intermediate Punishments in a Rational Sentencing System.* New York: Oxford University Press, 1990.

Murdoch, Iris. *Metaphysics as a Guide to Morals.* New York: Penguin Books, 1992.

- - -. *The Sovereignty of Good.* New York: Schocken Books, 1970.

Nagel, Thomas. *Mortal Questions.* Cambridge: Cambridge University Press, 1979.

- - -. *The View from Nowhere.* New York: Oxford University Press, 1986.

Nagin, Daniel S., Francis T. Cullen, and Cheryl Lero Jonson. "Imprisonment and Reoffending." *Crime and Justice* 38.1 (2009): 115-200.

Newsom, Carol. *The Book of Job: A Contest of Moral Imagination.* New York: Oxford University Press, 2003.

Niemeyer, Mike, and David Shichor. "A Preliminary Study of a Large Victim/Offender Reconciliation Program." *Federal Probation* 60.3 (1996): 30-34.

Nozick, Robert. *Anarchy, State, and Utopia.* Oxford: Blackwell Publishers, 1978.

Nugent, William R., and Jeff B. Paddock. "The Effect of Victim-Offender Mediation on Severity of Reoffense." *Mediation Quarterly* 12 (1995): 353-367.

Nugent, William R., Mark S. Umbreit, Lizbeth Wiinamaki, and Jeff B. Paddock. "Participation in Victim-Offender Mediation and Re-Offense: Successful Replications?" *Journal of Research on Social Work Practice* 11.1 (2001): 5-23.

Nussbaum, Martha. *Aristotle's* De Motu Animalium. Princeton: Princeton

University Press, 1978.

- - -. *Cultivating Humanity*. Cambridge: Harvard University Press, 1997.

- - -. *Love's Knowledge: Essays on Philosophy and Literature*. New York: Oxford University Press, 1990.

- - -. "Non-relative Virtues: An Aristotelian Approach." In *Ethical Theory: Character and Virtue, Midwest Studies in Philosophy, 13*, edited by Peter A. French, Theodore E. Uehling, Jr. and Howard K. Wettstein, 32-53. Notre Dame, IN: University of Notre Dame Press, 1988.

- - -. *Sex and Social Justice*. New York: Oxford University Press, 1999.

Nussbaum, Martha, and Amartya Sen, eds. *The Quality of Life*. Oxford: Clarendon Press, 1993.

Odem, Mary E. *Delinquent Daughters: Protecting and Policing Adolescent Female Sexuality in the United States, 1885-1920*. Chapel Hill, NC: University of North Carolina Press, 1995.

Office of Juvenile Justice and Delinquency Prevention. "Statistical Briefing Book." U.S. Department of Justice, Office of Justice Programs. http://ojjdp.ncjrs.gov/ojstatbb/ (accessed on May 14, 2009).

Orlando, Frank A. "Mediation Involving Children in the U.S.: Legal and Ethical Conflicts. A Policy Discussion and Research Questions." In *Restorative Justice on Trial: Pitfalls and Potentials of Victim-Offender Mediation—International Perspectives*, edited by Messmer, Heinz and Hans-Uwe Otto, 333-342. Dordrecht, the Netherlands: Kluwer, 1992.

Parenti, Christian. *Lockdown America, Police, and Prisons in the Age of Crisis*. London, New York: Verso, 1999.

Pate, Kim. "Victim-Offender Reconciliation Programs in Canada." In *Criminal Justice, Restitution, and Reconciliation*, edited by Burt Galaway and Joe Hudson, 135-144. Monsey, NY: Willow Press, 1990.

Peachey, Dean E. "The Kitchener Experiment." In *Mediation and Criminal Justice: Victims, Offenders, and Community*, edited by Martin Wright and Burt Galaway, 14-26. London: Sage Publications, 1989.

- - -. "Restitution, Reconciliation, Retribution: Identifying the Forms of Justice People Desire." In *Restorative Justice on Trial: Pitfalls and Potentials of Victim-Offender Mediation—International Perspectives*, edited by Heinz Messmer and Hans-Uwe Otto, 551-558. Dordrecht, the Netherlands: Kluwer, 1992.

Pepinsky, Hal. "Empathy and Restoration." In *Handbook of Restorative Justice: A Global Perspective*, edited by Dennis Sullivan and Larry Tifft, 188-197. New York: Routledge, 2006.

Pepinsky, Harold E. and Richard Quinney, eds. *Criminology as Peacemaking.*
Bloomington: Indiana University Press, 1991.

Perry, John G., ed. *Repairing Communities through Restorative Justice.*
Lanham, MD: American Correctional Association, 2002.

Peters, Edward. "Prison Before the Prison." In *The Oxford History of the
Prison,* edited by Norval Morris and David Rothman, 3-42. New York:
Oxford University Press, 1995.

Pettit, Peter, and John Braithwaite. "Not Just Deserts, Even in Sentencing."
Journal of the Institute of Criminology 4.3 (1993): 225-239.

Plato. *The Laws of Plato.* Translated by Thomas L. Pangle. Chicago: The
University of Chicago Press, 1980.

Pranis, Kay. "From Vision to Action: Some Principles of Restorative Justice."
Church and Society: Presbyterian Church Journal 87.4 (1997): 32-42.

- - -. "Promising Practices in Community Justice: Restorative Justice." In
Community Justice: Concepts and Strategies, 37-57. Lexington, KY:
American Probation and Parole Association, 1998.

Presser, Lois. "Justice Here and Now: A Personal Reflection on the
Restorative and Community Justice Paradigms." *Contemporary Justice
Review* 7.1 (March 2004): 101-106.

Price, Martin. *Forms of Life: Character and Moral Imagination in the Novel.*
New Haven, CT: Yale University Press, 1983.

Richard Quinney, *The Social Reality of Crime.* Boston: Little, Brown, 1970.

Reinganum, Jennifer F. "Sentencing Guidelines, Judicial Discretion, and Plea
Bargaining." *The RAND Journal of Economics* 31.1 (2000): 62-81.

"Residential Faith-Based Programs in State Corrections." In *Special Issues in
Corrections.* Washington, D.C.: U.S. Department of Justice, National
Institute of Corrections Information Center, 2005.

Rex, Sue. "A New Form of Rehabilitation?" In *Principled Sentencing:
Readings on Theory and Policy,* 2nd edition, 34-41. Oxford: Hart
Publishing, 1998.

Ricoeur, Paul. *The Rule of Metaphor: Multi-disciplinary Studies of the
Creation of Meaning in Language.* Robert Czerny, trans. Toronto:
University of Toronto Press, 1975.

- - -. "Imagination in Discourse and in Action." In *Rethinking Imagination:
Culture and Creativity,* edited by Gillian Robinson and John Rundell, 118-
135. New York: Routledge, 1994.

Rossi, Philip. "Moral Imagination and the Narrative Modes of Moral

Discourse." *Renascence* 31.3 (1979): 131-141.

- - -. *Together Toward Hope: A Journey to Moral Theology*. Notre Dame: University of Notre Dame Press, 1983.

Roy, Sudipto. "Two Types of Juvenile Restitution Programs in Two Midwestern Counties: A Comparative Study." *Federal Probation* 57.4 (1993): 48-53.

Schazenbach, Max M., and Emerson H. Tiller. "Reviewing the Sentencing Guidelines: Judicial Politics, Empirical Evidence, and Reform." *The University of Chicago Law Review* 75.2 (2008):715-760.

Schiff, Mara. "The Impact of Restorative Interventions on Juvenile Offenders." In *Restorative Juvenile Justice: Repairing the Harm of Youth Crime*, edited by Gordon Bazemore and Lode Walgrave, 327-356. Monsey, NY: Criminal Justice Press, 1999.

- - -. "Models, Challenges, and the Promise of Restorative Conferencing Strategies." In *Restorative Justice and Criminal Justice: Competing or Reconcilable Paradigms?*, edited by Andrew Von Hirsch, Julian V. Roberts, Anthony Bottoms, Kent Roach, and Mara Schiff, 315-338. Portland, OR: Hart Publishing, 2003.

Schofield, Malcolm. "Aristotle on the Imagination." In *Essays on Aristotle's De Anima*, edited by Martha Nussbaum and Amélie Rorty, 249-277. Oxford: Clarendon Press, 1992.

Schwarz, Ira M. and Laura Preiser. "Diversion and Juvenile Justice: Can We Ever Get It Right?" In *Restorative Justice on Trial: Pitfalls and Potentials of Victim-Offender Mediation—International Perspectives*, edited by Messmer, Heinz and Hans-Uwe Otto, 279-290. Dordrecht, the Netherlands: Kluwer, 1992.

Shaw, Clifford R., and Henry D. McKay. *Juvenile Delinquency and Urban Areas*. Chicago: University of Chicago Press, 1942.

Sherman, Lawrence W., and Heather Strang. *Restorative Justice: The Evidence*. London: The Smith Institute, 2007.

Sherman, Lawrence W., Heather Strang, and Daniel J. Woods. *Recidivism Patterns in the Canberra Reintegrative Shaming Experiments (RISE)*. Canberra: Centre for Restorative Justice, Australian National University, 2000.

Sherman, Nancy. *The Fabric of Character: Aristotle's Theory of Virtue*. Oxford: Clarendon Press, 1989.

Shiner, Roger A. "Aristotle's Theory of Equity." In *Justice, Law, and Method in Plato and Aristotle*, edited by Spiro Panagiotou, 173-191. Edmonton, Alberta: Academic Printing and Publishing, 1987.

Skotnicki, Andrew. *Criminal Justice and the Catholic Church.* Lanham, MD: Rowman and Littlefield, 2008.

- - -. "How is Justice Restored?" *Studies in Christian Ethics* 19.2 (2006): 187-204.

- - -. *Religion and the Development of the American Penal System.* Lanham, MD: University Press of America, 2000.

Smith, Paula, Paul Gendreau, and Kristin Swartz. "Validating the Principle of Effective Correctional Intervention: A Systematic Review of the Contributions of Meta-analysis in the Field of Corrections." *Victims and Offenders* 4.1 (2009): 148-169.

Smith, Polly Ashton. "William Godwin's Moral Education Theory of Punishment: Is it a Restorative Approach to Justice?" *Contemporary Justice Review* 1 (1998): 87-101.

Snyder, T. Richard. *The Protestant Ethic and the Spirit of Punishment.* Grand Rapids, MI: Wm. B. Eerdmans Publishing Company, 2001.

Spradley, James P. *The Ethnographic Interview.* Belmont, CA: Wadsworth, 1979.

Stevens, Edward. *Developing Moral Imagination: Case Studies in Practical Morality.* New York: Sheed and Ward, 1998.

Stewart, Charles. *Demons and the Devil: Moral Imagination in Modern Greek Culture.* Princeton, NJ: Princeton University Press, 1991.

Strang, Heather. *Victim Participation in a Restorative Justice Process.* Oxford: Oxford University Press, 2001.

Strang, Heather, and John Braithwaite, eds. *Restorative Justice and Civil Society.* Cambridge: Cambridge University Press, 2001.

Strang, Heather, and Lawrence W. Sherman. *The Victim's Perspective: RISE Working Paper 2.* Canberra: Law Program, RSSS, Australian National University, 1997.

Strang, Heather, Geoffrey Barnes, John Braithwaite, and Lawrence Sherman. *Experiments in Restorative Policing: A Progress Report.* Canberra: Australian National University, 1999.

Strawson, P.F. "Imagination and Perception." In *Experience and Theory*, edited by Lawrence Foster and J.W. Swanson, 31-54. Amherst: University of Massachusetts Press, 1970.

Sullivan, Dennis. "Mutual Aid: The Social Basis of Justice and Moral

Community." *Humanity and Society* 6 (1982): 294-302.

- - -. "Living Restorative Justice as a Lifestyle: An Interview with Fred Boehrer." *Contemporary Justice Review* 1 (1998): 149-166.

Sullivan, Dennis, Peter Sanzen, and Kathryn Callaghan. "The Teaching and Studying of Justice: Fostering the Unspeakable Vision of Cooperation." *Crime and Social Justice* 29 (1987): 128-135.

Sullivan, Dennis, and Larry Tifft. "Criminology as Peacemaking: A Peace-Oriented Perspective on Crime, Punishment, and Justice that Takes into Account the Needs of All." *The Justice Professional* 11.1/2 (1998): 5-34.

- - -. *Restorative Justice: Healing the Foundations of Our Everyday Lives.* Monsey, NY: Willow Tree Press, 2001.

- - -, eds. *Handbook of Restorative Justice: A Global Perspective.* New York: Routledge, 2006.

- - -. "Introduction: The Healing Dimension of Restorative Justice: A One-World Body." In *Handbook of Restorative Justice: A Global Perspective,* edited by Dennis Sullivan and Larry Tifft, 1-16. New York: Routledge, 2006.

Taylor, Mark Lewis. *The Executed God: The Way of the Cross in Lockdown America.* Minneapolis: Fortress Press, 2001.

Thomson, Douglas. "Can We Heal Ourselves? Transforming Conflict in the Restorative Justice Movement." *Contemporary Justice Review* 7.1 (March 2004): 107-116.

Tierney, Nathan L. *Imagination and Ethical Ideals: Prospects for a Unified Philosophical and Psychological Understanding.* Albany: SUNY Press, 1994.

Tilmouth, Christopher. *Passion's Triumph over Reason: A History of the Moral Imagination from Spenser to Rochester.* Oxford: Oxford University Press, 2007.

Tivnan, Edward. *The Moral Imagination: Confronting the Ethical Issues of Our Day.* New York: Simon and Schuster, 1995.

Tonry, Michael H. "The Fragmentation of Sentencing and Corrections in America," in *Sentencing and Corrections.* Washington, DC: National Institute of Justice, 1999a.

- - -. "Intermediate Sanctions in Sentencing Guidelines." *Crime and Justice* 23 (1998): 199-253.

- - -. "Proportionality, Parsimony, and Interchangeability of Punishments." In *Penal Theory and Penal Practice,* edited by R.A. Duff et al., 59-84. Manchester: Manchester University Press, 1992.

- - -. "Reconsidering Indeterminate and Structured Sentencing." *Sentencing and Corrections*. (Washington, DC: National Institute of Justice, 1999b).

Trenzcek, Thomas. "A Review and Assessment of Victim-Offender Reconciliation Programming in West Germany." In *Criminal Justice, Restitution, and Reconciliation*, edited by Burt Galaway and Joe Hudson, 109-124. Monsey, NY: Willow Press, 1990.

Trilling, Lionel. *The Liberal Imagination: Essays on Literature and Society*. New York: The Viking Press, 1950.

Tuan, Yi-Fu. *Morality and Imagination: Paradoxes of Progress*. Madison, WI: University of Wisconsin Press, 1989.

Umbreit, Mark S. "Violent Offenders and their Victims." In *Mediation and Criminal Justice: Victims, Offenders, and Community*, edited by Martin Wright and Burt Galaway, 99-112. London: Sage Publications, 1989.

- - -. "Mediating Victim-Offender Conflict: From Single-Site to Multi-Site Analysis in the U.S." In *Restorative Justice on Trial: Pitfalls and Potentials of Victim-Offender Mediation—International Perspectives*, edited by Heinz Messmer and Hans-Uwe Otto, 431-444. Dordrecht, the Netherlands: Kluwer, 1992.

- - -. *Victim Meets Offender: The Impact of Restorative Justice and Mediation*. Monsey, NY: Criminal Justice Press, 1994.

- - -. *Mediation of Criminal Conflict: An Assessment of Programs in Four Canadian Provinces*. St. Paul, MN: The Center for Restorative Justice and Mediation, University of Minnesota, 1995.

- - -. *Family Group Conferencing: Implications for Crime Victims*. Washington, D.C.: Office of Juvenile Justice and Delinquency Prevention, U.S. Department of Justice, 2000.

- - -. *The Handbook of Victim-Offender Mediation*. San Francisco: Jossey-Bass, 2001.

Umbreit, Mark S. and Robert B. Coates. "Cross-Site Analysis of Victim-Offender Mediation in Four States." *Crime and Delinquency* 39 (1993): 565-585.

- - -. *Multicultural Implications of Restorative Justice: Potential Pitfalls and Dangers*. Washington, D.C.: Office of Juvenile Justice and Delinquency Prevention, U.S. Department of Justice, 2000.

Umbreit, Mark S., Robert B. Coates, and Betty Vos. "The Impact of Victim-Offender Mediation: Two Decades of Research." *Federal Probation* 65.3 (2001): 29-35.

- - -. "Restorative Justice versus Community Justice: Clarifying a Muddle or Generating Confusion." *Contemporary Justice Review* 7.1 (March 2004): 81-89.

Umbreit, Mark S. and Jean Greenwood. *Directory of Victim-Offender Mediation Programs in the US.* Washington, D.C.: Office of Juvenile Justice and Delinquency Prevention, U.S. Department of Justice, 2000a.

- - -. *National Survey of Victim-Offender Mediation Programs in the US.* Washington, D.C.: Office of Juvenile Justice and Delinquency Prevention, U.S. Department of Justice, 2000b.

- - -. *Victim-Sensitive Victim-Offender Mediation: Restorative Justice Through Dialogue.* Washington, D.C.: Office of Juvenile Justice and Delinquency Prevention, U.S. Department of Justice, 2000c.

Umbreit, Mark S. and Ann Warner Roberts. *Mediation of Criminal Conflict in England: An Assessment of Services in Coventry and Leeds.* St. Paul, MN: The Center for Restorative Justice and Mediation, University of Minnesota, 1996.

United States Conference of Catholic Bishops. "Responsibility, Rehabilitation, and Restoration: A Catholic Perspective on Crime and Criminal Justice." 2000. http://www.usccb.org/sdwp/criminal.shtml.

Van Ness, Daniel W. "Perspectives on Achieving Satisfying Justice: Values and Principles of Restorative Justice." *ICCA Journal on Community Corrections* 8.1 (1997): 7-12.

- - -. "New Wine and Old Wineskins: Four Challenges of Restorative Justice." *Criminal Law Forum* 4:2 (1993): 251-276.

Van Ness, Daniel W., and Mara Schiff. "Satisfaction Guaranteed? The Meaning of Satisfaction in Restorative Justice." In *Restorative Community Justice: Repairing Harm and Transforming Communities*, edited by Gordon Bazemore and Mara Schiff, 47-62. Cincinnati, OH: Anderson, 2001.

Van Ness, Daniel W., and Karen Heetderks Strong. *Restoring Justice.* 2nd edition. Cincinnati: Anderson Publishing Company, 2002.

Von Hirsch, Andrew. *Doing Justice: The Choice of Punishments.* New York: Hill and Wang, 1976.

Von Hirsch, Andrew, and Andrew Ashworth. *Principled Sentencing: Readings on Theory and Policy*, 2nd edition. Oxford: Hart Publishing, 1998. Von Hirsch, Andrew, Julian V. Roberts, Anthony Bottoms, Kent Roach, and

Mara Schiff, eds. *Restorative Justice and Criminal Justice: Competing or Reconcilable Paradigms?* Portland, OR: Hart Publishing, 2003.

Von Leyden, W. "Aristotle and the Concept of Law." *Philosophy* 42.159 (1967): 1-19.

Wachtel, Joshua. "Colorado Children's Code Authorizes Restorative Justice Conferences for Adjudicated Youth (Parts 1 & 2)." *Restorative Practices eForum*. International Institute of Restorative Practices. www.iirp.org.

Wachtel, Ted, and Paul McCold. "Restorative Justice in Everyday Life." In *Restorative Justice and Civil Society*, edited by Heather Strang and John Braithwaite, 114-129. Cambridge: Cambridge University Press, 2001.

Walgrave, Lode. "Mediation and Community Service as Models of a Restorative Approach: Why Would it be Better? Explicating the Objectives as Criteria for Evaluation." In *Restorative Justice on Trial: Pitfalls and Potentials of Victim-Offender Mediation—International Perspectives*, edited by Messmer, Heinz and Hans-Uwe Otto, 343-354. Dordrecht, the Netherlands: Kluwer, 1992.

- - -. "Beyond Retribution and Rehabilitation: Restoration as the Dominant Paradigm in Judicial Intervention Against Juvenile Crime." Paper presented at the International Congress on Criminology, Budapest, Hungary. 1993.

- - -, ed. *Restorative Justice for Juveniles: Potentialities, Risks, and Problems for Research.* Leuven, Belgium: Leuven University Press, 1998.

Walker, Peter F. *Moral Choices: Memory, Desire, and Imagination in Nineteenth-Century American Abolition.* Baton Rouge: Louisiana State University Press, 1978.

Walsh, William. *The Use of Imagination: Educational Thought and the Literary Mind.* London: Chatto and Windus, 1959.

Walster, Elaine, G. William Walster, and Ellen Berscheid. *Equity: Theory and Research.* Boston: Allyn and Bacon, 1978.

Ward, Tony, and Robyn Langlands. "Repairing the Rupture: Restorative Justice and the Rehabilitation of Offenders." *Aggression and Violent Behavior* 14 (2009): 205-214.

Ward, Tony, and Shadd Maruna. *Rehabiliation: Beyond the Risk Paradigm.* London: Routledge Press, 2007.

Warnock, Mary. *Imagination.* Berkeley: University of California Press, 1976.

Watson, David, Jacky Boucherat, and Gwynn Davis. "Reparation for

Retributivists." In *Mediation and Criminal Justice: Victims, Offenders, and Community*, edited by Martin Wright and Burt Galaway, 212-228. London: Sage Publications, 1989.

Watterson, Kathryn. *Women in Prison: Inside the Concrete Womb*. Boston: Northeastern University Press, 1973/1996.

Wedin, Michael V. *Mind and Imagination in Aristotle*. New Haven: Yale University Press, 1988.

Weitekamp, Elmar. "The History of Restorative Justice." In *Restorative Juvenile Justice: Repairing the Harm of Youth Crime*, edited by Gordon Bazemore and Lode Walgrave, 75-102. Monsey, NY: Criminal Justice Press, 1999.

Weitekamp, Elmar, and Hans-Jürgen Kerner. *Restorative Justice: Theoretical Foundations*. Portland, OR: Willan Publishing, 2002.

Werhane, Patricia H. *Moral Imagination and Management Decision-Marking*. New York: Oxford University Press, 1999.

West, Heather C., and William J. Sabol. "Prisoners in 2007." *Bureau of Justice Statistics, Bulletin 224280*. Washington, DC: U.S. Department of Justice, 2008.

West, Traci C. *Disruptive Christian Ethics: When Racism and Women's Lives Matter*. Louisville: Westminster John Knox Press, 2006.

White, Alan R. *The Language of Imagination*. Oxford: Blackwell, 1990.

White Jr., Lynn. "The Historical Roots of Our Ecological Crisis." In *Western Man and Environmental Ethics: Attitudes toward Nature and Ecology*, edited by Ian G. Barbour. Reading, MA: Addison-Wesley, 1973.

Whitmore, Todd David. "Crossing the Road: The Case for Ethnographic Fieldwork in Christian Ethics." *Journal of the Society of Christian Ethics* 27.2 (2007): 273-294.

Williams, Bernard. *Moral Luck*. Cambridge: Cambridge University Press, 1981.

Williams, Oliver, ed. *The Moral Imagination: How Literature and Films Can Stimulate Ethical Reflection in the Business World*. Notre Dame: University of Notre Dame Press, 1998.

Worth, Marvin, and Spike Lee. *Malcolm X*. 40 Acres & a Mule Filmworks, 1992.

Wright, Martin. "What the Public Wants." In *Mediation and Criminal Justice: Victims, Offenders, and Community*, edited by Martin Wright and Burt Galaway, 264-268. London: Sage Publications, 1989.

- - -. "Victim-Offender Mediation as a Step Towards a Restorative System of

Justice." In *Restorative Justice on Trial: Pitfalls and Potentials of Victim-Offender Mediation—International Perspectives*, edited by Heinz Messmer and Hans-Uwe Otto, 525-540. Dordrecht, the Netherlands: Kluwer, 1992.

Wright, Martin and Burt Galaway, eds. *Mediation and Criminal Justice: Victims, Offenders, and Community*. London: Sage Publications, 1989.

Wynne, Jean. "Leeds Mediation and Reparation Service: Ten Years Experience with Victim-Offender Mediation." In *Restorative Justice: International Perspectives*, edited by Burt Galaway and Joe Hudson, 445-462. Monsey, NY: Criminal Justice Press, 1996.

Zehr, Howard. *Changing Lenses: A New Focus for Crime and Justice*. Scottdale, PA: Herald Press, 1990.

- - -. *The Little Book of Restorative Justice*. Intercourse, PA: Good Books, 2002.

- - -. "Fundamental Concepts of Restorative Justice." *Contemporary Justice Review* 1 (1998): 27-55.

Zellerer, Evelyn and Joanna B. Cannon. "Restorative Justice, Reparation, and the Southside Project." In *What is Community Justice: Case Studies of Restorative Justice and Community Supervision*, edited by David R. Karp and Todd R. Clear, 89-107. Thousand Oaks, CA: Sage Publications, 2002.

Index